Social Glimpses of Iraq's Modern History

IRAQ FROM 1920 – 1924
by
Ali al-Wardi, PhD

لمحات اجتماعية من تاريخ العراق الحديث

Translated from Arabic *by* Yasin T. al-Jibouri

LANTERN PUBLICATIONS

In the Name of Allāh,
the Most Compassionate, the Most Merciful

CONTENTS

Chapter 1

Chapter Two

Chapter Three

Chapter Six

Conclusion

Sociologist Ali al-Wardi [1]

1 By Unknown author - first page of the book;علي الوردي: شخصيته ومنهجه وأفكاره الإجتماعية by

Al-Jamal publishing, Public Domain,

https://commons.wikimedia.org/w/index.php?curid=60826230

Front cover of this book's Arabic text

Translators Preface

Born in al-Kadhimiyya City, northwest Baghdad, in 1913 and died in 1995 at 82, Ali Hussain Muhsin Abdul-Jalil al-Wardi, Iraq's top sociologist and historian, left behind a rich literary legacy unmatched in its style, genre and precision. He also left behind his sons Hassān حسّان, Ja`far جعفر, Faisal فيصل and daughter Sīnā' سيناء.

Ali al-Wardi was born to a traditional religious family but grew up defying his family's strict no-modern education policy. His father wanted him to learn a craft instead of reading books, but he grew up disliking physical work and had a strong liking for books. He left school in 1924 to work at a grocery shop but was fired because of being too busy reading books to tend to customers. After that, he opened a small shop which he ran himself

In 1931, he joined the evening study in the sixth grade of his primary school, which was the beginning of a new life for him. He completed his studies and became a teacher. He also changed his traditional dress in 1932 and became an *Effendi* or *Afandi*, a title given by Iraqis to one who wears a Western-style outfit. He managed to complete his high school studies and was awarded the recognition of being the top high school graduate in the then Kingdom of Iraq. Due to this recognition, he was awarded a scholarship to the American University of Beirut, where he received his Bachelor's degree in 1943. In the same year, he was appointed by Iraq's Ministry of Education as a teacher at the Central Preparatory School in Baghdad.

Later Al-Wardi travelled to the United States to earn his Masters (1948) and PhD (1950) degrees from The University of Texas. He was then appointed in 1950 as a professor of sociology at the College of Arts, Baghdad University, immediately after he graduated from the University of Texas. He retired in 1970 at his request, and Baghdad University awarded him the title "Expert Professor".

Upon his return to Iraq, Ali al-Wardi started his career by writing many books based on the theory of Ibn Khaldun about Al-Badawa (Nomadic society) vs Al-Hadhara (civil or urban society). In addition to the influence of Ibn Khaldun on Dr. al-Wardi, let us not forget that he was also influenced by al-Jahiz الجاحظ in his objective view, rational approach, social and psychological analyses of the human behavior.

Works

His published books which remain in Arabic, include the following with the date of publication in parentheses. These are the English translation of the Arabic titles:

- The personality of the Iraqi individual (1951),
- The supernatural of the subconscious (1952),
- The sultan's preachers (1954),
- The farce of the human mind (1956),
- Dreams between science and faith (1959),
- The logic of Ibn Khaldun (1962),
- A study in the nature of Iraqi society (1965),
- The myth of the sublime literature (1957).

In addition to the above, the following list of books was published after the author's death:

- A study in Islam's sociology (2013),
- A psychological analysis of Ibn Khaldun's theory of the science of sociology (2018),
- Knowledge (a book about general knowledge) (2018),

- Thus did they kill the apple of the eye (1997),
- The story of the Sharifs and Ibn Saud (2007),
- Ethics: What is lost of the moral sources (2007),
- Intellectual works of Dr. Ali al-Wardi in Iraqi and Arab magazines and newspapers (2018), From the inspiration of the 1980s (2007),
- Dr. Ali al-Wardi on the human nature: An attempt to comprehend what went on (1996), The human nature (2017),
- Ali al-Wardi on the psyche and the society (2011).

In 2014, the Iraqi Ministry of Culture, through its publishing house, Dar al-Mamoon, commissioned a team of translators (one of whom included Yasin T. al-Jibouri) to translate al-Wardi's major work لمحات اجتماعية من تاريخ العراق الحديث (Social Glimpses of Iraq's Modern History). Al-Jibouri's contribution is the translation of Volume Six and its supplement, which was renamed Volume Seven.

An abridged translation of the first volume of the seminal work on Iraqi social history by Ali al-Wardi, first published in Baghdad in 1969, is already in print. It was completed by Haydar al-Khoei (a researcher with the Centre for Academic Shi`a Studies), who had his 132 pages-page book published by Lambert (marketed at an exorbitant price and ill attributed to the author). The only other book translated is Iraq in Turmoil, translated by Youssef H. Aboul-Enein and edited by Cdr. Youssef Aboul-Enein.

The first volume of لمحات اجتماعية من تاريخ العراق الحديث Social Glimpses of Modern Iraqi History is a detailed analysis of Iraqi politics, history, culture and society between the rise of the Ottoman Empire to the demise of the Mamlukes in the mid-19th century. Influenced by Ibn Khaldun, William Ogburn and Robert MacIver, al-Wardi argues that the conflict between nomadic and urban norms of culture was due to change, and the Iraqi individual's dual personality, all combined to explain the nature of Iraqi society. Al-Wardi also argues that Iraq has always been plagued by sectarianism ever since the introduction of Islam itself, but the violence peaked during the Ottoman-Safavid war that raged for almost three centuries. Iraqis saw these powers not as foreign invaders but as vanguards of their respective faiths. Al-Wardi focused on the societal aspect of this turbulent era in Iraqi history. His arguments were informed by sociological theory, archival material and, most interestingly, personal experience and observation.

Al-Wardi's Methodology

Al-Wardi is known for adopting social theories that were considered "modern" while analysing the Iraqi social reality during his time. He also used those theories to analyse some historical events, as he did in the book وعاظ السلاطين *The Sultans' Preachers,* and he is one of the pioneers of secularism in Iraq. His family's nickname, Al-Wardi, refers to his great-grandfather, who worked in the rose water distillation industry.

Al-Wardi wrote many important research papers, books and articles and often did that at his own peril. He disagreed with the rulers in some matters, which often resulted in difficult situations. He wrote about Salamah Mousa, Abdul-Razzaq Muhid-Din, penned hundreds of newspaper articles, encyclopedias, and books, and supervised Master's and PhD theses. Up to the late seventies, he was busy writing his Memoirs to put them in book format.

Al-Wardi was heavily influenced by Ibn Khaldun's approach to sociology. This objectivity caused significant problems for him because he neither adopted the Marxist approach nor followed contemporary ideologies. This enraged followers of these ideologies who accused him of being an Arab nationalist, whilst the communists criticized him for not adopting the historical materialist method in his studies.

In his analyses of the structure of modern Iraqi society, Dr al-Wardi's study of the Iraqi personality was the most important of its kind, and whose research method is readily translatable to the rest of the Middle East. The impact of the make-up of Iraq's personality is that it is a country that allows the construction of civilization because of its rivers, but its proximity to the Arabian desert has made it vulnerable to large and numerous migrations throughout history, most recently in the past 250 years. He analysed the nature of the Iraqi mindset, including the notion that there is a duality in it that holds contradictory values. Ali al-Wardi describes Iraq as a melting pot of immigrant Bedouins integrated with the settled and urbanized population that preceded them. His outlook creates two values for them: an urban value and a Bedouin value. The Iraqi individual advocates the values of dignity and dominance, but his life forces him to submit to the values of civilization. He analyses most of the regions of Iraq except for the Kurdish region because of his self-confessed lack of knowledge of the Kurdish language.

Dr. Al-Wardi's contribution was a unique scientific analysis of the nature of the emergence and structure of modern Iraqi society. His analysis of the sociology after the Mamluke era, the floods of the Tigris and Euphrates, and the waves of plagues that either killed huge numbers of citizens who lived in the Iraqi states during the era of the Ottomans was particularly relevant. This led to the migration of large numbers of Iraqi citizens to Ottoman states and emirates east of Najd and the Gulf or to the Levant, Syria, Lebanon, Jordan, Palestine, and Egypt. Indeed, many families of Iraqi origins still maintain their Iraqi surnames.

Dr. Ali Al-Wardi brings the reader through his books to topics that we fly with and through in the atmosphere of the soul and its hidden and beyond, topics that approach or move away with their titles from psychological analysis, but when they touch on their parts the doors of pink thought, they take another curve to review the laboratory of his interpretations, to come out wearing dimensions that often surprise the mind with their titles. In The Myth of Lofty Literature, the title takes the reader to the extent of literature labelled as such by Al-Wardi, and to an analytical space of another kind. This book contains beautiful intellectual discussions between two schools, the first being proud of poetry and language to the point of fanaticism, and the second represented by the writer criticizing poetry, royal literature and the complex grammar rules set by grammarians. He presents and discusses the impact of literature and language on the Arab society, placing the reasons behind the interest of the caliphs and sultans in particular so that the Arabs became one of the nations that are the most interested in poetry. In his book The Sultans' Preachers, al-Wardi posits various issues, including the logic of Platonic preaching as being the one of the affluent and the dark, and that history does not proceed based on logical thinking but, instead, it proceeds on the basis of the original tendencies in the human nature that do not accept change, and ethics are only the outcome of the results of social conditions. Through his books "The Paranormal" and "Dreams between Science and

Faith," Al-Wardi takes readers through psychological analyses to areas that affect all people.

His other significant contribution was the analysis of the origins of immigrants. His writings and research were characterized by an anthropological nature, specifically, the customs and traditions that stem from the eras of the Abbasid Caliphate, around religious occasions and their importance in the life of the Baghdadi individual, such as the birth of the Prophet and the Ashura memorial, etc.

Al-Wardi launched a relentless campaign against some members of the clergy, especially in his book titled *The Sultans' Preachers* and the farce of the human mind. He accused them of siding with the rulers and ignoring the nation's interests at the expense of the narrow interests of their duty as the custodians of the creed. Additionally, he called for rejecting the sectarian dispute between Shi`as and Sunnis, demanding the issue of the dispute between Imam Ali and Mu`awiyah be viewed as a historical dispute that has outlived time, and that Muslims must instead draw inspiration from the positions and opinions of these historical leaders.

Al-Wardi believed that the doctrine of Zaid bin Ali is the middle faith in Islam, and some say that he declared his embrace of this Zaidi doctrine. He wrote describing the rulers of Islamic countries using preachers to justify their oppression, stating the reason behind the preachers being led to go along with the sultans as self-love, and egotism. In contrast, the preachers claimed that they were doing it "in the interest of Islam and Muslims".

Dr. Ali al-Wardi was Iraqi to the core in everything. He was reproaching the Iraqi historians who attributed Abu Hanifa to the country of the Afghans, saying that he was an Iraqi man from the "Nabt (Nabateans) of Iraq" who settled in the Arab lands before the advent of Islam, that al-Hallaj was born white in the south and not the white of Persia, and Abd al-Qadir al-Jilani was born in Iraq, not in Jilan (or Gilan), Tabaristan, in the light of historical narrations that are "intentionally neglected" that stress their Iraqi birth. He adds that the ratio of al-Jawahiri to Faris, Persia, who is the Iraqi of the heart, and he was saddened by the ratio of the symbols of Baghdad to others.

His Books

Ali Al-Wardi is considered to be the pioneer of sociology in Iraq, and he is one of the few who wrote about this society, dedicating his life to it. So far no one has succeeded him. He stated in an interview shortly before his death that he wrote several books and asked his heirs to publish them after his death. Despite the passage of more than ten years, these are yet to be published.

Al-Wardi is known to have written eighteen books and hundreds of research articles. Five of these books were written before the July 14, 1958 revolution, and were of a literary-critical style and had new enlightening and satirical content that the Iraqi reader was unfamiliar with. Therefore, his bold social ideas and opinions faced sharp criticism, especially in his book "The Preachers of the Sultans," which relies on the logic of Platonic preaching and guidance on the premise that human nature cannot reform by preaching alone and that preachers themselves do not follow the advice they preached to. At the same time, they live at the tables of the affluent. He emphasized that he criticizes preachers of religion, not religion itself.

It is narrated on the authority of Professor Hussein Ali Mahfouz; when asked in his late days about his friend and companion Ali al-Wardi, Was al-Wardi secular and not religious? And what does he remember about him? Mahfouz replied, "In al-Wardi, a trait that I hope everyone possesses is that he did not get upset with criticism and did not hate anyone. Instead, he rejoiced when someone criticized him... He definitely believed in God... But he transcended loyalty to narrow identities... He used to provoke people who criticised him... and had his own world... I don't think he did not pray..., maybe he was negligent with the obligatory duties..., but I remember when he was walking on the bridge reciting this verse from the Qur'an: *...and the night when it is quiet* always as an indication of his relationship with God.

As for the books he wrote post the July 14, 1958 revolution, they were characterized by a scientific nature. They represented his project to develop a social theory about the nature of Iraqi society. The foremost of these books was his study of the nature of the Iraqi society, Ibn Khaldun's logic and social glimpses of Iraq's modern history in eight Volumes. Al-Wardi benefited from Ibn Khaldun's proposals and considered him a true theorist and a careful study of Arab society at that time. Ibn Khaldun was the subject of his doctoral thesis. Al-Wardi was the first to call for an "Arab sociology" that studies Arab society in light of its geographic and cultural peculiarities, based on Ibn Khaldun's proposals. Al-Wardi focused on the Bedouin factor, its values, and its impact on the formation of the Arab personality.

Al-Wardi predicted the explosion of the current situation, as well as the roots of the fanaticism that control the personality of the Iraqi individual, which is a societal reality whose roots extend to values, social norms, sectarian, clan and partisan fanaticism whose remnants are still latent. As well as to the authoritarian tyranny, temporal and simultaneous, which encouraged and still encourages the reproduction and re-establishment of the old traditional social and cultural deposits, is still apparent to date.

In most of his propositions, he strongly carried on the classic style of rhetoric and enthusiasm that glorified and elevated the self without looking at its negative aspects and humiliation, which the elites used to do and spread even among the intellectuals.

No Iraqi writer or thinker like Ali Al-Wardi, has raised bold critical ideas. It is evident that he was subjected to criticism, defamation, and attack from the far right to the far left (where fifteen books and hundreds of articles were published around his ideas), until the well-known Iraqi proverb "like a reprehensible eaten fish" was applied to him.

Most of his proposals that filled his books and delivered in his lectures disturbed the ruling authority, which gradually restricted him. This started with withdrawing the title of "expert professor" and ended with withdrawing most of his books from libraries and banning them, doing so in the pretext of what the government termed "intellectual safety", thus marginalizing him. He gradually felt financially strapped and finally died, forgotten, in July 1995 due to illness despite the treatment he had received in Jordanian hospitals. A modest funeral was held for him in which government officials were absent, and the mourners who attended did so at their own risk.

His social vision of the Iraqi individual

Ali Al-Wardi was the first Iraqi sociologist who studied the personality of the Iraqi individual and the nature of the Iraqi society with boldness and frankness, analysed hidden social phenomena and individual and collective behaviours, and drew attention to their study, analysis, and criticism. This prompted the reconsideration of intellectual, social, and political discourse and to the need to come down from our ivory towers and be aware of reality with all its positives and negatives.

More than half a century ago, Ali al-Wardi said that Iraqis should change themselves and reform their minds before starting to reform society because their harsh experiences taught them eloquent lessons. The Iraqis must get used to practising democracy so that it allows them freedom of opinion, understanding and dialogue without a group, tribe or sect imposing its opinion on others by force. He also said: "The Iraqi people are divided among themselves and have more tribal, national and sectarian strife than any other country. There is no way but to implement democracy, and the Iraqis should consider their past experiences, and if this opportunity slipped from our hands, it would have been lost for a long time." Ali al-Wardi believed that Iraq today stands at a crossroads. It has no choice but to practice (real) democracy, even in its simplest forms and mechanisms, as it is the only way out of this difficult crisis.

His Death

Ali Hussein Al-Wardi died on July 13, 1995, after a struggle with cancer. Doctors could not treat him because the Iraqi hospitals at that time lacked medicine and medical supplies due to the economic blockade imposed on Iraq, so he travelled to Jordan to receive treatment at Al-Hussein Medical City and then returned to Iraq, where he passed away.

At the time, the United States of America was accused of killing al-Wardi because of the unjust siege it had imposed on Iraq, which caused a dearth of food and medicine.

About the Translator

Yasin T. al-Jibouri is not only a translator but also a writer, published author, editor and simultaneous interpreter. He started his Islamic propagation activities in 1973 when he founded in Atlanta, Georgia, U.S.A. the Islamic Society of Georgia, Inc. while studying for his graduate degree. In January of the following year, he started editing and publishing *Islamic Affairs.* This bimonthly newspaper developed from a 4-page newsletter to a full 12-page bulletin. Its circulation at its peak covered all 50 American states in addition to 67 countries abroad. This popular newsletter ceased publication in 1989 when the financial support which maintained it weakened and weaned, becoming too inadequate to sustain it. Al-Jibouri kept translating and quoting the literary legacy of Ahlul-Bayt (as), incorporating what he translated into his bimonthly newsletter and translating and serializing books of martyr Muhammed-Baqir al-Sadr.

We can put al-Jibouri's works into three categories: the ones he wrote, others he edited and still others which he translated, the third category is the largest in number.

As for the ones he wrote, these include 1) his two-volume book titled *Allah: the Concept of God in Islam.* The original first edition in a single volume of 744 pages was published in Qom, the Islamic Republic of Iran, by Ansariyan, in 2001, then reprinted in 2007. This book has been translated into the Indonesian language, as have another he wrote about the fast of the month of Ramadhan and his translations of some of Muhammed-Bāqir al-Sadr's early works. Other editions of this book, including electronic ones, have been published by different Muslim organizations.

The two-volume new edition of his book titled *Allah: the Concept of God in Islam* was published by AuthorHouse of Bloomington, Indiana, in hardcover and later in softcover electronic editions. Volume One, published in 2012, falls in 532 pages, and Volume Two, published in 2013, falls in 631 pages. This is one of Yasin Publication's international books; it is available in as many as eighty countries.

Another book al-Jibouri wrote is titled *Fast of the Month of Ramadhan: Philosophy and Ahkam*. It is one of his earliest books. It was published in 1998 in both the U.S. by the author and in Iran by Ansariyan Publications of Qum.

Al-Jibouri also wrote *Mary and Jesus in Islam,* which was first published by Ansariyan in 2009 in modest 127 pages. The author published it in 2011 in the U.S. in 519 pages through AuthorHouse Publishers of Bloomington, Indiana, adding to it a Glossary of Islamic Terms. Another major original work is his book, *The Ninety-Nine Attributes of Allah* (470 pages). It is quite popular and is available in many formats.

Among his most important works are two books about Imam al-Hussain (as). One of them is titled *Kerbala and Beyond,* and the other carries the title *The Master of Martyrs* in two editions, one in print, one in full colour. The original edition of this book, published in hardcover by AuthorHouse, is 740 pages and is being marketed worldwide.

Another major work that al-Jibouri wrote together with Mr. Haider al-Jammali in three languages is *A Pictorial Tour of Imam Ali's Shrine in Arabic, English and Chinese.* In 2015, this book was showcased in China at the Beijing International Book Fair. Al-Jammali did the Chinese translation, edited by a Chinese university professor, Dr. Yufeng Chen, who works as a Professor at the School of Ethnology and Sociology at the Minzu University of China. She graciously edited the Chinese text free of charge and refused to let her photo be included in this excellent book... It fell in 441 colour pages and was published in 2015 by "Yasin Publications" in coordination with Amazon's CreateSpace.

Another major book al-Jibouri wrote is the 576-page book titled *Muhammed: Messenger of Peace and Tolerance.* Its first edition was published by AuthorHouse in hardcover, and now there are many editions of it in softcover and electronic editions. In 2016, this book was showcased at the London International Book Fair. This book is one of al-Jibouri's best. It was written in response to the rash of Islamophobia throughout the West which is funded, organized and fuelled by the Zionist news media and some Christian fanatics, the so-called Evangelicals, and has resulted in killing a number of Muslims in different countries for no reason other than being Muslim. Muslim women have been targeted more than others.

Fairly recently, al-Jibouri wrote a book about Khadija titled *Khadija Daughter of Khuwaylid: Wife of Prophet Muhammed* in English, Chinese and Spanish in 480 pages in two editions, one of which is in full colour. The date of its publication is June 16, 2016. Another book he wrote is titled *The Battle of the Camel of A.D. 656 When Muslims Killed Muslims for the First Time* in 480 pages; its date of publication is September 3, 2016. September 3, 2003, was when the author returned to his homeland, Iraq, 32 years after his last departure from it (in 1971).

Additionally, Yasin al-Jibouri has written some essays, which some Muslims published in booklet forms. Two examples are 1) his essay on the late Abul-Qāsim al-Khoei, which falls in only 26 pages, and 2) his essay titled Fatima (ع), the Daughter of Muhammed (ص): a Brief Biography which Talee published in 2014 and which e-Bay still markets globally.

The most important of the books he has edited is the Holy Qur'ān. He edited Muhammed-Habib Shakir's English translation of the Holy Qur'ān and the one done by SV Mir Ahmed Ali, and they have both been in print for many years. Another book al-Jibouri edited by Mr. Tahir al-Bayati is titled English in a *Simplified Way*, which Amazon has been marketing globally. Yasin al-Jibouri also edited a number of editions of *Noor al-Islam* magazine, which at the time was being published in Beirut, Lebanon, a series about the Fourteen Infallibles published in Beirut, Lebanon, by Imam Hussain Foundation, in 14 volumes, one volume per Ma`soom (Infallible) Imām.

Among al-Jibouri's most influential English translations is a book written by the late Muhammed-Jawad Fadhlallah, two editions of which are now available, one in black-and-white and one in full colour. One of al-Jibouri's translations was done for the office of late Grand Ayatollah Sayyid Muhammed Saeed al-Hakim, titled مُرشد المُغترب *Expatriate Guide* in 372 pages. This translation was published by "Talee" publishers on October 25, 2014, and has been marketed by Amazon since then. Another book al-Jibouri translated is titled *Originality of Humanity and Peace,* 134 pages which was written by an Iraqi scholar, Ayatollah Dr Fadhil al-Māliki, and Amazon has been marketing it since June 25, 2015.

Another translation al-Jibouri completed and is now being globally marketed by Amazon is titled *The Pristine Judiciary of Commander of the Faithful Ali ibn Abi Talib* in 258 colour pages. Al-Jibouri has also translated the first two Chapters (Suras) of the Holy Qur'ān in a new way, heavily applying punctuation marks to both Arabic and English texts and employing present-day English, bringing the meaning closer to the comprehension of the average English-speaking individuals in general and non-Muslims in particular. This translation of Al-Fatiha and Al-Baqara was first published on October 14, 2014, by Talee, and Amazon is still marketing it globally. It falls in 108 pages and contains both original Arabic text and al-Jibouri's English translation.

His translated works are numerous. The first book al-Jibouri translated was نظرة عامة في العبادات *A General Outlook at Rites* by Martyr Muhammed-Baqir al-Sadr which was published in Tehran, Iran, in 1979 by the World Organization for Islamic Services (WOFIS) when the revered martyr was still alive. The following year, WOFIS published another book by al-Sadr, which al-Jibouri translated, and which was initially written by martyr Muhammed-Baqir al-Sadr, namely الانسان المعاصر و المشكلة الاجتماعية *Contemporary Man and the Social Problem.* Some Iranian brothers in London, who then were operating under the business name "Talee", published it, and Amazon has been marketing it since 2014. Al-Jibouri translated two other works by al-Sadr: 1) ماذا تعرف عن الاقتصاد الاسلامي؟ *What do You Know about the Islamic Economy?* and 2) الأسس العامة للبنك في المجتمع الاسلامي *The General Bases for the Bank in the Islamic Society* which unfortunately was lost when the translator changed his residence from Maryland to Virginia in 1982. The first of these titles on Islamic economics was published in 1990 by the Imamia Center in Lanham, Maryland, U.S.A. Later, the translator thought of combining all the translations he completed of martyr al-Sadr's books into one volume with biographies of three prominent Sadr martyrs: the first and the second Sadr martyrs in addition to the martyred "Bint al-Huda", namely Āmina al-Sadr, sister of Martyr Muhammed-Baqir al-Sadr, together with the biography of the Second Sadr Martyr, Sayyid Muhammed Muhammed-Sadiq al-Sadr, in a book he wrote titled *A Tribute to the Sadr Martyrs*. This Tribute book was published first in hardcover by AuthorHouse in 2014 in 346 pages.

The list of books al-Jibouri translated includes less famous titles which Ansariyan of Qum, Iran, published. They have the following titles: *The Truth about the Shi`a Ithna-`Ashari Faith* by a Palestinian doctor, As`ad Wahid al-Qāsim أسعد وحيد القاسم (160 pages, 2004), *Al-Siraj: the Lantern on the Path to Allah* by Sheikh Hussain ibn Ali ibn Sadiq al-Bahrani (151 pages, 2004), *Pretension and Conceit* by Sayyid Ahmed al-Fahri, *Kashf al-Reeba an Ahkam al-Gheeba* (removing doubt from backbiting-related rulings) by Taqi ad-Din Ibrahim ibn Ali al-`Āmili (104 pages, 2008), *Soothing the heart of the bereaved* (*Musakkin al-Fuad*) of "Second Martyr" Zayn al-Din Ali ibn Ahmad al-Jab`i al-`Āmili (271 pages, 2022) **(Published by Lantern Publications)**, and *The Model of the Gnostics* (*Uswat al-`Ārifeen*), biography of Ayatollah Bahjat (181 pages, 2008) and many others.

The translator now spends his last years in his hometown, Holy al-Kādhimiyya, northwestern Baghdad, Iraq.

Lantern Publications **September 2022**

Introduction

This volume covers four years, namely, from 1920 to 1924. This is a period of great importance in Iraq's modern history because during these years, the Iraqi government was established, and the foundations of the government were laid down according to a particular way. I would like here to reiterate what I had stated in the Introduction to Volume One of this series, which is: I am not a historian. My objective behind narrating historical events is to discover behind them the features of the social phase through which Iraq passed. As a result, the reader may notice in this volume, as he did in previous volumes, many specific details, and interesting incidents which historians generally do not mention. From the social standpoint, however, (such details and incidents) are of significant importance because they reveal the nature of the values and traditions that prevailed during a specific period of time, as well as the level of thinking of people at the time.

I have here to briefly talk about the sources on which I have relied in the study of this period. Primarily, I have relied on the research of historians, but I have also relied on other sources as follows:

1.   **British Documents**: They include top-secret correspondence between the British government and its representatives abroad, such as ambassadors, consuls, delegates, residents and others. The British government only permitted the publication of these documents 50 years after their (original) dates. It recently decreased the period to 30 years, placing them in a special directorate in London which is open for researchers and calling it the "Public Records Office." I visited that office

in the summer of 1973 and became familiar with many of its files. I also obtained copies of some of them. I do not hide from the reader the fact that I found in them secrets that made me change my mind about many issues which I was in the past confident that I was right about.

2.	**Letters of Ms. (Gertrude) Bell**: This lady used to occupy the post of eastern secretary to the (British) high commissioner in Iraq. She used to record her memories in 1927 in the form of letters. One year after her death, i.e. in 1928, it became clear that another portion of her letters was kept hidden, and its publication was banned. This portion remained hidden until 1961, when it was published in two large volumes. In fact, the part that was published later contains secrets that are no less important or unusual than the secrets (found within) the British documents. I prefer Ms Bell's letters over the British documents from some aspects and consider them to be more factual in depicting reality. (The official British) documents usually follow a dry, formal style and do not touch on events except from

Gertrude Margaret Lowthian Bell
(Courtesy: Verve pictures)

their formal aspect. As for Ms Bell's letters, they are alive and full of warmth and give us many psychological and social images, the like of which we seldom find in documents. This is the reason that made me rely on Ms Bell's letters and quote them in this Volume.

3.	**University Theses**:
These are dissertations submitted by some students of graduate studies at Baghdad University and elsewhere in order to obtain a Master's or a PhD degree in history. I admit that these theses benefitted me in writing this volume immeasurably, especially the theses from the History Department of the College of Arts, Baghdad University.

4.	**Memoirs of Iraqi Politicians**: These are many in number. Their memoirs may contradict each other in the narration of events, but their contradiction provides us with different viewpoints about those events, and this may help us understand some of their hidden matters. We must not forget that some Britons who took part in the events of that period also recorded their memoirs, thus giving us other viewpoints.

5.   **The Views of Contemporary Elders**: They are many, but unfortunately, their number is shrinking as time passes by. In fact, the words and views of elders are indispensable for understanding past events and disclosing some of their neglected aspects. In my opinion, the words of illiterate elders may sometimes be more useful to the researcher than those of educated folk. An educated person may try to depict the events in a way that suits his ideological trends or political affiliation. As for the illiterate one, he narrates them as he witnessed them and without embellishments. Although his narration may be superficial and naïve, it may reveal some hidden aspects of those events. These aspects are usually ignored by educated people.

6.   **Old Local Newspapers**: We do not have to state the significance of these newspapers while studying past events. Many more advanced countries have invested in preserving collections of old newspapers and enabling researchers to easily access them. Unfortunately, we [Iraqis] - and until only recently - did not care about safeguarding newspapers. Some of our cultural institutions, such as the [National] Museum's Library, the Scientific Assembly, the Central Library, the National Records Center and the National Library, have exerted great efforts in buying collections of newspapers available from private individuals, paying huge sums of money for them. Despite all of this, they could not get all of them. Presently, a researcher may sometimes face difficulty in finding the newspaper they are looking for.

7.   **Iraqi Records**: We now have a directorate for public records called the "National Records Center," but this directorate is new; it was only established in 1963. It contains half a million files collected from various government directorates. The most important among them are the royal palace's files. But this directorate, unfortunately, suffers from an acute shortage of specialists and staff. File folders have been piled up in unfit rooms, posing a serious danger to them. Many of them have actually

been damaged. We do not deny the fact that they are now in a much better condition than previously. I have recently come to know that the Iraqi government has set a budget of three million dinars for building a document assembly (archives), and we hope that it will soon be built because records form a wealth of their own. I was able to review some files of the royal palace, especially those related to the time period which I am researching, and I found remarkable things in them. Had all Iraqi records been accessible to researchers, unknown pages of great significance in Iraq's modern history would have been unveiled.

About Grammatical Rules

In my introduction to the fourth volume of this series, I criticized Arabic grammar, demanding the shrinking of its rules because they are numerous (and often) useless. This criticism created a [negative] reaction among many readers. I have to explain here my position in relation to grammar once more.

I wish the reader would come to know that I am not the only one who demands the shrinking of the rules of grammar. It is, in fact, an urgent civilizational necessity that many people have realized. The Moroccan "Al-`Ilm" newspaper made this point on March 30, 1974, by saying: "Despite efforts of more than half a century, [Arabic] grammar remains un-simplified and is still debated; therefore, the Union of Arab Linguistic Assemblies has invited Egypt, Syria and Iraq to hold a seminar in Cairo this year to discuss the topic of simplifying grammar."

I do not know what happened to this invitation and whether the seminar was held or not, but I, at any rate, categorically believe that keeping grammar as it is severely harms our civilizational march. It leads to much waste of our intellectual efforts without yielding any benefit. A grammar specialist said to me once that three-quarters of the grammatical rules - which are currently being taught at schools - can be discarded without causing any harm. In fact, I do not understand why some educated people amongst us are so fanatical about grammar while knowing that most grammatical rules were created by mercenary grammarians in the Abbasid age and in the one that followed it in order to turn it into a tool for class distinction, i.e. so that the affluent class would be able to be pedant in its language to the extent it would be difficult for commoners to cope with it.[1]

I do not deny that grammatical rules exist in all world languages and that there is no language in the world without grammar, but languages vary amongst themselves in terms of how easy or difficult their grammar is. During a visit to Poland, I found its language to be distinguished because of numerous complicated grammatical rules. However, what I noticed is that the Polish people do not have great difficulty in this regard because they apply rules in the colloquial language which people speak in their everyday life and in which a child is born, so he becomes used to it and, as time passes, he finds it to be normal. Here is the source of the difference between that and our own [Arabic] grammatical rules: our child is not born into them; rather, he learns them only at school. After he is tested on them in an exam, he then forgets them. For this reason, we do not find - except quite rarely - among our educated people those who are capable of extemporarily delivering a speech while fully adhering to all the rules of grammar. When such an individual appears, he feels as if he has a very precious talent, and he may race to ascend the podium on every occasion - and sometimes without any occasion - in order to demonstrate his "brilliant genius" to the public.

As the reader knows, I decided to violate two grammatical principles that are taught in our schools: 1- the parsing of modern proper nouns such as "Faisal", "Abul-Ḥassan", "Muḥammad-'Ali", etc.; 2- the eliminating of the "y" [or "i"] from shortened proper nouns such as "Sami", "Kafi", "Radhi", "Sari", etc. What is strange is that some grammarians came to me to tell me that the violating of both of these principles was licensed by ancient grammarians and that I did not bring about anything new. I answered them by saying, "If what you say is right, why are both of these principles taught at schools? Why does a student flunk if he violates them?" This means that modern grammarians are more rigid and fanatical than the ancient ones, and I do not know when Allah the Almighty will save the nation from this dilemma!

---

[1] I have discussed this subject in detail in my book titled *Ustūrat al-Adab al-Rafī'* (myth of the lofty literature) which was published in 1957.

Appreciation

On this occasion, I have to express my appreciation of those who helped me write this volume and those whom I forgot to thank in the previous volumes. In particular, I would like to mention those in charge of the Library of the College of Arts and those of the Central Library, the Museum's Library, the National Records Center, the National Library, the Library of the Scientific Assembly, the Library of Higher Studies at the College of Arts, and the Library of the Sociology Department of the College of Arts. I also thank Sheikh Mahdi al-Khalisi Junior, who lent me all the documents and draft memoirs in his possession. I (also) thank the following honoured gentlemen: Salmān al-Safwāni, Sami Khundah, Abdul-Razzaq al-Fadhli, Ahmed al-Rawi, Abdul-Hamīd al-Yasiri, Ṣahib Shawkat, Abdul-Hādi al-Zāhir and both late Ahmed Zaki al-Khayyat and Maḥdi al-Basīr, for allowing me to review their memoirs, or to talk to me about some events which they witnessed. To all of these men and to others whose names fail my memory at this moment, I express my sincere thanks.

Chapter 1

The Forming of The Iraqi Government

We pointed out in the fifth volume of this series that Sr. Percy [Zachariah] Cox was summoned to London on June 6, 1920, when he was minister plenipotentiary of Britain in Tehran, for a consultation about setting up a temporary administration in Iraq. On Cox's way to London, a revolution erupted in Iraq, and when he reached London, he found in (the city) a storm (that had formed) in relation to this revolution. In his report, Cox says the following:

> "Few days after reaching London, I found out that English public opinion was greatly upset about the conditions in Iraq. A great deal of agitation took place at a team of British newspapers which demanded the government to withdraw from Iraq and to end the losses it was suffering there. The British government itself was very upset because of the disturbing telegrams that it was receiving from Baghdad. There was great difference of opinion about the best plan which must be followed. Anyhow, it was clear that the revolution had to be quelled before implementing any plan in Iraq. The question in mind became: what do we do after stability returns to Iraq? Should we stop our losses, abandon the mandate and withdraw from Iraq? Or should we install a national government if it is (even) possible that such a

government will succeed? When I was asked about my opinion in this regard, and in my capacity as the officer who was present in the location where events were taking place, I answered that the thought of withdrawing from Iraq could not be entertained. (Such a step) would not only lead to abandoning Iraq and [wasting] seven or eight million pounds of capital which we spent in Iraq but at the same time, it would by itself be a serious breach of all pledges which we made to the Arabs during the World War. Also, the country would return to chaos and to Turkish rule as soon as we leave Iraq. Finally, our evacuation from Iraq would stir active hatred towards us among the population we betrayed, and we would need another military division to secure our evacuation from the country. With regards to the question of the possibility of the success of installing a national government, my answer was that the matter deserved the risk if we regarded it as the only option instead of the evacuation, although I was not fully confident of it. After lengthy discussions, I was asked if I was ready to bear the burden of setting up a national government in Iraq if opinion settles on it. I answered affirmatively."[1]

Farewell And Reception

The British government accepted Cox's proposal and commissioned him to set up a national government in Iraq. On August 20, 1920, Cox left Britain by sea route accompanied by his wife and three men to assist him in his mission; one of them was [Harry St. John Bridger] Philby[2].

---

[1] Lady Bell, *The Letters of Gertrude Bell* (London: E. Benn, 1947), pp. 426-427.

[2] His full name is Harry St. John Bridger Philby (April 3, 1885 – September 30, 1960), also known as Jack Philby or "Sheikh Abdullah," the name given to him by some Arabs. He was an Arabist, explorer, writer and British colonial intelligence officer educated at Westminster School and Trinity College, Cambridge, where he studied oriental languages. Philby was a friend and Cambridge classmate of late Indian prime minister Jawaharlal Nehru. – Tr.

On his way to Iraq, Sir Arnold Wilson - who was occupying the post of acting general political governor - was getting ready to leave. On September 19, Sayyid Talib al-Naqīb held a farewell party for Wilson in Baghdad, during which [poet] Jamīl Sidqi al-Zahawi delivered a speech in which he praised Wilson's services to Iraq, denouncing the revolution and the revolutionaries. Sayyid Talib delivered another speech carrying the same meaning. Wilson finally stood up and thanked the host and attendants, expressing his regret for being unable to continue to serve Iraq.

On the next day, another party was held at the Railroad Office in which Wilson delivered a lengthy speech the text of which he recorded in his memoirs. In it, he attributed the reason behind the revolution first to the British policy, which encouraged nationalism in Iraq without sending specific orders to set up a local government at the right time, and second, to the leaders of the opposition, whom he described as being short-sighted, fanatical and anarchist.[1]

On September 24, Wilson left Baghdad by train to Basra. After him, Talib [al-Naqeeb] left it in order to welcome Cox. In the evening of October 1, Cox and his entourage reached Basra. A large crowd of people was there to welcome them in the vanguard of which were Wilson and Talib. On the next day, a big party was held in Basra's gardens to honour Cox, which was attended by Sheikh Khaz`al[2] [photo of the sheikh above]. In the evening of the same day, Sayyid Talib threw a luxurious banquet in his mansion, which overlooks Shatt al-Arab in the Sabīliyyat area. In that banquet, Basra's dignitaries gifted an honour

---

[1][A.T.] Wilson, *Loyalties,* Vol. 2, London, 1932, pp. 318-320.

[2]His name is: Sheikh Khaz`al son of Jabir al-Ka`bi (1863 – 1936), governor of al-Muhammara sheikhdom in Ahwaz, Iran, from 1897 to 1925 and the last of its emirs. It is said that he was poisoned in 1936 after Iran had arrested him in 1925. – Tr.

sword to Wilson on the occasion of his leaving Iraq, and Abdul-Latīf al-Mandīl and Muzahim al-Pachachi delivered speeches praising the services which Wilson rendered to Iraq. Wilson recorded in his memoirs a portion of al-Pachachi's speech, an excerpt of which we would like to quote here:

> "I very much regret the foolishness of the Arab individuals who disturbed the English nation in its honourable mission. These actions were committed because of dreams which, on the one hand, cannot be realized and, on the other hand, for personal gains. The present movement - meaning the revolution - is not purely Arab. Rather, it is a movement in which a foreign element is mixed, one which quite regrettably has been successful in taking advantage of fame, wealth and Arab blood for its own self-interest in order to weaken the position of Great Britain in other countries. So, do not let appearances deceive you, which mostly are deceptive, especially in the East, and do not regard the present revolution, which some bedouin tribes are carrying out, as a truly nationalist revolution seeking independence, for such a movement cannot be regarded as representing the sentiments of the entire society. The influential families in Baghdad do not sympathize with a movement that has ruined their homeland. These are the sentiments of people whose opinions carry weight, and they are eager to transmit their thoughts and sentiments to those who in Britain demand the withdrawal from this land. They cannot realize that withdrawal does not mean anything less than violating the sanctity of the law and destroying the people and whatever follows the spread of chaos throughout the country, something which implies the eruption of an Asian war from which Britain cannot be isolated."[1]

---

[1] *Ibid.*, Vol. 2, p. 321.

In the morning of the next day, honor guards stood in a line on the port's wharf to bid Wilson goodbye. In his memoirs, Philby says this about Wilson:

"I talked to him before his departure. I found him bitterly disappointed with how things in general went on, particularly with the newly proposed government system. This meant the end of his embellished dreams about Iraq as a shining jewel in the English crown. In the end, sorrow overwhelmed me when I saw him leave. His great characteristics, which are not debated, were now shattered because of a worn-out, deranged opinion. The structure which he tried to erect had collapsed, becoming worn-out ruins at an ear's shot from him. A disappointment of this sort has no room in it for mercy."[1]

Philby And Sayyid Talib

Cox stayed in Basra for a few days. He flew to Nasiriyya, Imara, Qurna and Qal`at-Salih, where he discussed with city dignitaries and tribal chiefs the mission for which he had come. Having finished his discussions, he left Basra with his entourage on board a river ship heading to Baghdad. On board the ship, Sayyid Talib al-Naqeeb was in his company.

A meeting and a special talk took place on board the ship between Philby and Sayyid Talib. Philby had already become acquainted with Sayyid Talib before then in Alexandria, Egypt. When they met on board the ship, Sayyid Talib revealed his secret to him; that is, he was ambitious to become Iraq's king under British auspices. Philby kept this secret to himself without revealing it to anyone, not even to his boss Cox.

I imagine Philby at that time, wanted to undertake a role similar to the one undertaken by Lawrence [of Arabia] in Hijaz during the war. Perhaps Philby was looking for an Iraqi dignitary who would somehow

---

[1]John Philby, *Philby's Days in Iraq* (translated by Ja`far al-Khayyat), Beirut, Lebanon, pp. 38-39.

help him perform this role as Faisal did with Lawrence. It can be said that Philby found what he was looking for in the person of Sayyid Talib. In other words, Philby probably aspired to earn international fame of the type that Lawrence had won in his adventures across Arab lands. We can see this from what Philby wrote in his memoirs when describing Sayyid Talib following his meeting with him on board that ship. In this regard, he says the following:

> "In fact, I had great hope in his future. It was clear that he was the most distinguished personality in Iraq in terms of brilliance and strength of character. But he was greatly reckless and conceited; therefore, he was feared by the public and disliked by most. If his good qualities could be utilized and fully put to use, I predict that his role will be to administer Iraq's future destiny for many years, which most likely comes from the positions which circumstances and conditions dictate, such as the post of head of an administration for example, or president of a republic. Since then, I kept leading him to assume one of these two roles. I must admit here that he was a qualified and able student provided the hand that trains him must have some affection and friendship. Perhaps we could have succeeded with him had certain circumstances not stood in the way."

What is strange is that at the time when Philby discovered Sayyid Talib and decided to train him, Ms Bell started entertaining fears about Sayyid Talib in Baghdad and tried to destroy him. It is thought that Sasson Hisqail (Ezekiel) is the one who caused her to have concerns about Sayyid Talib, for this man used to fully hold Sayyid Talib in contempt, and Ms Bell — from her end — very much admired Sasson Hisqail and was influenced by his views.

On October 10, Ms Bell wrote saying that she kept meeting with Sasson Hisqail for a number of days, and a nice chat went on between them about Sayyid Talib in which he frankly said to her:

> "People hate Sayyid Talib, but they pretend they love him for

fear of him; therefore, if they come to know that the British support him, they would pretend that they accept it regardless of what they hide in their hearts towards him."

Sasson narrated to her an incident that he personally witnessed when he and Sayyid Talib were returning to Basra on the same ship late during the Ottoman period. He said:

"Believe me, Khatoon, all people of Basra went out to Muhammara to welcome Sayyid Talib, and they all, without any exception, hated and feared him. Those who hated him the most were the most to show affection to him, for they were that day afraid of him, and they remain to be so till this very day."

Ms Bell did not like Sayyid Talib reaching Baghdad accompanied by Cox because if Sayyid Talib reached it with Cox, the latter would exert his effort to appear as though he was flattering him, introducing him to the public under his auspices; therefore, Ms Bell sent a telegram to Cox and suggested to him to dispatch Sayyid Talib to Baghdad before him. Cox did as Ms Bell had suggested. He and his entourage stayed in Kut for one day, sending Sayyid Talib to Baghdad by train. Train service was then available between Kut and Baghdad.

Cox's Arrival

Cox and his entourage arrived on October 11 at 5:30 pm. A splendid reception was prepared for him at the Bab al-Sheikh (train) Station. On top of those who welcomed him were Sayyid Talib and Gen. Holden. 17 artillery rounds were fired, and the military music played the "God save the King" piece, referring, of course, to King George V.

After the welcoming party had been introduced to Cox, poet Jameel Sidqi al-Zahawi stepped forward and delivered a 43-line poem praising the English people and denouncing the revolution. The following are sample verses from it:

Go back to Iraq to repair what has been damaged,
Spread in it justice and grant its people prosperity.
Iraq is pleased to see him
A father to it coming from the land of justice,
Have compassion on a nation sought by evil seekers
Intending to spread evil in it which it does not seek.
They thought that guidance lies in what they brought
But it may be misguidance, not guidance at all
They said: perhaps the revolution will gain for the people
Happiness, but the people gained no happiness at all
So what a blind rebellious sedition it is,
One that has tormented the soul and the body of its people!
Be supported by people who saw sedition in their land
But they did not support those who were behind sedition.[1]

Having finished reciting his poem, al-Zahawi delivered a speech in which he denounced the revolution. From what he said was this: "After you, O' compassionate father, the security which you established in the lands of Iraq has disappeared, seditions, turmoil and fears have unfortunately now replaced it, so do provide full comfort."[2]

Once al-Zahawi finished his speech, Cox stood up to speak. He said:

> "Jameel Afandi, delegates, the government of England sent me to help, to make an agreement with Iraq's chiefs and men of honour to achieve the goal which both sides seek and to form the Arab government, an independent government overseen by the government of England, and I have come for this purpose. But deception continues. Of course, this cannot

---

[1] Ibrahim al-Wā'ili, *Thawrat al-'Ishrin fil Shi'r al-Iraqi* (the 1920 Revolution in Iraqi poetry), Baghdad, 1968, pp. 153-158.

[2] *Al-Iraq* newspaper of October 12, 1920.

be done; I am available when the opportunity is there, and this is in your hands."[1]

It seems that the reception did not go well. Ms Bell pointed this out in one of her letters, saying that the reception party at the [train] station angered many Baghdadi dignitaries and tribal sheikhs who were invited. Some of those men went to her in her office the next day complaining about the insult inflicted upon them there because only a small number of those who were invited were allowed to enter the station. As for most of them, they were crowded outside the fence in the dusty weather, so they could not shake hands with Sir Percy Cox. A respected tribal sheikh, in his extreme anger, said to her, "We came to express our love and obedience, but when we tried to get close to His Excellency, they pushed us far away." This happened even to al-Naqeeb's brothers.[2]

Angry Britons

Since the moment he reached Baghdad, Cox started being called the "high commissioner". Before then, he used to be called the "general political governor" which was meant to point out that he was no longer ruling Iraq but was delegated by Britain to set up a national government in it.

Cox appointed Ms Bell as his "Eastern Secretary". In cooperation with Philby, Ms Bell started working on preparing a list of 100 dignitaries to meet Cox. She also prepared another list of elite names of men with whom Cox should personally consult about the system of government to be established in Iraq. *Al-Iraq* newspaper made reference to the meeting which was held by Cox with the elite folks. That meeting took place on the morning of October 13 when Cox talked about forming a caretaker government; therefore, Sayyid Ibrahim al-Rawi stood up and talked about the need to assist the English government. Then Sheikh Kadhim al-Dujaili stood up and delivered a lengthy speech in which he explained the

---

[1] Abdul-Razzaq al-Hassani, *Al-Thawra al-Iraqiyya al-Kubra* (the great Iraqi revolution), Saida, Lebanon, 1972, p. 252.

[2] Lady Bell (cited above), pp. 455-456.

ongoing incidents of turmoil — meaning events of the revolution — and said that they resulted from the misunderstanding that extremists from both sides had created. Had both sides been lenient and understanding, it would have brought happiness to Iraq.[1]

As Cox was carrying out his deliberations, a large group of British officials in Iraq were not pleased with these deliberations and with the new policy which the British government began following in Iraq. Ireland says the following in this regard:

> "Many administrative officers were sceptical about forming an Arab government, so much so that they did not hide their feelings against it. Most of them were supportive of and loyal to Wilson and to his opinion about the role which Britain should undertake in Iraq, and they could not accept the new viewpoint which Cox had brought."[2]

The Britons who opposed Cox's plan were immersed in what is called the "message of the white man" in modernizing nations. Their opinion was that if full independence was granted to the Iraqis to rule themselves, they would consume each other; therefore, it was the obligation of Britain to continue to rule Iraq for a sufficient period of time till the Iraqis became accustomed to modern civilian life and abandon their old tribal customs in raiding, avenging and bloodshedding.

In 1923, a book was published in London which reflected the viewpoint of an author named Thomas Lyell, who was in those days a government employee in Iraq. This man was not satisfied with saying that the Iraqis were not competent to rule but generalized his statement to all Muslims, particularly the Shi`as. He says the following in the Introduction to his book:

> "I am strongly convinced as a result of my personal knowledge that the Islamic religion is not progressive and

---

[1] --*Al-Iraq* newspaper of October 17, 1920.

[2] Philip Willard Ireland, *Iraq: A study in Political Development* (translated by Ja`far Khayyat, Beirut, 1949), p. 217.

that it weakens one's personality and destroys any patriotic inclination, social cohesion or national ambition. This conviction has prompted me to say that the Muslim individual, particularly the Shi`a, must remain for several years completely unfit for self-rule. He seeks self-rule because he finds in it an opportunity to get rid of law and order."[1]

Lyell directed his blame at Cox and at his aides, who were distorting Cox's image and regarding his policy as the main reason for the revolution. Lyell regarded Wilson as a great man and rendered the reason behind the revolution to the tribes being in a continuous revolution against every government and that they found themselves during Wilson's time surrendering to law and order for the first time in their history. Lyell says that the revolution was supposed to take place before the time when it actually did and that the reason behind this delay is all due to the persistent efforts which Wilson exerted. Then Lyell goes on to say:

"There is no man who deserves the essential support of the citizens of his country like Sir Arnold Wilson. But they, despite that, abandoned him time and time again, and hence those who are in England defamed him, even those who used to work under him. It is unfortunate that the new board — meaning Cox and his aides — encourages people's sentiments against the administration of Sir Arnold Wilson. Hence, the first of this board's measures was to summon the polluting Suweedi and to issue an amnesty for those whom Wilson had punished. As for those who ran away for fear of being punished, he demanded their return, lowering the taxes for everyone, so the Arabs started loudly praising the government."

Lyell says that this new policy of lowering taxes, especially for the sheikhs who led the revolution, will have an impact on the English tax

---

[1]Thomas Lyell, *The Ins and Outs of Mesopotamia* (London, 1923), p. 7.

payer without having behind it any justification. Then he demonstrates his pain due to statement of an enthusiast from among Cox's supporters who spoke before a crowd of Baghdadis, criticizing Wilson rashly without stopping for a moment to think of the impact of his speech on Eastern minds.[1]

Cox kept walking along his path, heedless of the opposition of these folks. He knew what they did not. Ireland says, "Since Sir. Percy Cox was convinced that the situation required either the forming of an Arab government or the evacuation of the British from the country, he walked along his path despite the pleas in the official circles."[2]

Choosing A Head Of Administration

Cox set his mind on first forming a caretaker government. With regards to the subject of choosing an emir or a king for the country, he put it off for later.

The first problem that faced Cox in this regard was: who would be in charge of presiding over the presumed caretaker government? In the beginning, Cox was of the view of nominating Sayyid Talib to preside over the government, but the consultations he held with his advisers made him change his mind.[3]

Cox and his advisers were of the view that the best (person) to preside over the government would be the *naqeeb*, the chief of Baghdad's dignitaries, namely Abdul-Rahman al-Gailani[4], but the problem was: will this *naqeeb* agree?

---

[1]*Ibid.*, pp. 204-210.

[2]Philip Ireland (opt. cit.), p. 217.

[3]*Ibid.*, p. 218.

[4]Abdul-Rahman al-Gailani, head of the first Iraqi cabinet of ministers (ministerial council), was born in Baghdad on Sunday, Rajab 1, 1261 A.H./July 6, 1845 and died in it on Monday, the second day of Eidul-Adha (Feast of Sacrifice), i.e. Thul-Hijja 12, 1345 A.H./June 13, 1927. He presided over three cabinets: The first he put together on October 25, 1920 which resigned on August 23, 1921; he formed the second on September 10, 1921 and it resigned on August 19, 1922. The third and

This *naqeeb* was at the time 78 years old, (suffered from) arthritis, and moreover, his mind was not set on this world and its positions. He usually described himself as being a *darvish*. Add to this the fact that he regarded accepting positions under the shade of the English rule as demeaning to his religious status in the eyes of his followers throughout the world. In a report which she wrote in 1919, Ms Bell says that she offered that year to make him the emir of Iraq, but he strongly refused. She says in this report that she visited him at his house on February 6, 1919. After a lengthy talk with him, she asked him:

"If the necessity of the political reasons, which cannot be predicted in advance, dictates that an emir is to be installed as head of the Iraqi state, will you be able to accept such a responsibility with our help and support so that we may avoid having to choose an emir from Hijaz?"

His answer was accompanied by a strong emphasis:

"How can you ask me such a question? I am a *darvish*; will this habit of mine not protect me?" He kept making the well-known signal of moving his black *jubba* (cloak). Then he went on to say, "If they make me a political head of the state, it is against the most deeply rooted principles of my faith. During the days of my grandfather, Abdul-Qadir, the Abbasid caliphs used to consult him just as you and your fellows are now asking for my advice, but he never agreed to participate in public affairs, and neither I nor any of his grandsons shall agree to do that. This is my answer from a religious standpoint. But I am going to give you an answer based on personal reasons. I am advanced in age, and I wish to spend the last five or six years of my life studying and contemplating, for they both continuously occupy my time."

---

last cabinet he put together started its official work on July 28, 1922, and resigned on November 16, 1922. – Tr.

After remaining silent for a short while, he raised his voice as he said, "I shall never go back on what I have just said, even if it means saving Iraq from complete destruction."[1]

Whatever the case may be, Cox decided to try his luck and to go to the *naqeeb* in person to offer him the presidency of the administration. He actually went to him on October 23. Ms Bell says that as she was sitting in her office with Philby on that day, Sir Percy Cox entered, panting with excitement and saying, "Yes, he has accepted it!" Ms Bell comments saying:

> "Thus did the first success take place, and there was nobody there other than Sir Percy who could do it. In fact, convincing the *naqeeb* to participate in public matters is close to a miracle. The elation of Sir Percy about this success equalled our own, so we remained for half an hour flying with pleasure and with praise of the *naqeeb* as we praise the high commissioner."[2]

Here, we are faced with an important question: how was Cox able to convince the *naqeeb* to bear the responsibility of presiding over the administration? In other words, what is the reason that made the *naqeeb* accept to preside over the administration in 1920, whereas in the previous year, he used to categorically reject being the emir of Iraq?!

We do not find in all the references before us that which reveals the secret of this amazing shift in the *naqeeb's* position, and it is a secret that researchers ought to study and discover.

Some evidence indicates that Cox was able to convince the *naqeeb* by playing on some sensitive chords in his heart. It is known that the *naqeeb* held the revolution and those who were behind it in strong contempt. He also held in contempt the *mujtahids* who supported the revolution with their *fatwas* (religious edicts). He also loathed putting the

---

[1]Ms. Bell, *Chapters of Iraq's Recent History* (translated by Ja`far al-Khayyat, Beirut, Lebanon, 1971), pp. 480-481.

[2]Lady Bell (op. cit.), p. 460.

reins of government in the hands of anyone from among the common people. Actually, his opinion was that placing these reigns it should be in the hands of the nobility from among the sons of renowned families, people of lineage and distinction. It is thought that when Cox went to the *naqeeb* to talk to him about forming the administration, he kept playing on such sensitive chords, and he may have mentioned to him that his acceptance of the responsibility was an obligation imposed by customs and traditions, (and) that if he did not do so, he would fall short of performing his duty towards his homeland as well as religious beliefs. I imagine that Cox warned him that if he did not accept the responsibility, he would be forced to place it in the hands of people from the group which he very much held in contempt, and this would lead to the country's destruction. Ireland says, "Cox pleaded to the *naqeeb* via his duty towards the country, hinting to him about others' personal ambitions and the extent of damage that would take place if he did not form the administration."[1]

Choosing Cabinet Ministers

After the *naqeeb* had accepted to preside over the government, another problem surfaced: choosing its members. This was not an easy concern under those circumstances. Some well-known men did not accept to participate in the government due to their belief that doing so would tarnish their image in the eyes of the public. Also, other men had other reasons which prevented them from joining the administration. Ms Bell talks to us in her letters about the difficulty which she faced in trying to convince some candidates. For example, she talks about Ja`far al-`Askari, who was nominated for the defence ministry. Only a few days had passed since his return from Syria. He went to her and asked for her opinion about whether his participation in the cabinet would ruin his national reputation because people would regard the cabinet as an English game.

---

[1]Philip Ireland, p. 219.

Ms Bell strongly rebuked him for saying so, and she kept arguing with him until she convinced him to agree.[1]

After Ja`far al-`Askari, the role of Sayyid Talib [al-Naqeeb] came: he was nominated for interior ministry. But Sayyid Talib was indignant, feeling that this was an insult because he could not rank as second to anyone else, not even to the *naqeeb* himself. Therefore, Ms Bell, in cooperation with Philby, tried to convince him. He was not convinced except after asking them to announce that he came directly after the *naqeeb* in rank. So, if the *naqeeb* was sick, or if he died, Sayyid Talib would take his place. Anyhow, Talib wanted to be awarded the highest honours and be surrounded by a large number of bodyguards[2]. Philby says in his memoirs that he was at the time in continuous contact with Sayyid Talib, whom he advised to be patient. He also advised him to go along with Cox's plans so the caretaker government could be formed.[3]

When Sayyid Talib was convinced, Sasson Hisqail, who was nominated for the ministry of finance, declared his refusal. This man did not like to be a minister together with Sayyid Talib in one cabinet. Ms Bell describes the efforts that she, Philby and Clayton exerted to convince him. She says the following in this regard:

> "Major Yates visited me for tea in the afternoon accompanied by Mr Todd and his wife. Mr Todd surprised us by saying that when he went to congratulate Sasson Afandi for his nomination for the ministry of finance, both he and Hamdi Pasha Baban (who offered him the position of minister without a portfolio) found him in a status of refusal. So I left the tea beaker without drinking tea and rushed back to the office to tell Mr Philby. He was not there, but I noticed that there was light in Sir. Percy's room; therefore, I went and told him. He ordered me to go immediately to Sasson Afandi,

---

[1][Elizabeth] Burgoyne, *Gertrude Bell: From Her Personal Letters 1914 - 1926* (op. cit.) [Abe Books, 1958], Vol. 2, p. 175.

[2]*Ibid.*, Vol. 2, p. 177.

[3]John Philby, p. 46.

commissioning me to try to let him change his mind. I, therefore, went to Sasson feeling as though I was carrying all of Iraq's future on my shoulders. When I reached Sasson's house, I felt at ease because I found Mr Philby and Captain Clayton present there. (My source of ease was) because when the *naqeeb* received Sasson's letter of refusal, he immediately sent both men to him, so I arrived at the right time, for they had exerted their effort to convince him but to no avail. I think that my serious concern must have inspired me something to convince him because he was noticeably moved for one hour after a concerted effort with him, although his brother Shaul (whom I respect and admire) had come and exerted his effort to oppose us. We were finally able to make Sasson Afandi agree to reconsider and meet Sir Percy the next day. I was certain at heart that we had won the game, and I slept that night very little, for I was turning in my mind the evidence with which I argued with him, wondering if I could bring about anything better. The next morning, a Thursday, Sasson Afandi came to me at 10 o'clock. I immediately took him to Sir Percy and left him there. Half an hour later, he [Percy Cox] came out and told me that he [Sasson] had agreed."[1]

The forming of the cabinet was announced on October 25, and its members were of two types: one type was comprised of nine working ministers, and the other type numbered 12 who were described as being ministers without ministerial positions, or according to the French expression, "ministers without portfolios."

The working ministers were: Sayyid Talib for the interior, Sasson Hisqail for finance, Ja`far al-`Askari for the defence, Hassan al-Pachachi for justice, Izzat al-Karkukli for education and health, Mustafa al-Alusi for endowments, Abdul-Lateel al-Mandeel for trade, and Muhammed Ali Fadhil for benefits (rations). Mr Hassan al-Pachachi asked to be excused for not participating in the cabinet, so he was replaced in the ministry of

---

[1]Lady Bell (op. cit.), p. 460.

justice by Mustafa al-Alusi. Muhammed Ali Fadhil replaced al-Alusi in the ministry of endowments, and the benefits ministry remained vacant till January 29, 1921, as will be stated later.

With regards to the ministers without portfolios, they were: Hamdi Baban, Abdul-Jabbar al-Khayyat, Abdul-Ghani Kubba, Abdul-Majeed al-Shawi, Abdul-Rahman al-Haidari, Fakhri al-Jumail, Muhammed al-Saihood, ʿAjeel al-Samarmad, Ahmed al-Saigh, Salim al-Khayun, Hadi al-Qazwini and Dawood al-Yousfani. Both Hamdi Baban and Hadi al-Qazwini apologized for not participating in the administration, so they were replaced with Dari al-Saʿdoun and Najm al-Badrawi.

It is said that the appointment of these non-working ministers was the idea of the *naqeeb* because he wanted to gather in his cabinet the largest possible number of sons of old families. One interesting incident narrated about him in this regard is that when he wanted to nominate Fakhri al-Jumail as one of these ministers, Cox hesitated about accepting him, so the *naqeeb* said to him, "My *mawla*[1], he is the son of so-and-so. With what face shall I meet his ancestors in the next world if I do not get him in the cabinet?!"[2]

For each minister, a British operational adviser was appointed to steer and direct him, and it was decided that the minister must submit all official businesses to the ministerial council through the adviser and that all decisions of the ministerial council must be referred to the minister also through the adviser. The adviser has the right to attend the sessions of the ministerial council when there is a discussion of works of his own particular administration and he participates in the discussion without having the right to vote.[3]

In reality, the adviser was the real authority in almost every ministry, and the minister could not bid or forbid except within a very limited scope. Some ministers started grumbling about it while others kept

---

[1]This word, *mawla* مولى, is used loosely in everyday conversation in Iraq and must not be understood to literally mean "master," since it is only an expression of courtesy, respect or high regard and nothing more. –Tr.

[2]Khayri al-Omari, *Hikayat Siyasiyya* (political anecdotes), Cairo, 1969, p. 43.

[3]Philip Ireland (op. cit.), p. 222.

quiet and obeyed. The civilians realized the reality of the new system; therefore, they preferred to take their transactions [directly] to the adviser rather than to the minister, for they were confident that their needs would not be met except through such a route. Sati` al-Husari narrates about one minister, namely Izzat al-Karkukli — who was during the Ottoman period a military commander — as saying this to him: "In all previous positions which I assumed, I was the absolute authority. But after becoming a minister here [in Baghdad], my command does not go beyond this partition."[1]

Ma`ruf al-Rusafi composed two verses of poetry that speak to this meaning titled "the ministry's bathroom" (verses), which remained in circulation at the time, and they were:

Convey on my behalf to the minister a statement
In it there is for him a reprimand:
I envision you as a marble in the ministry's bathroom
But in the presence of the adviser, you are arsenic.[2]

To such a meaning did Baqir al-Shibeebi point out when he said the following in a poem which he later composed:

The adviser is the one who drank the wine,
So why is this minister revelling?!

The Beginning's Paradoxes

The Qashla [barracks] was chosen to house the ministries, but it was at the time occupied by the British army. Cox asked Gen. [Sir Percival Otway] Hambro (1870 – 1931) to vacate it, but the general procrastinated

---

[1]Sati` al-Husari, *Muthakkarati fil Iraq* (my memoirs in Iraq), Beirut, 1967, Vol. 1, p. 51.

[2]Ma`ruf al-Rusafi, *Diwan al-Rusafi*, Beirut, Lebanon, p. 514. [The poet apparently contrasts the solidness of marble with the flimsiness of arsenic in order to depict an image of such a cabinet minister. – Tr.]

and dragged his feet, and it was not vacated until a good period of time later.

When the ministries moved to the Qashla, Sayyid Talib took for himself the best wing, so it would be the quarters for his ministry, which is the wing located above the central gate. Sayyid Talib set aside a spacious room beside his own for Philby, who was appointed as his adviser. He also set aside another spacious room to be his office, where he would host his ministers and serve food to them during lunchtime. Sayyid Talib, at the time, used to live in a house near the Qashla in the Jadeed Hassan Pasha Quarter. Excellent food used to be brought from his house every day to the office's room for him and his guests.

What is odd is that the worst Qashla wing was allocated for the defence ministry. What is also odd is that he [Talib] wanted the Qashla wing which was set aside for the defence ministry, but the defence minister, Ja`far al-`Askari, was very indignant about that. Philby says the following in his memoirs: "Ja`far Pasha came to me complaining with tears in his eyes because he was a very sensitive and excitable man, about who lodged him and his adviser, Col. Eddy, in a room which looked like an animal stable without furniture suitable for an office; was he not a defence minister with nothing to defend himself or [anything] to defend?"[1]

A salary of 7,000 rupees was earmarked for the prime minister, and each minister and adviser was to receive 3,000 rupees. In fact, this salary used to be considered in those days as quite huge. It was not common during the Ottoman period for anyone to receive such a salary, save in rare cases. It is narrated that when the minister of justice, Mustafa al-Alusi, went to the Ottoman bank to receive his first salary, and when he saw the large bundle of paper money which the teller gave him, he asked him, "Is this bundle all for me?!" When the teller answered him in the affirmative, he unconsciously raised his hands to the heavens and said, "O Allah! Grant victory to the religion and to the state!"[2]

---

[1]John Philby (op. cit.), pp. 48-49.

[2]Khairi al-Omari (op. cit.), p. 45.

Anyhow, Sayyid Talib did not relish the thought that his salary would be similar to those of the rest of the ministers; such would be a violation of the condition that he imposed on the British when he accepted to participate in the administration. On February 22, 1921, the high commissioner sent a proposal to the ministerial council to let the salary of the interior minister be 5,000 rupees, as is the case with that of the interior minister in Istanbul. On the 27th of the same month, the ministerial council met to look into the proposal. It decided unanimously to accept it plus an additional 1,000 rupees as well, making the salary of Sayyid Talib 6,000 rupees[1], that is, twice the salary of the rest of the ministers and topped only by that of the *naqeeb*.

In this regard, a very interesting anecdote is narrated: the ministers had agreed among themselves, before the cabinet could convene, about opposing the proposal when submitted to them. They encouraged each other to stand firm in the face of Sayyid Talib. But when the council convened, they cowered as they faced the terrifying looks of Sayyid Talib. The first of those who cowered was Sasson Hisqail, who quickly said "muwafiq" (agree), then the rest of the ministers kept saying one after one the same till the turn reached Abdul-Majeed al-Shawi, who was known for his sarcasm. Instead of saying "muwafiq," he said, "munafiq"[2] (hypocrite). Thus, he proved to be the most honest among them!

It is worth mentioning that the ministerial council used to convene at the *naqeeb*'s house, which was located on the bank of the [Tigris] river next to the present Agricultural Bank building. The reason is that the *naqeeb* could not leave his house because of being afflicted with arthritis. The cabinet used to convene twice a week on Saturday and Monday. The ministers would go there after the noon prayer service. Some of them would go there riding in a car, another group in a carriage and others on horseback. When they were all present, and after they had sipped their coffee, the naqeeb would signal to the cabinet's secretary,

---

[1] Abdul-Razzaq al-Hassani, *Tarikh al-Wizarat al-Iraqiyya* (history of Iraqi administrations), Saida, 1965, Vol. 1, pp. 21-22.

[2] Khayri al-Omari, *Ibid.*, pp. 45-46.

Hussain Afnan, saying, "Read, son." Hussain would start reciting the incoming letters. Once the cabinet commenced its deliberations, the *naqeeb* would invite them to eat lunch at his house, accepting no excuse. Once they had finished eating and wanted to get out, Mahmoud al-Gailani, the oldest son of the *naqeeb*, would stand at the door according to the banquet tradition: they would say upon leaving, "May your table always be ready, and may your home always be inhabited," and he would respond to them with suitable statements.[1]

Bahr Al-`Uloom Al-Tabatabai

From the beginning, Cox desired to assign a ministerial post to a man from among the Shi`as, but two obstacles stood in his way: the first was that the *naqeeb* and some influential ministers did not agree. The other was that the Shi`as themselves would hold in contempt any man among them who agreed to take part in the administration. If any of them dared to join the administration, they would treat him as a social pariah and might even insult him. If this man happened to be a theologian, they would give him the title of "`alim al-hafeez," i.e. friend or agent of the British.

Cox was finally able to convince the *naqeeb* and the influential ministers to agree to assign a ministry with a portfolio to a man from among the Shi`as. On November 14, 1920, Ms Bell wrote, saying, "It is surmised that the positions in the administration would be reorganized in order to let a Shi`a man join it."[2] What is noteworthy is that what Ms Bell stated about the redistribution of ministerial posts did not materialize except more than two months later. Apparently, this delay resulted from the difficulty of finding a man from among the Shi`as who had (the necessary) social status and who would agree to take part in the administration.

Finally, a man from among the residents of Karbala who would agree was found. His name is Sayyid Muhammed-Mahdi Bahrul-Uloom al-Tabatabai. The *naqeeb* sent him a letter on January 24 in which he wrote

---

[1]*Ibid.*, pp. 43-46.

[2]Lady Bell (op. cit.), p. 4646.

that the ministry of education and health was assigned to him. On February 4, al-Tabatabai answered him with a letter full of resonating traditional statements as follows:

> "To the honourable, the most perfect and the very best of men, His Excellency the Prime Minister, the naqeeb of the men of nobility and the great one from among the choicest descendants of Abd Manaf, may his shade and exaltation perpetuate.

> "After saluting you and all those who win the honour of serving you, the mercy of Allah and His blessings, my fingers were honoured today by receiving your order issued to me on Jumada I 14, 1339 [Monday, January 24, 1921] which delighted me because it did, on my behalf, address your niceties to the man who is sincere to you. I am proud of serving the homeland and the creed of which you have become the leader and the great one. Had there been in it anything but the honour of obeying your orders, it would suffice me as a source of pride. Here I am anticipating the procedure of your high command to rush to you on my eye rather than on my foot."

Jumada I 25, 1339 Bahrul-Uloom Zadeh: Muhammed-Mahdi[1]

Izzat al-Kirkukli was at the time in charge of the ministry of education and [public] health, so he was transferred to the services ministry after changing its name to the "[public] works and transports ministry". On February 22, the ministry of [public] health and education was assigned to al-Tabatabai.

What is worth mentioning in this regard is that al-Tabatabai used to serve in government jobs at the beginning of the [British] occupation. His name appeared on lists that Wilson mentioned in his memoirs. The British had appointed him as an aide to a political governor in Karbala on

---

[1]Abdul-Razzaq al-Hassani, *Ibid.*, Vol. 1, p. 9.

February 1, 1918[1]. This means that al-Tabatabai was one of those "hafeez" theologians.

Administration Crisis

In late November of 1920, a crisis took place in the administration, which was considered to be the first in Iraq's modern history, and the one behind it was Sayyid Talib. Ms Bell analyzes the cause of the crisis by saying that when Sayyid Talib lost hope of the British helping him win the Iraqi crown, he started faking his patriotism, so he announced his resignation. Ms Bell says the following in a letter to her father dated November 29:

> "We are at the peak of an administration crisis. Sayyid Talib resigned and asked that we permit him to go to London in the company of his children. He provided for his resignation with very flimsy excuses. His real motives, I believe, is that he realized that we did not intend to impose him on people against their wish, so he wanted to attract towards him the extremists and even the real nationalists; therefore, he delivered a lengthy speech at the ministerial council in which he asked for a general amnesty. He expected the *naqeeb* to reject this request so he would then show himself to the public as a true patriot and that he was ready to work with the British, but he found it impossible to do so. Anyhow, the *naqeeb* and several ministers had come to know about the matter in advance. Ja`far and Sasson spent most of the morning talking to me. I imagine they will adopt Sayyid Talib's way with some adjustment; thus, they would take the wind from his sails. We agreed that his resignation was regretful, for it would lead to shaking up the administration, which is already in an uncomfortable condition. At the same time, if Sayyid Talib insisted on resigning, we should face it with stiffness: if we could stand firm in the face of this fuss,

---

[1]Wilson (op. cit.), Vol. 2, p. 388.

our getting rid of Sayyid Talib would undoubtedly be of great benefit for us."[1]

Sayyid Talib was not satisfied with announcing his resignation but contacted *Al-Istiqlal* newspaper which at the time was speaking on behalf of the nationalists. This newspaper published an interview with him which it said was conducted with one of its editors. The editor inquired about reports of his resignation, so Sayyid Talib answered him, saying, "Public opinion is against the present administration. It is believed that if the government is not supported by its people, it cannot succeed in its mission." In his statement, he submitted legitimate and moderate demands for the benefit of the nation and the homeland, but there was some hesitation in accepting those demands, so he had to resign so that his slate would remain clear as it used to be during its early inception. When the editor asked him about those demands, he said, "This is a secret which I cannot reveal, but the public opinion would become familiar with them at the right time." Then he said that most ministers supported him, so the editor asked him, "Is your resignation final?" He answered, saying that the resignation was not final and that he could retract it when he was sure his demands would be accepted.[2]

On December 4, Ms Bell wrote her father another letter in which she mentioned something about the resignation of Sayyid Talib and its effect on public opinion. She said:

> "Sayyid Talib's clowning is most interesting to us. I told you about the resignation of Sayyid Talib and how it was withdrawn. His only goal was to flatter the nationalists. He explained his position clearly in another interview with the editor of the extremist *Istiqlal* newspaper, which appeared after the withdrawal of his resignation, where he said that he closely monitored public opinion and found it against the present administration. On his part, he submitted a series of

---

[1]Burgoyne (op. cit.), Vol. 2, pp. 185-86.

[2] -- *Al-Istiqlal* newspaper dated December 1, 1920.

demands which the cabinet must submit to Sir Percy Cox. Among those demands was the return of those exiled and the refugees, and the granting of more freedom to the ministers in doing their jobs, etc. But his fellow ministers did not view those demands with approval; therefore, he found it his duty, as a patriot, to resign, and he hoped his fellows would follow in his footsteps and resign if they loved their homeland. Then he hinted in an ambiguous way that he would reconsider his stance in case the cabinet agreed to his demands. In fact, Sayyid Talib's maneuvers did enhance his stance among Arab youths who used to hold him before in contempt."

Ms Bell added, saying, "Sasson Hisqail and Abdul-Hamid al-Shawi were the only ones who truly stood against Sayyid Talib in the cabinet. As for Ja`far al-`Askari, he went along with his game." She explained this by saying that al-`Askari did so in order to find a way for him later on, especially when the Iraqis returned from Syria. Ms Bell quoted a statement by Hussain Afnan describing Sayyid Talib's game which was: "Sayyid Talib spent 30 years before now scheming with the Turkish officials and learned everything big and small in the art of this game."[1]

Anyhow, Sayyid Talib did not continue his game for long. On December 18, Ms Bell wrote saying:

"Sayyid Talib came to me today, Sunday, and I must admit that he created within me a good impression. He told me frankly that he desired to be Iraq's emir. We kept discussing his situation in detail, and I thought that he demonstrated wisdom and sensibility. After that, we started talking about the violent nationalist newspaper — meaning *Al-Istiqlal* — which now had become completely Bolshevik, and it is likely that it received financial aid. He was thinking that we should

---

[1] *Ibid.*, Vol. 2, pp. 188-89.

shut it down, and I think that his opinion is sound and I shall convey it to Sir Percy Cox tomorrow."[1]

The *Istiqlal* (Independence) Newspaper

As we have already pointed out, the *Istiqlal* newspaper was the spokesman of the nationalists. In fact, this newspaper was not ordinary; rather, it was like a political organization at the house in which nationalists would meet and take part in writing it. It was the first newspaper that opposed British policy in Iraq.

The newspaper's owner was Abdul-Ghafour al-Badri. During the war, he was an officer, and he later joined the Arab Revolution. He could not get a concession to publish the newspaper except after hesitation and procrastination from the officials. Its first issue came out on September 28, 1920, and its administration was located on the river bank in the Risafa flank near the present-day Shari`a Court.

Abdul-Ghafour al-Badri was not a good writer, or he could not write, as it was said, but he was a man of resolve and opinion, and he was able to lobby round him a number of writers to participate in editing his newspaper. For his part, he was bearing the consequences of what they were writing, and he was protecting them. In the beginning, the newspaper's editor-in-chief was Qasim al-Alawi, who was assisted in editing (the paper) by many men, including Ali Mahmoud al-Shaikh Ali, Talib Mushtaq, Mahdi al-Baseer, Sami Khundah, Rasheed al-Sufi, Awni Bakr Sidqi, Hussain al-Rahhal, Mustafa Ali, Baqir al-Shibeebi, Salman al-Shaikh Dawood, Ahmed Jamal ad-Deen, Fahmi al-Mudarris, Abdul-Lateef Habeeb, Khayri Hammad al-Filistini (the Palestinian) and others. Rafael Batti describes this newspaper thus:

---

[1] *Ibid.*, Vol. 2, p. 129.

"One would have the sense, as he was in the administration of this newspaper, that it was a popular and patriotic forming, a political club crowded with strugglers, an active movement in which groups of civilians from among the people's classes participate. One donates money, another writes, yet others donate by managing the newspaper, some individual there expresses views and provides direction etc. Everyone is overwhelmed with enthusiasm, so much so that the sign of the newspaper's name on the door of its administration office was written in these four colours: white, black, green and red, the colors of the Arab flag which was hoisted during the revolution's early days in Hijaz before an Iraqi flag was flown in Iraq's sky."

Rafael Batti adds saying:

"There is a fact which must be recorded: the government of the British occupation was patient about what was written in the *Istiqlal* newspaper, awarding it a good deal of freedom of the press which we did not find on a sustained level during the period of independence."[1]

Miss Bell has provided us, in one of her letters, with an amazing description of the group which was rallying behind the *Istiqlal* newspaper. She said:

"The progressive nationalists here, those who do not want the Turks but are not pleased with their status quo, use the myth of the Turkish prattle: hopefully the Turks will come to get us [the British] out of the country, they, in turn, will come to get the Turks out of it. Those who think like that make up a small but boisterous group, and they have a newspaper that speaks for them called *Al-Istiqlal*. Most of its writers and followers are individuals whom no government can use. If we

---

[1]Rafael Batti, *Al-Sahafa fil Iraq* (press in Iraq), Cairo, 1955, p. 60.

get out of the country, they will be against those who would come after us."[1]

The *Istiqlal* newspaper used to quite often mention the name of Prince Faisal on its pages, profusely praising him and expressing its agony at what happened in Syria following his expulsion from it. Moreover, it used to directly or indirectly point out that Faisal is a suitable candidate for Iraq's throne. On August 11, 1920, it posted a telegram that originated in London, the gist of which was that Faisal was on his way to Switzerland to meet the British Prime Minister, who was present there in order to discuss placing him on Iraq's throne. We do not need to say that this persistence from the newspaper in referring to Faisal used to provoke Sayyid Talib and make him angry. In his memoirs, Talib Mushtaq says, "Sayyid Talib offered Abdul-Ghafour al-Badri 12,000 rupees in exchange for seizing to mention Faisal's name, an offer which al-Badri rejected."[2]

Salman al-Shaikh Dawood, who was one of the newspaper's editors as we have already stated, narrates that when Sayyid Talib submitted his resignation, he called him in and showed him papers which included his resignation and complaint about the [British] advisers' interference, telling him that Philby and Ms Bell talked to him and convinced him to withdraw his resignation and that he promised them to do so. Then Sayyid Talib asked Salman to write in the newspaper an article praising him and lauding his patriotism. But Salman did not do what Sayyid Talib had asked him; rather, he did exactly the opposite.[3] The newspaper came out the next day bearing an article under the heading "I want him to live, he wants me to die", which contained a severe implicit attack on Sayyid Talib without mentioning his name but clearly making a reference to him.[4]

Sayyid Talib started looking for an opportunity to bring down the *Istiqlal* newspaper. Finally, he got such an opportunity on February 9,

---

[1]Burgoyne (opt. cit), Vol. 2, p. 205.

[2]Talib Mushtaq, *Awraq Ayyami* (my days' leaflets), Beirut, 1968, Vol. 1, p. 96.

[3]Khayri al-Omari, *Shakhsiyyat Iraqiyya* (Iraqi personalities), Baghdad, 1955, Vol. 1, p. 38.

4 -- *Al-Istiqlal* of December 22, 1920.

1921. On that day, some of those who were banished to Hungam Island [in Iran] had returned to Baghdad after their release. Among them were: Ahmad Sheikh Dawood, Ja`far al-Shibibi, Arif al-Suweedi, Muhammed Mustafa al-Khalil, Nouri Fattah and others. The newspaper, therefore, published a special issue on the occasion under a broad heading saying:

> "We congratulate the Iraqi nation on the arrival of some of our good people who were banished, and we demand the return of all banished people without any exception; we also continue to demand the implementation of the rest of the seven articles."

This newspaper outlined under this heading a program for the political struggle, which contained seven articles, including the freedom of the press and (freedom to) hold meetings, a general amnesty, and the abolishment of the martial (law) administration. As soon as this issue was circulated among the public, an order was issued by the interior ministry to shut the newspaper down and to arrest its owner together with eleven of his aides.

The prisoners did not linger long in jail. Justice adviser Bunham Carter mediated in their regard and was able to get seven of them released. Then the government expelled two of them. As for the remaining three, namely Abdul-Ghafour al-Badri, Mahdi al-Baseer and Qasim al-Alawi, they were taken to court. Their trial is regarded as the first press-related trial in Iraq's modern history. The court sentenced al-Badri to one year in prison with hard labour, sentencing al-Baseer to nine months and al-Alawi to six months. The court also decided to suspend the *Istiqlal* newspaper for one full year.

It is narrated that Sayyid Talib passed by Abdul-Ghafour al-Badri as the latter was smashing street rocks with ordinary prisoners and said to him, "Do you like this, Abdul-Ghafour?!" Al-Badri answered him, "There is nothing that I like more than suffering in the cause of my homeland and people. Go on tormenting others for as long as you please. Woe unto you all from the people!"[1]

The Returnees

In Syria, there were many Iraqi army officers and government employees who were employed by Faisal's government. When this government collapsed following the Maysalun Battle, these men lost their jobs, and many of them started suffering from harsh living conditions.

Ja`far al-`Askari was the first among them to return to Iraq, arriving on October 16 1920, when he took charge of the defence ministry, as we have already stated. Al-`Askari kept insisting in the ministerial council that the government should help the speeding up the return of the others due to their bad living conditions on the one hand and due to Iraq's need for their services on the other.[2]

The government obtained from the French attaché in Baghdad a list of 240 names of Iraqi officers who were then present in Syria. On October 27 1920, Cox sent a telegram to London seeking permission to facilitate their return. In mid-February of 1921, the first group of them reached Baghdad. In their vanguard was Nouri al-Sa`eed who was appointed as deputy to defence minister Ja`far al-`Askari. We must not forget in this regard that Nouri and Ja`far were brothers-in-law; each of them married the other's sister.

On February 24, Ms Bell wrote, saying, "Last week saw the first arrival of new elements: the Iraqi officers who were in Syria and who began returning [home]. The first of them to arrive was Nouri Pasha, husband of Ja`far's sister.

"One day after his arrival, Ja`far called me to ask me when Nouri could meet Sir Percy [Cox]. Sir Percy, therefore, asked them both to have lunch with him. They both came at 12:00

---

[1] Faiq Batti, *A`lam fi Sahafat al-Iraq* (renown personalities in Iraq's press), Baghdad, 1971, p. 173.

[2] Philip Ireland (cited in the previous reference), p. 225.

o'clock and sat with me for a while. I invited Capt. Clayton knew and liked Nouri, and Maj. Murray came too. A very important talk went on among them."[1] Ms Bell kept comparing in her letter Ja`far al-`Askari with Nouri al-Sa`eed, saying, "Ja`far is a good man who is motivated by the highest principles, but he lacks strength. He is good-natured, a man of tolerance, very fat with a shining smile, and he immediately responds to friendship and affection, granting you his trust immediately. It is amazing how a man who has these physical and mental features is so enthusiastic in his political beliefs. But he has nothing that makes him known as such by the public, for he did not succeed in attracting the extremist youths in Baghdad and in convincing them of our integrity the way he himself was convinced of it. As for his brother-in-law, Nouri, he is totally different from him. The moment I saw him, I realized that we were facing a strong and flexible energy and that we had to either cooperate with him or enter into a very tough struggle with him in order to subdue him."[2]

Ja`far and Nouri kept working together to facilitate the Iraqis' return from Syria and to find the jobs that would suit them. On March 6, 111 Iraqi officers and their family members arrived by sea route. On the 14th of the same month, Naji al-Suweedi arrived by land route with 15 persons. On October 3, Tawfeeq al-Suweedi arrived, and on the 21st of the same month, the ministerial council decided to earmark 75,000 rupees to repatriate the rest of the Iraqi officers who remained in Syria because they could not afford the travel expenses.

At the same time, the Iraqis who were present in Turkey started returning to Iraq.[3] They were former government employees, officers, businessmen or students.

---

[1]Lady Bell (op. cit.), p. 476.

[2]Burgoyne (op. cit.), Vol. 2, pp. 209-210.

3 -- Report on Iraq Administration, October 1920 – March 1922, p. 7.

Before then, the first batch of Iraqi doctors who had studied medicine in Istanbul had arrived. They were: Hashim al-Watari, Fa'iq Shakir, Sami Shawkat, Shakir al-Suweedi, Isma`eel al-Saffar, Sa'ib Shawkat, Shawkat al-Zahawi and others.[1]

Filling Positions

At the inception of the British occupation, government jobs used to be filled mostly with British and Indian officials, and a few were Iraqis. When the *naqeeb*-led interim administration was formed, the policy started going in the direction of shrinking the number of the Britons and Indians and increasing that of the Iraqis. In his memoirs, Philby says that when he undertook the position of adviser to the interior ministry, he found the number of the British administrative officers to be 130; therefore, he worked to decrease it to 40, granting those who were released from their jobs generous bonuses so they could manage their affairs till they got other jobs.[2]

On January 6, 1921, the Iraqi army's command was set up at the defence ministry quarters with 10 officers. Since then, the army kept growing in its positions and formations. The officers who returned from Syria started gradually filling those positions. At the same time, the ministerial council started issuing successive job placements in order to fill the administrative positions in its governorates. Ms Bell wrote on February 7, saying, "The [ministerial] council took decisions (regarding) a number of job placements in the governorates' administrative positions, such as governors and mayors. Many of them were good to a certain extent, and Sir Percy agrees to the placements when the *naqeeb* insists, and I think that he is right, for we have to sit and see how they make mistakes. All the appointments were issued by the interior ministry."[3]

---

[1] Hashim al-Watri and Mu`amar Khalid al-Shabandar, *Tarikh al-Tibb fil Iraq* (medicine's history in Iraq), Baghdad, 1939, p. 50.

[2] John Philby, *Ibid.*, pp. 46-47.

[3] Lady Bell (op. cit.), p. 474.

On February 27, the ministerial council agreed to gradually lay off the Indian employees and to appoint Iraqi officials in their place[1]. Thus, the doors of government jobs became open for the Iraqis; therefore, those who returned from Syria and Turkey rushed to seize this opportunity. Former employees who had lost their jobs following the withdrawal of the Turks from Iraq also did likewise. Ms Bell stated that Sayyid Talib talked to her about the immediate need to silence café-goers from among the old government employees and officers. He said about them that they were now in abject poverty, so they had to be silenced by placing them in government jobs. Ms Bell fully endorsed his opinion[2].

What is generally observed is that those who returned from Syria received the lion's share of high-level positions, stirring the ire of sons of renowned families who monopolised many of those positions during the Turkish era. The returnees were mostly from middle-class or poor families, and a hidden struggle took place between them and the sons of the renowned families, a struggle that went on for a long period of time, as we will discuss.

We must not forget in this regard that the Jews were able to get a large share of jobs at that time. This is due to two reasons: First: the Jews had their own schools, which had a good educational level where they learned foreign languages, bookkeeping and other subjects which at the time were rare in Iraq; therefore, the government regarded them as being competent to fill the positions which needed experience in those areas. The second reason was that the British regarded the Jews as their supporters who were loyal to their rule in Iraq, so they helped them fill those positions. We can add a third reason which is the personality of their leader, Sasson Hisqail, who was in charge of the finance ministry and whom the British very much respected. This man worked hard to fill many positions in his ministry and elsewhere with members of his Jewish community. Sati` al-Husari says the following in describing Sasson: "I do not doubt that he was the most shrewd minister and the most knowledgeable of government affairs, but he was the furthermost of all of

---

[1]Abdul-Razzaq al-Hassani (previous reference), p. 21.

[2]Burgoyne (op. cit.), Vol. 2, p. 192.

them from thinking about the country's interests. The interest of his Israelite group occupied the first place in his thinking and action."[1] A man whom I trust told me how he once witnessed a violent verbal altercation between Sasson and Abdul-Muhsin al-Sa`doun about appointing the Jews. Al-Sa`doun was extremely angry and outraged about Sasson's persistence and about various mediations in this regard.

The Shi`a *Marji`iyya*

When the 1920 Revolution erupted, the Shi`as' religious *Marji`iyya*[2] was confined to Mirza Taqi al-Shirazi, who used to reside in Karbala. This man effectively assisted the eruption of the revolution and its leadership, as is well known. He died on August 17, 1920, when the Revolution was at its peak. The Marji`iyya, therefore, was transferred to Sheikh Fath-Allah al-Isfahani, who was called "Sheikh al-Shari`a" [Mentor of the Islamic legislative system], and he used to reside in Najaf. He assisted the revolution and oversaw it till his last days; he died on December 18 of the same year.

There were three *mujtahids*[3] who were candidates for the Marji`iyya at the death of the Mentor of the Shari`a. Two of them resided in Najaf, namely Sayyid Abul-Hassan al-Isfahani and Mirza Hussain al-Naeeni, and one resided in al-Kadhimiyya, namely Sheikh Mahdi al-Khalisi. Al-Khalisi was the oldest of the three men, and both his fellows recognized his status among them and respected his opinion quite often.

---

[1] Sati` al-Husari (former reference), Vol. 1, p. 52.

[2] The word "Marji`iyya" refers to the highest religious juristic authority in Shi`a Islam. The "marji`" usually holds the degree of "Ayatollah" or "Grand Ayatollah". He has to have a published set of instructions, known as *risala*, that are relevant to various rules and regulations about implementing daily religious and secular practices. These rules and regulations are in accordance to what he believes, according to his *ijtihad*, personal opinion, and which he derives from both of Islam's major sources of the Shari`a, namely the Qur'an and the Sunnah. – Tr.

[3] A *mujtahid* is a Muslim clergyman who is recognized as having the ability to derive edicts based on his own understanding and level of Islamic knowledge. – Tr.

He had the distinction over them in lieu of the fact that he was an Arab from a staunch Iraqi family, but he obtained Iranian citizenship during the Ottoman period in order to escape enlistment in the army, just as many others had done, remaining in his way of dressing himself, in his conduct, and [with his] accent as an Iraqi Arab.

Al-Khalisi is also distinguished for his intense interest in politics, which he regards as an indivisible part of religion. He regards religion as having an outer and an inner context. Its outer form is comprised of expressions of worship and rituals, while it's inside is restricted to an effort to rid the Islamic lands of the infidels' hegemony. He used to prefer the Turks' rule over that of the British: these are Muslims, and those are unbelievers. A Muslim ruler, in his view, even if he may be unjust, is better than a just unbeliever. Al-Khalisi, thus, differs in his opinion from Ibn Tawoos, who in old times had issued his edict that a fair unbeliever is better than an unfair believer (Muslim).

Sheikh Mahdi al-Khalisi (Courtesy: Ali Jaafar Al-Khalisi)

When jobs became available for the Iraqis in the first month of 1921, al-Khalisi issued an edict that banned taking them, regarding them as means of cooperating with the unbelievers. It is worth mentioning that this edict by al-Khalisi banning such jobs received a broad circulation in Shi`a circles; therefore, many of them refused the jobs they were offered. It can be said that the economic boom which used to prevail in the country at the time helped support and disseminate that edict: a Shi`a individual preferred to make money which is "halal" (lawful according to Islam) at the market over the "haram" (unlawful) money of such a job.

Cox was keen about giving the Shi`as jobs, especially in the mid-Euphrates area and areas of the holy shrines, but he found two obstacles before him obstructing his path. The first was this edict by al-Khalisi, and the other was the reluctance of the *naqeeb* and some ministers to give the Shi`as jobs. Finally, Cox was able to convince the *naqeeb* and the ministers to hire a limited number of Shi`as, but he could not convince al-Khalisi to rescind his edict.

Someone I trust told me that Cox asked Sayyid Ja`far Utayfah, head of the al-Kadhimiyya municipality, to arrange a meeting for him with al-Khalisi to talk with him, so Ja`far suggested that al-Khalisi could be met when he came to the Shrine (of Imam Kadhim (as)) to pray. An agreement was made between Cox and Sayyid Ja`far about that, and they both stood together at a small Shrine door that al-Khalisi was accustomed to using when entering to pray. When al-Khalisi came, Sayyid Ja`far advanced and said to him, "Honorable Sheikh, the high commissioner desires to greet you." When al-Khalisi hardly heard the name "high commissioner", he quickly put his cloak over his head and hurried to enter the Shrine without saying one word. Of course, Cox could not enter the Shrine after him. Thus, the attempt failed!

Chapter Two

The Monarchy Recipe

Having completed the formation of the first administration in Iraq as we have already detailed in the previous chapter, Cox began thinking of looking for a king for Iraq who would be suitable to British interests on the one hand and acceptable to the Iraqi people on the other.

The Iraqis who returned from Syria — on top of which stood Ja`far al-`Askari and Nouri al-Sa`eed — were publicizing Prince Faisal, son of [Sharif] al-Hussain [of Mecca], whom they regarded as the best candidate for Iraq's throne, and Ms Bell supported and indirectly encouraged this notion.

It is worth mentioning in this regard that Wilson was the first British official who thought of Faisal as being suitable for Iraq's throne. On July 31, 1920, that is, following Faisal's exit from Syria as an outcast, Wilson sent a telegram to London in which he suggested [the idea] of offering Iraq's emirate to Faisal, hinting at his talents and implicitly referring to Faisal's disappointment in Syria as having a psychological impact that would make him more aware of the reality and more reasonable in dealing with matters.[1] This suggestion was met with

---

[1] Arnold Wilson, *Loyalties Mesopotamia* (London, U.K., 1936), Vol. 2, pp. 305-306.

acceptance in London, but the British policymakers were apprehensive of the French opposition to it.

On August 8, 1920, Lord Curzon, the British foreign minister, initiated talks with the French government, asking it if it had any objection to installing Faisal in Iraq. The French government responded by saying it fully opposed it, and the French began defaming Faisal to the British in order to cause them to be averse to him, charging him of having two faces. They said to the British, "Do not trust Faisal, for he used to negotiate with us behind your backs while ruling Syria in order to cooperate with us against the British authority in Iraq."[1] The French foreign minister said to the British prime minister, "Faisal's manners are weak, and he is dangerous." The British prime minister responded to him, saying, "Faisal is just as you describe, but Iraq's tribal sheikhs want him. If the French government agrees to install him in Iraq, we can do away with the 70,000 soldiers who now control security in Iraq."[2]

On November 11, when Faisal was in seclusion in northern Italy, he received a letter from Lord Curzon inviting him to visit London. At the end of the month, Faisal went to London. Faisal himself narrates that the next day following his arrival in London, he visited Lord Curzon. The latter noticed that Faisal was not wearing the Arabian cloak which he used to wear before, so he asked him, "Where is your beautiful cloak?" Faisal answered him, "They stripped me of my homeland, Lord; therefore, I took off my cloak." Curzon said, "Rather, you will wear a better one." Faisal understood from this statement that they [the British] would compensate him for Syria's throne with that of Iraq."[3]

Anyhow, it can be said that the British government remained hesitant about Faisal for fear that France would be angry with it, so it was taking one step forward and another backwards. On December 26, it received a message from Cox in Baghdad, a telegram in which he said that

---

[1]Sulayman Mousa, *Al-Haraka al-Arabiyya* (Arab movement), Beirut, Lebanon, 1970, p. 575.

[2]Elie Kedourie, *The Chatham House Version and Other Middle Eastern Studies,* London, U.K., 1970, p. 240.

[3]Khayriyya Qasimiyya, *Muthakkarat Awni Abdul-Hadi* (memoirs of Awni Abdul-Hadi), Beirut, Lebanon, 1974, p. 51.

Faisal was the most fit person to rule Iraq, and that France's objection can somehow be managed.[1] This telegram had its impact on the British government and was an additional factor that increased the government's inclination towards Faisal.

On January 7, 1921, Curzon sent Maj. [Sir Kinahan] Cornwallis[2] to Faisal to open non-official talks in this regard. Cornwallis was a close friend of Faisal in Syria, where a personal friendship was established between them since then. Curzon instructed him that his talk with Faisal would include two conditions: first, Faisal must accept the British mandate [over Iraq], and second, he must avoid any hostile action against France in Syria. Curzon also told him to explain to Faisal that he should pretend before people that he was independent and was not a puppet in the hands of the British government.[3]

Prince Abdullah (Courtesy: Wikipedia Commons)

The meeting between Cornwallis and Faisal took place at 1:00 am (after midnight) following his return from the theatre, and it went on for two hours.[4] Apparently, it did not go well, for Faisal said that his father, King Hussain, did not accept his nomination for Iraq's throne but wanted it for his other son, Prince Abdullah [photo to the right], and that if he, Faisal, accepted Iraq's throne, his father and all people would consider him as being selfish and seeking his own personal interest in cooperation with Britain, that he was seeking a throne

---

[1]Ghassan al-Atiyyah, *Influential Voices from the Arab World* (Beirut, Lebanon, Arab Institute for Research and Publishing, 1973), p. 364.

[2]The references I, Translator of this Volume, checked indicate that Cornwallis was a colonel. Most likely he was gradually promoted from a major to a colonel by token he received the title "Sir" as well. – Tr.

[3]*Ibid.*, p. 365.

[4]Philip Willard Ireland, *Iraq: A study in Political Development*, Beirut, Lebanon, 1949, p. 241.

at the expense of his brother. Cornwallis wrote his report about the meeting, and in conclusion, he said that there were two open paths to solve the Iraq problem: Abdullah should go to Iraq, or Cox should try to get the Iraqis to calmly and discreetly choose Faisal. Cornwallis says that the first path is easier, but the second one is more beneficial because Faisal is by far better than his brother, Abdullah, and that "He will serve us with sincerity and competence."[1]

Lloyd George commissioned Lord Winterton to make another attempt to convince Faisal. Winterton was a close friend of Faisal, so he invited him over to his house and invited with him Jibraeel (Gabriel) Haddad Pasha, representative of King Hussain [of Mecca] in London. He also invited Lawrence and others. These men talked with Faisal for long hours in order to convince him, and the meeting went on till two o'clock in the morning. Faisal used the opportunity to direct a bitter criticism of the unfair treatment meted to him by the French as well as the British, and he articulated injurious remarks about the manners of the British in general.[2] Finally, Faisal accepted Iraq's throne provided that his brother Abdullah be convinced to surrender his right to the throne.

On February 14, 1921, Churchill moved from the war ministry to the ministry of colonies, becoming responsible for solving Middle East problems. Churchill established in his new ministry a special Middle East office, making his friend, Lawrence, his adviser in it. Then Churchill decided to hold a conference in Cairo to look into Middle Eastern issues in general and the Iraq issue in particular. Churchill travelled to Cairo to attend a conference in the company of Lawrence. The conference convened on March 11 and was attended from Iraq by Sir Percy Cox, Gen. Holden, Ms Bell, Ja`far al-`Askari, Sasson Hisqail and three British advisers: Slater, Eddie and Watkinson. There was an agreement in the conference about the same view which was decided in London before, that is, Faisal was the suitable person for Iraq's throne. Lawrence suggested that the Air Force should undertake the reins of controlling the country instead of the occupation army which is more costly, and the conference endorsed it.

---

[1]Ghassan al-Atiyyah (op. cit.), pp. 363-366.

[2]Sulayman Mousa (op. cit.), p. 580.

On the 16th of the same month, while the conference was still convening, a telegram reached Churchill sent by Lloyd George reminding him of Faisal's stance with regard to Iraq's throne and how he would not accept it except after his brother, Abdullah, gave it up.[1] Churchill, therefore, pledged to go in person accompanied by Lawrence to convince Abdullah to forfeit it.

Convincing Abdullah

Prince Abdullah had reached the Trans-Jordan area on November 21, 1920, coming from Hijaz accompanied by a small Bedouin force and three Iraqi officers.[2] He announced that he had come in response to relief cries from leaders of Syria, which they sent to his father, and that he was determined to liberate Syria and save it from aggressor Frenchmen and avenge his brother. Many men and leaders of Syria who had fled away began to go to him, and he intended to form a government in exile. Then he circulated a statement to the Syrian public in which he said, "How do you agree that the Umayyad capital would become a French colony? If you agree to it, the Jazeera [Arabian Peninsula] will not agree, and my anger will reach you. Our only objective, Allah knows, is to support you and to get the aggressors out. Here I am saying it without any hesitation that I have accepted to renew the oath of allegiance to your King Faisal I on behalf of the overwhelming majority which renewed such an oath before me."[3]

The Trans-Jordan area at the time was populated by no more than a third of a million, and it did not have a central government; instead, it had several small local governments according to the tribal norm, and each of them had a British adviser. The advisers did nothing about Abdullah's movements which made people think that Britain was pleased with them, or that they were of its own doing.

---

[1]*Ibid.*, p. 594.

[2]Those three Iraqi officers were: Hamid al-Wadi, Rauf al-Shahwani and Sa`eed al-Kallak.

[3]Khayr ad-Deen al-Zurakli, *Aamaan in Amman* (two years in Amman), Cairo, 1925, p. 16.

In March 1921, Prince Abdullah settled in Amman. It came to his knowledge that the British government intended to install his brother, Faisal, as king of Iraq, so he was very upset about it and became angry. Awni Abdul-Hadi, who was at the time among the protégés of Prince Abdullah, says, "Prince Abdullah thundered and revelled, opening his chest to all his visitors and those in his company, casting sparks and fire at Faisal who had agreed to his nomination for Iraq's throne, insisting that this matter should be discussed with Mr Churchill because the throne was his, and that he did not agree to abdicate." Awni adds to this saying, "I insisted upon His Highness not to discuss the subject of Iraq's throne with the British minister, and His Highness was bursting in rage and periodically repeating these words: 'How can I keep silent about the loss of a throne which was sanctioned for me by the Arab nation?'"[1]

Khayr ad-Deen al-Zurakli narrates that Prince Abdullah summoned him during those days and said to him that he was not confident that his brother, Faisal, would accept Iraq's throne. Then he brought him proof that he was the legitimate owner of the throne and that anyone who would take it away from him would be only a usurper. Then he said in rage, "Why would you not write for us a series of articles on this subject, Khayr ad-Deen?" Al-Zurakli says that he thus was placed in an embarrassing situation and kept asking himself if the issue of al-Ameen and al-Mamoon [sons of Harun al-Rasheed] would return to Iraq once more, and whether it would bring people another joke: two brothers fighting over a throne made in London.[2]

A few days later, Prince Abdullah was summoned to Jerusalem to meet Churchill. When the prince was passing by the Salt Town on his way to Jerusalem, Lawrence met him, so they spent the night together over there, and Lawrence kept talking to the prince in order to convince him to surrender Iraq's throne [to his brother]. He said to him, "You are well known for sacrificing your own ambitions for the sake of the nation; therefore, you have to stay in Trans-Jordan to establish a civilian administration free of any violence in its political objectives. If you

---

[1]Khayriyya Qasimiyya (op. cit.), p. 44.

[2]Khayr ad-Deen al-Zurakli (op. cit.), p. 44.

succeed in so doing, you will win six months later the unity of Syria, God willing, and we will then visit you in Damascus to congratulate you."[1]

On March 29, a meeting took place in Jerusalem between Prince Abdullah and Churchill, and it was attended by Lawrence, Awni Abdul-Hadi, the high commissioner of Palestine, Sir Herbert Samuel, and his secretary, Windham Deeds. In his memoirs, Awni Abdul-Hadi provides us with a detailed picture of that meeting of which we would like to [share] the following:

"After Churchill had welcomed the Prince, he immediately spoke in a way that demonstrated toughness. He said that when he reached Cairo, he was surprised about the Prince being in Amman, and he was overcome with amazement when he came to know that the Prince wanted to take by force the areas which Faisal was ruling, although the Prince was not ignorant of the fact that France is an ally of Britain, [and] that any attack on France was regarded as an attack on Britain itself." Then Churchill raised his voice, and his tone became more intense as he said that he did not want to imagine that such an attack would take place by some descendants of Hashim, allies of Britain, and that it was the pleasure of the British government to work with full understanding with the offspring of Hashim in all political and international fields, but it wanted to work with all of them, not just with some of them. "I shall be frank with Your Highness to the extreme limits of frankness, for the British government has decided to work with either all descendants of Hashim or with none of them at all." Then Churchill said in a strict tone, "Faisal has sailed from London, and he is now on his way to Cairo, and after visiting his father, he will go to Baghdad where he will be installed as king over Iraq. However, Faisal will sit on the throne of Iraq, and these two shoulders — and he pointed to his right and left shoulders — will challenge the trouble makers."

---

[1]Sulayman Mousa, *Lawrence*, London, 1967, p. 240.

This statement stunned the Prince, who wanted to change the subject of the talk, so he said, "But, Your Excellency the minister, the matter that concerns the Arabs before everything else is Palestine. I have come to know that the Jews are ambitious [in that they aim] to establish their Jewish state in this precious Arab spot and expel the Arabs from it, and the Arabs, as you have pointed out, are allies of Great Britain; so, does the British government regard the Arabs in Palestine as trees that can be cut off?" Here Samuel came close to Churchill and whispered in his ears, asking his permission to answer the Prince, then he said, "It is not the policy of the British government, Your Highness the Prince, to cut off the trees of Palestine; on the contrary, it is determined to increase its trees with other species that increase its value."

Now the Prince looked at Churchill with remonstrating looks, and then he started talking about his past efforts to make an alliance between Britain and the Arabs, since it was his own idea and the first person to try to realize it, and he was also the intermediary between Lawrence and Faisal. The result was: that the British government preferred someone else to undertake Iraq's throne, even when this someone was his own brother, Faisal. Then the Prince said, "This preference has weighed heavily on me, especially since the Iraqis who represented Iraq in the Syrian conference of 1920 are the ones who invited me to be the king of Iraq. And it surprised me, Your Excellency, the minister, to hear you say that my brother, Faisal, sailed from London on his way to Iraq to ascend the throne, and you said that there would be some people who will oppose him and that your shoulders will bear such an opposition. Perhaps you have counted me among such opponents. God forbid that I should do anything which opposes the policy of the British government."

It was then that Churchill started soothing his intensity. He admitted the services which the prince had rendered during the war [World War I] then said, "If the present circumstances necessitate that your brother should ascend the throne of Iraq, it may not be distant that you — and this may take place shortly — may ascend the throne of Syria, probably this year. I shall exert all my efforts to remove the misunderstanding between you and France, which will help restore things to the way they should be among you. Since France does not desire to establish any relationship with Faisal, the path becomes paved for Your Highness in this case. I warn Your Highness about permitting anyone or any board to assault Syria from the borders of the area which I wish Your Highness will temporarily rule, and I say the temporary rule of Your Highness because my government must agree about the policy which will be applied to this area, and also the nations of the area must agree, too, which requires waiting until such a final agreement is concluded in the next six months."[1]

Prince Abdullah accepted Churchill's plan. He says in his memoirs that Churchill threatened him saying, "If you do not do this, you will lose everything, and it is likely Ibn Saud can reach Mecca in three days; England has done what it can." Then the prince said that he consulted with the Syrian leaders who were with him in this regard and that they unanimously agreed. Thus, it was agreed that Sir. Herbert Samuel should visit Amman in order to set the foundation for the desired civilian administration.[2]

Abdullah's Sighs

Faisal left London by sea route on March 31, 1921, and headed to Hijaz. On his way, he passed by Cairo, where he stayed for a few days at Shepherd Hotel. Abdullah sent him from Amman to Awni Abdul-Hadi carrying two letters, one for him and the other for his father. Awni says the following in his memoirs: "Having read both letters, Faisal commented about them saying, 'My brother thinks that I have usurped Iraq's throne from him, that I have torn to pieces the resolution which the Iraqis had issued at the Syrian conference. I have come to know everything which he has been saying about me, and I have always been saying, 'May Allah forgive him.'" Faisal kept telling Awni how the British wanted to assign Iraq's throne to him and how he did not agree and wanted the throne for his brother, Abdullah, but the British strongly insisted. Then Awni says that during his return from Amman, he tried to convince Abdullah to accept the matter of assigning Iraq's throne to Faisal, and his answer was, "I know my brother, Awni. He had ascended the throne of Syria, becoming

---

[1]Khayriyya Qasimiyya, *Muthakkarat Awni Abdul-Hadi* (memoirs of Awni Abdul-Hadi), Beirut, Lebanon, 1974, pp. 46-48.

[2]Abdullah ibn al-Hussain, *Memoirs*, Jerusalem, 1945, pp. 180-182.

the head of the state, so now nothing is sweeter for him than ascending thrones. My brother Faisal is no different from the rest of the heads of state in this regard. History has taught us that any Arab who becomes head of state insists on staying at the top even if it means his annihilation; therefore, my brother has preferred to ascend Iraq's throne even if this throne belongs to his brother, and I have no choice here but to plead to Allah to forgive him."

Awni says that when he went again to Cairo and conveyed to Faisal his brother's regards, Faisal said, "I know my brother, Abdullah, and I sense his pain because of losing Iraq's throne. I am sure he will not forget his loss of this throne. His grudge against me because of this throne will not disappear easily, and he has pointed this out clearly in his statement which you carried to me and which I read to you."[1]

Abdullah continued to suffer over the loss of Iraq's throne, and his pain intensified when it became clear to him that the British were unable to fulfil their promise to him to install him on Syria's throne. Sati` al-Husari narrates an interesting anecdote in this regard: four Iraqi officers who came out of Syria went to Amman, where they stayed for some time. Whenever they attended the meeting place of Prince Abdullah, he always used to speak on every occasion about his right to Iraq's throne and say, "My father asked me to relinquish my right, but I did not respond to his request; I did not relinquish, and I shall not relinquish my right to Iraq's throne. I shall maintain my right, however, so that [it may be etched in] history." He used to quite often repeat the phrase "for history, for history," and he would ask the Iraqi officers for some details about Iraq. Whenever he heard them praising Iraq, his sighs and moans would intensify, and he would resume his talk about his "right" to Iraq's throne and openly state his determination never to relinquish this right but to hold on to it, for history's [sake]. His repeated sighs for Iraq prompted a Syrian leader who was present there to say this to the Iraqi officers: "Stop praising Iraq; let the man work here." Sati` al-Husari says, "Abdullah's talks about his "right" to Iraq's throne spread widely, so much so that they were reflected

---

[1]Khayriyya Qasmiyya (op. cit.), pp. 50-53.

on the pages of newspapers. Even a Turkish newspaper used this as a pretext to cast doubts about the Arab revolution."[1]

What is strange is that Abdullah did not forget his "right" to Iraq's throne even after Faisal's death. It is narrated that he went to Iraq after Faisal's death, so a party was thrown for him during which a poet said the following verse of poetry in his praise:

He relinquished, due to his goodness, Iraq's throne,
Thus he honoured Iraq's throne when he let it be bygone.

When Abdullah heard this verse, he became angry and interrupted the poet saying, "Fie on you! I never relinquished it, and I shall never relinquish it!"

Sayyid Talib's Activity

Sayyid Talib [al-Naqeeb] was in Baghdad when he felt that the winds were blowing against him and that the British did not want him. His feeling intensified when the delegation that travelled to attend the Cairo conference was formed; he was not invited to participate in it, whereas Sasson Khadhouri, Ja`far al-`Askari, Ms Bell and others were not inclined to him. Ms Bell wrote in a letter dated February 24, 1921, after her departure from Baghdad with the said delegation on board a boat, saying the following:

> "We are leaving. Ja`far and Sasson Afandi were glad to participate in the delegation. But Sayyid Talib from the other side is very angry for not being in the delegation. We ate with him supper the night before leaving to Baghdad the next morning, and I was sitting beside him and kept encouraging him to talk. When Whisky glasses were circulated, he whispered in my ear in a sad drunk tone that he regarded me as his sister and obeyed my advice, and he regarded me as his only support." Ms Bell comments about this saying, "Since I

---

[1]Sati` al-Husari, *My Memories in Iraq*, Beirut, Lebanon, 1967, Vol. 1, pp. 24-25.

was deeply convinced that his ambition will never materialize, I kept muttering cordial statements that had no color."[1]

Sayyid Talib seized the opportunity when Cox was away from Iraq during his participation in the Cairo Conference and kept exerting great efforts, spending huge sums of money to publicize himself, and his motto in that [regard] was "Iraq belongs to the Iraqis." In his memoirs, Sulayman Faydhi, then governor of Baghdad, wrote in his memoirs that Sayyid Talib visited him in the courtroom and asked to talk to him alone. He said to him, "I have decided to nominate myself for Iraq's throne. Due to the love which I have known in you, I request you to publicize for me in the judicial circles and to get the governors, lawyers, law students and ministry of justice staff to vote for me." When Sulayman reminded him that his effort would fail, Sayyid Talib said, "You are wrong, for Mr. Philby is on my side, and he has promised me to exert the greatest efforts. He promised me to convince Sir Percy Cox, who remains hesitant about the matter of the new king and to get Ms Bell to tone down her enthusiasm for Prince Faisal. He also wrote to the political governors in the southern governorates advising them to assist me; therefore, I have decided to tour these governorates and to conduct a broad electoral publicity campaign there. I, therefore, ask you to publicize in the field in which I think you are influential and loved." When Sayyid Talib lost hope of convincing Sulayman Faydhi, he left him angrily.[2]

Aziz al-Qassab narrates in his memoirs that as he was sitting at the meeting place of Abdul-Aziz al-Zi'baq one afternoon, Sayyid Ibrahim al-Shawaf and his brother Ali entered the place, holding in their hands a folder containing an order from the high commissioner to appoint Sayyid Talib as ruler of Iraq, and al-Qassab protested. Then the attendants passed it around without signing it. The café's owner beat his head with his hand

---

[1]Burgoyne, *Gertrude Bell,* London, 1961, Vol. 2, p. 209.

[2]Sulayman Faydhi, *Fi Ghamrat al-Nidhal* (in the thicket of struggle), Baghdad, 1952, pp. 262-263.

as he sarcastically said, "Is this the appointment of a quarter's mayor?!" Those present laughed.[1]

On March 8, Sayyid Talib began his 13-day tour of the southern governorates accompanied by a group of his supporters such as Salim al-Khayun, Abdul-Razzaq al-Meer, Abboud al-Mallak, Ahmad al-Rawi, Shakir al-Ni`mah and Ahmad al-Salim. Sayyid Talib spent huge sums of money on his tour, and his supporters held for him a huge reception and many banquets, and he used to address people [in such a way as to] try to make himself loved by them. He kept disseminating the principles which ran in harmony with their beliefs and inclinations. One of the interesting incidents narrated in this regard is that a tribe released this chant as it welcomed him:

A third is for Allah, two-thirds are for Talib,
And Allah's third is demanded by Talib.

During his tour, Sayyid Talib kept announcing to people that he would exert his effort to release all the political prisoners who participated in the 1920 Revolution. When he passed by Hilla, he visited the prisoners in it and assured them that they would shortly be released. His speech in al-Najaf was an example in this regard. In it, he struck on the hearts' sensitive chords. Here below, we quote an excerpt from what he said there:

"I have seen that it is my duty to derive from the opinions and views of the good men and *mujtahid* scholars what should be done to bring to life the legacies of the straightforward religion, to seek the paths of civilization and progress for our common homeland, especially al-Najaf al-Ashraf and Karbala. I have endeavoured first of all to perform the first duty upon me before the preliminary matters, which is: repatriating all those who are exiled, forgiving the criminals and repatriating my Iraqi brothers who migrated to Syria and other lands. But my firm belief causes me to think well of the

---

[1] Abdul-Aziz al-Qassab, *Min Thikrayati* (from my memories), Beirut, 1962, pp. 207-208.

supporters of the auspicious Shari`a and of their lofty determination. I plead to Allah by the sanctity of my pure grandfather, especially my greatest ancestor, my master and chief, the Commander of the Faithful, peace be upon him, that I promise you to realize your hopes in front of his [Imam Ali's] sacred mausoleum. I have appointed for you a rational, well-cultured and strict governor and a mayor who has expertise and experience, and it will please me if you disclose to both of them everything that concerns you so they may recommend to me what should be done about various matters. I would like to convey to you the glad tiding that the prime minister in the capital — His Highness Baghdad's chief of chiefs, my master, Sayyid Abdul-Rahman Afandi [al-Naqeeb], has expressed to me — that he greatly depends upon you and greatly trusts you, and he has commissioned me to convey his kindness and directives to you all in particular."[1]

Al-Rusafi Summoned

Public opinion in Baghdad was at the time split into two groups: one of them advocated the principle of "Iraq belongs to the Iraqis", and it was headed by Sayyid Talib, as we have already stated. The second called for choosing one of the sons of King Hussain [of Mecca] to ascend Iraq's throne. This second group was called the "Sherifi Party".

The first group mainly included the sons of staunch families and those who were inclined to the Turks. They were the ones who, in our days, were called "reactionaries". The second group, i.e. the Sherifi Party, it included most of those who participated in the 1920 Revolution and the advocates of Arab nationalism. Nationalism was regarded in those days as a progressive movement. In a letter that she wrote after her return from the Cairo Conference, Ms Bell stated the following:

---

[1]'Hussain Hadi Sheela', *Talib al-Naqeeb* (a non-published university thesis), pp. 258-260.

"The prominent figures, who are proud of their lofty class affiliation, loathed the possibility that they would see the youths who ruled Syria under Faisal, those who mostly do not belong to renowned families, also ruling Iraq. The thinking of these figures did not agree with that of those youths who are very progressive and are ready to speak openly and continuously about the necessity of getting rid of the reactionary sheikhs and about introducing new ideas."[1]

It is worth mentioning that the *naqeeb*, Abdul-Rahman al-Gailani [right photo], supported the first group. Due to his class way of thinking, he held in contempt the revolutionary youths who rose to fame and who do not belong to deeply rooted families. In addition to that, he held in contempt the Hashimi [Hashemite] family. He declared this opinion frankly to Ms Bell in 1919 when he said to her, "I prefer a thousand times the return of the Turks to Baghdad overseeing the Sherif or his sons installed here."[2]

Abdul-Rahman al-Gailani
(Courtesy: Wikipedia Commons)

One day, the leaders of the first group met. They were headed by the *naqeeb*, Sayyid Talib, Hikmat Sulayman and Tawfiq al-Khalidi. They decided to launch a newspaper that would speak for them, provided poet Ma`ruf al-Rusafi would be its editor-in-chief. At that time, al-Rusafi was in Jerusalem studying Arabic literature at the Teachers House, so Hikmat Sulayman sent him a telegram asking him to return to Baghdad. The ministry, too, sent a telegram to the high commissioner in Palestine asking

----

[1]Burgoyne (op. cit.), Vol. 2, p. 212.

[2]Ms. Bell, *From Iraq's Recent History* (translated by Ja`far al-Khayyat), Beirut, Lebanon, 1971, p. 480.

him to send al-Rusafi at its own expense. Thus, al-Rusafi travelled to Cairo and waited for a ship to transport him from the Suez. Al-Rusafi met some members of the delegation that attended the Cairo Conference. When Cox came to know that al-Rusafi was going to Baghdad, he suggested to him to go with them on the same ship. Cox did not know that al-Rusafi was going to Baghdad for the opposite goal of the one decided in the Cairo Conference.

In his memoirs, al-Rusafi says,

"When I reached Baghdad and met *naqeeb* Abdul-Rahman Afandi, I came to know thereafter that they wanted to oppose Faisal based on 'Iraq belongs to the Iraqis'. Then we met at the *naqeeb*'s place with Sayyid Talib, and I was among those who supported this idea. I suggested to them, after carefully discussing the subject, that this job, I mean the publicity, could not be undertaken except on the basis of money. I said to them that this could not be done for less than 100,000 Ottoman liras. The *naqeeb* thought the sum was huge. Then Talib Pasha said that he was ready to put twice the sum the *naqeeb* would put. The meeting did not result in an agreement about any opinion. It was concluded with the decision to meet again. I contacted Tawfiq al-Khalidi —who was present during the meeting — who said to me that we would go together in a small ship, 'I, you and Talib Pasha, and we would discuss the subject there.' But before this meeting could take place, the British banished Sayyid Talib Pasha."[1]

Shrewdness

Cox reached Baghdad on April 9, but he did not announce what was decided in the Cairo Conference, i.e. that Faisal was chosen [to be Iraq's king]; rather, he let people argue and discuss the candidates for the throne as he kept watching them as if he had nothing to do with it. On April 12,

---

[1]-- *Al-Thaqafa al-Jadeeda* (new culture) magazine in its issue dated April of 1954.

Cox announced a statement about the matters which the Cairo Conference had discussed, pointing out the issue of minimizing military expenses, issues of domestic security, border protection and the issuing of general amnesty, but he did not talk at all about the subject of choosing Faisal which was, in fact, the most important matter the Conference had discussed.

Philby had written before Cox's arrival a memorandum protesting the rumour that Faisal was chosen in the Cairo Conference, stating that he had to resign from his post if the rumour proved to be true because this, in his view, violated the past British promises to let the Iraqis be free to choose for themselves whoever they wanted. Philby submitted this memorandum to Bunham Carter, who supported his viewpoint. When Cox arrived, Carter presented the memorandum to him. Then Philby came to meet him. Cox answered him thus: "The British government does not intend to renege on its promises to the people of Iraq."[1] Apparently, Philby was convinced of this answer and quietly left, not knowing what fate had in store for him and for his fellow.

Cox left Philby free in his activity of inviting people to support Sayyid Talib while also leaving Ms Bell from the other side to be free in her activity of calling for [support of] the Sherifs. He stood between the two almost neutrally or, as he himself described it, "friendly neutrally." Whenever people went to him to ask him about his opinion, he would say to them, "The British government supports the nomination of a Sherif prince for Iraq, but people are free to accept or reject him." At the same time, Cox sent a telegram to his government warning it against imposing Faisal on the Iraqis, advising it to leave Faisal to personally undertake the task of convincing the Iraqis, when he reaches them, that he is the man who is suitable for their throne.[2]

It can be said that from the social standpoint, Cox was, in his position, a shrewd person of a high order: had he announced to people the British government's desire to choose Faisal, a reaction would have

---

[1] John Philby, *Philby's Days in Iraq* (translated by Ja`far al-Khayyat), Beirut, Lebanon, 1950, p. 51.

[2] Philip Graves, *Sir Percy Cox*, London, 2nd edition, p. 287.

resulted among the circles of the nationalists, and this might have led to weakening or crushing the Sherifi party.

We must not forget that days before and during the [1920] Revolution, the nationalists were demanding to choose a Sherif prince for Iraq's throne, and they did that in order to defy the British authority, which at the time did not desire it. Had the authority desired this choice and called for it, the nationalists would, of course, have responded contrarily.

This is one of the secrets of Iraqi society. Apparently, Cox realized the implication of this secret and wanted to avoid the mistake that his predecessor, Wilson, had made; therefore, we found him pretending to be neutral despite his knowledge that he was ordered by his government to install Faisal as king anyway.

Sayyid Talib Threatens

Sayyid Talib was accustomed, in his early days during the Turkish era, to use kindness and flattery to get what he wanted. If he found this useless, he would resort to intimidation, and he might sometimes resort to killing and bloodshed when intimidation failed. Sayyid Talib succeeded in his method a great deal. It seems that he now wants to follow the same method with the British, forgetting that the British are not the Turks, and that Cox is different from the Turkish *wali* (provincial governor) a great deal.

In April of 1921, Sir Perceval Landon — the special envoy of London's *Daily Telegraph* newspaper — reached Baghdad. This man knew Arabic, so Sayyid Talib decided to take the opportunity to deliver a speech threatening the British. He, therefore, threw a lavish dinner banquet at his house in honour of Landon.

The banquet was held on the eve of April 13 and was attended by the French consul, the Iranian consul, Arthur Todd, director of the Lynch Company, and his wife, Sheikh Muhammed al-Ameer, head of the Rabi`ah tribe, Sheikh Salim al-Khayun, head of the Bani Assad tribe in Chibayish, and others. Philby apologized for not attending the banquet as if he realized that it would have political repercussions, so he did not want to be involved in it. As for Hussain Afnan, he attended the banquet in order to translate the speech which Sayyid Talib was to deliver to the British.

We have two reports about what went on during that banquet. One of them exists in the memoirs of Philby, and the other is stated in Grave's book, where the biography of Cox is recorded. Perhaps it is useful to review excerpts from each report:

Describing the banquet, Philby says, "The talk was, in fact, political. Liquor flowed like water, including the best Champaign brands. The host was merry like any other guest, perhaps merrier than all others. At the end of the invitation, he stood up to lighten from his heart some of the political burdens which were more than he could bear. The gist of his talk was that there were rumours about appointing Faisal as king of Iraq, rumours which started filling up [the talk of] assemblies and gatherings, and he wanted to explain to the attendants and to the British government in particular that the people of Iraq did not want Faisal and would not tolerate imposing him on them. 'If you have doubts about my statement, we have among us at this table Sheikh Muhammed, the emir of Rabi`ah, who has 40,000 strong, and sheikh so-and-so as head of a tribe that provides 30,000 men. Ask them so they may tell you what people think in this regard, that the British government had promised we would freely choose the form of government which we want, and I protest against any change about this promise.'"[1]

As for Graves, his report is clearer and more detailed. He says, "Sayyid Talib's statement was not casual; rather, it was already very well prepared. Sayyid Talib started it by repeating his statement that he was not pleased with the stance of the high commissioner and believed that the British government intended to completely stay neutral. Then he turned to Landon, asking him for a confirmation. Landon answered him, saying that this is what he, too, believed; therefore, Sayyid Talib asked him, "Are you fully sure about it?" Landon felt a little bit annoyed by this question, then he answered that he had obtained an assurance from the high commissioner (in this regard). Sayyid Talib, therefore, went on to say, "Some British officials in the retinue of the high commissioner tilt towards the Sherif, and they are now trying to use their influence in this direction in an unsuitable way." Then Sayyid Talib directed a question to Landon, saying, "Does Landon advise me to submit a complaint to King George or to the high commissioner against these officials so they may be

---

[1]John Philby (op. cit.), p. 52.

transferred from their positions?" Answering him, Landon pointed out that there were some British officials who were known for their bias to the *naqeeb*; therefore, transferring the biased officials to a particular side must be accompanied by transferring the officials who are biased to the other side. Here, Hussain Afnan whispered in the ears of Sayyid Talib, pointing out to the precision of this point and to the repercussions it implied. Sayyid Talib roared a little, abandoned that point and shifted his talk to another: he turned to Sheikh Muhammed al-Ameer, asking for his support. He said, "The people of Iraq are determined that the British government should fulfil its promises, and if it does not do that, there is Muhammed al-Ameer who has 30,000 rifles desiring to know why. There is also the sheikh of the Chibayish and all members of his tribe." Then Sayyid Talib went on to say that if there was the slightest indication of bias from the British government towards one of the sides, the *naqeeb* was ready to submit his complaint to the Islamic world, to India, Cairo, Istanbul and also to Paris.[1]

The banquet had hardly come to an end when Arthur Todd rushed to the house of Ms Bell in the Sinak quarter [of Baghdad] to tell her about what went on. He was followed by Landon, who told her of the same. Ms Bell, therefore, sent a detailed report to Cox about what she had heard, including in it a warning to Cox that Sayyid Talib had gathered around him gang members who would help him in Basra to intimidate people, including the man who had killed the Turkish commander shortly before the war. Ms Bell also said in her report that Sayyid Talib might kill Faisal when he [Faisal] came to Iraq.[2]

Sayyid Talib's Banishment

When Sayyid Talib delivered his threatening statement, he wanted Cox to hear it through Todd. Due to his conceit, he thought that Cox would be apprehensive of his threat. But Cox was exactly the opposite[3]: He regarded Sayyid Talib's statement as a threat to declare revolution or

---

[1]Graves (opt. cit.), pp. 288-289.

[2]Burgoyne (op. cit.), Vol. 2, p. 214.

[3]Monroe, *Philby of Arabia*, London, 1973, p. 108.

jihad; so, if he remained silent about it and its report would spread among the people, this would be seen by the public as an indication that Sayyid Talib became strong enough to defy Britain and to do whatever he pleased without anyone to deter him.

Cox decided to arrest Sayyid Talib and to banish him as soon as possible, and he sent a telegram to London in this regard. Cox did not commission the police to carry out the arrest for fear they would fail. Instead, he contacted Gen. Holden, commander of the military forces, asking him to arrest Sayyid Talib with his forces.

On the morning of April 15, Holden held an emergency military meeting at his command's quarters to put the arrest plan together. After deliberations, he decided to commission Maj. Bouville carried out the arrest because the latter was a friend of Sayyid Talib and knew him very well, so he could not make a mistake in identifying him at the time of the arrest. Bouville protested and opposed his being commissioned to perform this task saying, "Sayyid Talib is my personal friend, and for so long I enjoyed his hospitality and food; so, it is not appropriate that I should be the one who arrests him." Bouville suggested the mission be undertaken by policemen, so Holden answered him by saying that his past experiences proved that the policemen could not be relied upon. Moreover, they would hesitate to arrest Sayyid Talib, who was their respected chief. Then Holden addressed Bouville saying, "You must forget your personal sentiments and carry out the mission as a military duty."

Holden planned the arrest to take place in the afternoon of that day, that is, April 15. The reason is that Sayyid Talib had an arrangement at that time to visit Cox's wife at her house and have tea there. Upon coming out of the house, he would immediately be arrested. Bouville protested to this, too, saying that the matter could be misunderstood by people who would regard it as a violation of the etiquettes of hospitality, and Cox's wife would be blamed for it. But Holden insisted on his opinion because he did not like any possibility of failure in carrying out this plan.

Cox and his wife used to live in the same famous house which later became the quarters of the British Embassy in Baghdad. They had moved into it shortly after its construction had been completed, and it overlooked the Tigris River bank in the Kraimat Quarter of the Karkh flank. Cox's wife made preparations to welcome Sayyid Talib at the house's garden without knowing anything about the arrest plan. She had also invited Ms Bell so she would interpret the talk between her and Sayyid Talib. As for Cox himself, he did not attend but went to the horse race track to watch!

Sayyid Talib arrived at the house in his car at 4:30 pm and sat in the garden to drink tea with Cox's wife and Ms Bell. Shortly after that, Maj. Bouville came accompanied by a young officer named Capt. Cookes, who both drank tea, then left. Ten minutes later, Sayyid Talib stood up to say goodbye because he had been invited to have dinner at Sayyid Ja`far Utayfah in al-Kadhimiyya. Ms Bell stood up and escorted him to the door to bid him goodbye. Sayyid Talib rode in his car, which took him in the direction of the bridge. But the car hardly drove before it suddenly found itself blocked by a large cargo truck stopped in the middle of the road as though it had malfunctioned. There was another cargo truck loaded with soldiers behind Sayyid Talib's car. When Sayyid Talib was about to protest and ask about the reason for that truck parked there, Maj. Bouville and Capt. Cookes suddenly came out, apologized about the road being blocked and asked him to consider himself their prisoner. Then they took him to the [Tigris] river shore where the general commander's steamboat was waiting. The boat carried Sayyid Talib southward.

Because of his extreme care that the plan should succeed, Holden ordered to cut off Philby's phone line; therefore, Philby did not know at the time about the incident.[1] He says in his memoirs that he did not know about the incident till in the evening when he and his wife went to the ``Ilwiyya Club to have dinner due to a previous invitation from Capt. Cookes. When he reached the club, he did not find Capt. Cookes; another officer was there representing him as the host. The officer talked to him about what happened to Sayyid Talib, so Philby became very angry when he heard the story, and so was his wife. In the morning, Philby went to meet Cox determined to submit his resignation immediately. But Cox kept pacifying him and apologizing to him for not informing him of the matter at the time for fear Sayyid Talib would know about his arrest and thus foil the plan. Cox assured him once more that there was no intention to

---

[1]Monroe (op. cit.), p. 109.

impose Faisal on the people. Then he told him that he had appointed an interior minister to replace Sayyid Talib. Philby came out pleased.[1]

On April 19, a statement was announced from the high commissioner justifying the banishment of Sayyid Talib. Its summary was that the British government maintained its pledge to ensure full freedom for the Iraqis to express their desire about the type of government they sought. But Sayyid Talib articulated shameful threats about raising arms in the face of the British government, something which the high commissioner could not tolerate, especially since it came from a man who occupied an important job such as Sayyid Talib.[2]

Sayyid Talib's banishment did not produce any effect in Baghdad, where people met it with calm as though it was normal. When some ministers talked to the *naqeeb* about this matter, he was satisfied by saying, "I advised that he should be treated with respect and politeness."[3] In London, the matter was to the contrary: the press published the story and kept calling for doing away with the mandate in Iraq, describing it as a "nightmare."[4] Cox wrote to a friend in London saying that his wife could not help crying over "poor" Sayyid Talib.[5]

Sayyid Talib's Fate

Perhaps it is appropriate here to talk briefly about Sayyid Talib's fate after his arrest in Baghdad. A steamboat carried him away to Kut. From there, he boarded a river tugboat to Fao where he boarded a ship that sailed to Ceylon Island [now Sri Lanka]. There, he was placed in custody. The British government set aside for him a monthly salary of 2,500 rupees.

---

[1]John Philby (op. cit.), pp. 53-55.

[2] Abdul-Razzaq al-Hassani, *Tarikh al-Wizarat al-Iraqiyya* (history of Iraqi administrations), Saida, Lebanon, 1965, Vol. 1, pp. 29-30.

[3]Khayri al-Omari, *Hikayat Siyasiyya* (political anecdotes), Cairo, Egypt, 1969, p. 48.

[4]Monroe (op. cit.), p. 109.

[5]Graves (op. cit.), p. 308.

Sayyid Talib remained in jail in Ceylon till after Faisal's coronation, after which he was released. When Ibn Saud attacked Hijaz in 1924, Sayyid Talib went to Jeddah to participate in the mediation between both sides. There, he met Lebanese writer Ameen al-Rayhani. Describing his meeting with Sayyid Talib, al-Rayhani wrote, "I remember our meeting in Jidda in the fall of 1924, and I remember a talk about Iraq. He (Talib) narrated to us some of his days' incidents as we were sipping Whisky and soda, then he put the cup on the table, raised his hand to that honourable shiny head to rub and to pat, saying, 'There is here something that cannot be beaten. It cannot be beaten.' He was considering his return to Iraq and to politics. He was still entertaining golden dreams. Resuming his talk, he said, 'Everything has its own timing. You will hear when I return what will surprise and please you, God willing, and I shall send for you, Professor, and appoint you minister of education.'"[1]

It seems that Sayyid Talib lost all hope after the Hijaz war, so he started trying to return to Iraq. I found, among the royal palace's documents, letters from him to King Faisal pleading to permit him to return. Philby kept trying to get the London government to lift the injustice meted upon him.[2] He was finally permitted to return. On May 1, 1925, Sayyid Talib reached Basra by ship, where a crowd of about 1,000 Basris waited on the dock to welcome him.[3]

Sayyid Talib secluded himself at home in the Sabeeliyyat on the bank of Shatt al-Arab (water estuary) near Basra and kept drinking too much Whisky, and he avoided meeting the public or attending parties. Whenever he went to Basra, he took an empty route, dodging the looks of passersby.[4] Apparently, he suffered from a severe psychological complex as a result of his hopes being dashed. His personality stood on the basis of love for power and broad glory, and it is difficult for a man like him to be normal like all other people.

---

[1] Ameen al-Rayhani, *Faisal al-Awwal* (Faisal I), Beirut, Lebanon, 1958, p. 84.

[2] Monroe (op. cit.), p. 109.

[3] -- *Al-Iraq* newspaper of May 5, 1925.

[4] Khayri Ameen al-Omari, *Shakhsiyyat Iraqiyya* (Iraqi personalities), Baghdad, Iraq, 1955, Vol. 1, p. 40.

In the spring of 1925, Sayyid Talib went to Baghdad to meet King Faisal after Abdullah al-Midhyafi had mediated on his behalf in this regard. Several banquets were held in Baghdad in his honour, the latest of which was that of the Gailani *naqeeb*. When Sayyid Talib entered to meet the *naqeeb*, the latter stood up to welcome him and to describe him as his "son", "loved one", and the "apple" of his eyes. Sayyid Talib kept remonstrating with the *naqeeb* for not helping him when he was arrested, then he bent on his hand and kissed it.[1]

Sayyid Talib stayed in Baghdad for only one week, after which he returned to his Sabeeliyyat home. In 1929, he became seriously sick, so he travelled to Munich for treatment at one of its hospitals. On June 16, he breathed his last, and his body was taken to Basra.

Sayyid Talib's coffin received an unprecedented send-off; the markets shut down, mourning him, and the masses wept around his coffin. After his death, Sayyid Talib turned into a loved Shi`a leader, and this is not odd![2]

Success Of The Call For The Sherifs

Sayyid Talib's banishment in April of 1921 was a reason for supporting the Sherifi party and a devastating blow to its opponents. Ja`far al-`Askari, Nouri al-Sa`eed and other men of the Sherifi party doubled their efforts, supported by those who returned from Syria on the one hand and by Ms Bell on the other.

A few days after the banishment of Sayyid Talib, another incident took place that led to increasing the support for the Sherifi party: a group of clergymen and tribal chiefs met in al-Kadhimiyya headed by the then

---

[1] *Ibid.*, pp. 43-45.

[2] Sayyid Tālib al-Naqeeb was not a Shi`a, he and his family were Sunnis. I, Translator of this book, heppened to know Lady Su`ad al-Naqeeb, cousin of Sayyid Talib al-Naqeeb, when I lived in Falls Church, Virginia. She at the time lived in a Mount Vernon, Virginia house a few yards from the house where George Washington used to live during the American Civil War at a curve of the Potomac River which I visited once. It is open to tourists. She was then trying to sell her house. She told me a good deal about Sayyid Talib, joking about him being called "Sayyid" although he was not a Shi`a. –Tr.

senior *mujtahid*, Sheikh Mahdi al-Khalisi, and decided to send a telegram to Sherif Hussain in Mecca to ask him to send his son, Faisal, to be the king of Iraq who would be tied to a parliamentary council. But when they sent their telegram to the telegram office, the official in charge of receiving it refused to accept it, providing some excuses and pretexts.

We do not know the reason that made the official in charge to refuse to accept the telegram, but this refusal, at any rate, led to people becoming more enthusiastic and to their insistence on sending the said telegram and considered the refusal of the official as a challenge to their patriotic wish and as a British plot against them.

The clergymen and tribal chiefs returned to meet with al-Khalisi again and decided to organize a protest to submit to the high commissioner, but al-Khalisi advised them to wait. He sent a letter to Nouri al-Sa`eed asking him to help them in their bid to send the telegram to Sherif Hussain. This is the text of the letter:

To the Honorable and Respectful Nouri al-Sa`eed:

After praying for your success, the British have refused to grant the Iraqis the freedom to do anything, including their right to choose their own king for whose sake they have sacrificed what is dear and precious. They instructed the officials in charge of sending telegrams to reject telegrams addressed to King Hussain son of Ali in which they ask him to send one of his sons to be king over Iraq. This undoubtedly has dire repercussions; therefore, I see it obligatory upon you to officially or personally interfere to remove this restriction and to give the Iraqis the full freedom in this regard. Anything else is up to them, and peace be upon you.

Sha`ban 10 [September 12], 1339 (A.D. 1921)
On behalf of Mahdi al-Khalisi

Al-Khalisi sent his letter through a special envoy who got it to reach Nouri al-Sa`eed in the defence ministry. When the messenger got the letter to reach Nouri, the latter said to him that he would investigate and send the answer as soon as possible, adding that he thought the British government in London had no knowledge of this plot; rather, it is the game of some British officials in Baghdad together with a group of Iraqis who do not wish to coronate one of the sons of King Hussain (of Mecca) as King of Iraq.

The next day, al-Khalisi received a letter from Houri al-Sa`eed; as below:

The Defence Ministry – Sha`ban 11 [September 13] 1339 (A.D. 1921)

To the great `allama and greatest mujtahid, His Eminence Sheikh Mahdi al-Khalisi, may Allah grant the nation the enjoyment of his sustained stay,

Peace of Allah, His mercy and blessings be upon you. I present to my master mentor that I discussed with those in the British government (in an official way) who are concerned with this matter in regards to the telegrams which are desired to be sent to His Majesty King , requesting him to send (to Iraq) one of his honourable sons, and they answered me saying that there is no objection in so doing, so I liked to write my master about this matter. If His Eminence wishes to wait till the high commissioner issues a circular [in this regard], there is no harm in it. The telegram offices are ready at all times to accept telegrams of this type. Please accept in conclusion my extreme respect and regards, master.[1]

When this answer reached al-Khalisi, he declared his thanks for Nouri al-Sa`eed and advised people to send their telegrams to Sherif Hussain as they wished. This announcement was echoed by jubilation among the public. People felt that they had achieved victory in their national demands. Throughout Iraq, people kept going to telegram offices to send Sherif Hussain telegrams asking him to send his son, Faisal. The

---

[1]Gen. al-Mizhir Al Fir`awn, *Al-Haqa'iq al-Nasi`a* (glittering facts), Baghdad, Iraq, 1952, Vol. 2, pp. 517-58.

telegrams kept reaching Mecca one after the other in an unprecedented way.

Ms Bell wrote on June 12 commenting on the above, saying,

> "Deep in my mind, there is a firm belief that there is no nation that must be permanently ruled by another nation. Last year, when they all were shouting the name of Abdullah, they did not want him because he was the best man or because they were under the impact of national zeal; rather, they regarded shouting his name as being against the wish of the British. It has been political short-sightedness to leave the notion to crystallize with them that nationalism is opposition to the British. Now we are trying to nourish nationalism. But I admit that the nationalism which is not against the foreigners, may grow weak. When Faisal comes and walks side by side us, he will not be a loved person had he led a *jihad* movement against us. He will not lead a *jihad* movement; this is not his temper; so, can we provide him with the spirit that enables him to inspire an Arab state, a true inspiration? This depends on his character. It is the wisdom of Sir Percy Cox to stay hiding, working from behind a curtain."[1]

Stance Of The Baghdadi Newspapers

Following the shutting down of the *Istiqlal* newspaper on February 9, 1921, no Arab newspaper remained in Baghdad other than *Al-Iraq* newspaper which is owned by Razzooq Ghannam. This newspaper used to support British policy in Iraq. When the Sherifi party was actively publicizing Prince Faisal, the *Al-Iraq* newspaper adopted the same stance undertaken by Cox, i.e. that of "friendly neutrality".

On May 5, the *Al-Iraq* newspaper published an article by (poet) Ma`ruf al-Rusafi under a borrowed signature, "an Iraqi contemplating", in

---

[1]Burgoyne (op. cit.), Vol. 2, p. 220.

which he called for the principle of "Iraq belongs to the Iraqis". In it, he responded to those who called for a Sherifi prince for Iraq. This is an excerpt from that article in which the writer says, "As regarding what one of our Iraqi brothers said, that is, the sun of the recent Arab Renaissance rose in the Hijazi country, especially in the house of the Sherif King of Hijaz, so only one of them should sit on the king's throne, he does not reach the truth because, in the said Renaissance, many sons of Iraq and Syria have participated, sacrificing everything that is precious and truly struggled for the sake of freedom and independence. Therefore, we can say that the Renaissance itself did not take place as it has except through these Iraqis and their likes from among the Arabs, not only through the Hijazis. Hence, the emirs of Hijaz do not have such a right."

When this article appeared, the Sherifis responded to it. *Al-Iraq* newspaper welcomed their responses as if it was discreetly encouraging them to do so as the British policy at the time required. It, therefore, published a response by Abdullah al-Dulaimi on May 11, another by Rasheed al-Hashimi on the 12th of the same month and a third by Sulayman Zuhair on the 13th.

On June 20, a newspaper called *Al-Falah*, which was owned by Abdul-Lateef al-Falahi, appeared. He was a graduate of the military college in Istanbul. He openly advocated choosing Faisal. In its first issue, he wrote, saying, "When the nation openly invited Prince Faisal, it did so because it sees him incorporating the attributes that qualify him to be a king over them. It recognizes the great services which he rendered to the Arab nation, in addition to the political experiences which he gained due to being in contact with the West's politicians and the lofty station he gained with those who tie and untie."

On June 23, a third newspaper appeared, *Lisan al-Arab,* owned by Ibrahim Hilmi al-Omar. This man was then publishing the same newspaper in Damascus, and he became famous there by quickly shifting from one stance to another. Ibrahim declared his political stance in the first issue of the newspaper, which he published in Baghdad. He said that people should not expect his newspaper to be biased to one party over another. It is believed that he undertook this stance in response to the "friendly neutrality" stance which Cox had adopted.

On June 25, a fourth newspaper appeared bearing the name *Dijla* (Tigris), owned by Dawood al-Sa`di. It undertook a trend indirectly opposing that of the Sherifi Party. It was said that Philby had something to do with this newspaper[1]. This newspaper started diversifying its discussions in order to weaken the Sherifi trend in Iraq: at times, it would point out the despotism and injustice the monarchist system contains, and at other times it would urge the Iraqis to stick to their allegiance to Abdullah about which an agreement was already made in Syria.[2]

What is noteworthy is that public opinion started looking at the *Dijla* newspaper with an attitude that was not without suspicion and accusation, regarding it as speaking on behalf of the British or those who are loyal to them. Serious criticism started being directed at this newspaper from every side till the matter prompted the newspaper's owner one day to write an editorial in which he responded to his critics under the headline, "A free man is tested by the sons of adulteresses."[3]

Khaz`al Nominates Himself

Since the end of the war [World War I], Sheikh Khaz`al, emir of al-Muhammara, hoped that he would rule over Iraq. He rendered the British a great service during the war, so he hoped they would install him as emir over Iraq as a reward for his service. On December 22, 1918, Sheikh Khaz`al wrote Cox the following:

> "It seems that the British government is looking for an emir for Iraq. There is no suitable candidate at hand. Nine-tenths of Iraq are Shi`as, so the emir must also be Shi`a, and I am an Iraqi citizen. I was born and raised on the [banks of] Shatt al-Arab and proved my sincerity [to the British], and I shall work in all matters according to the wishes and orders of the High Commissioner just as I have been in the past."

---

[1]Rafael Batti, *Al-Sahafa fil Iraq* (press in Iraq), Cairo, Egypt, 1955, p. 86.

[2]Khayri al-Omari, *Hikayat Siyasiyya* (political anecdotes), p. 73.

[3]Rafael Batti (op. cit.), p. 86.

Cox did not support this request of Sheikh Khaz`al. Cox was of the view that choosing Khaz`al to be the emir of Iraq would have a bad impact on the Sunnis who had the greatest influence in Iraq.[1]

Sheikh Khaz`al did not lose hope but kept seeking the appropriate opportunity to demand Iraq's throne again, and he kept strengthening his relationships with the Iraqis through various means, especially Shi`a theologians, poets and speakers, spending money lavishly on them and endearing himself to them. In 1920, he ordered the publication of a book in Egypt that contained a biography of Imam Ali and a very long poem in his praise written by Abdul-Maseeh al-Antaki, (Christian) owner of the *Imran* newspaper of Cairo. The publication of this book was completed on April 30, so its copies were sent to Muhammara and from there to Iraq to distribute to people free of charge by way of giving Khaz`al publicity. But the British authority did not permit its dissemination, so copies of the book remained stored at the homes of those who were put in charge of its distribution, and it was not disseminated except years later, that is, when it was too late!

In early 1921, when the British were looking for a suitable candidate for Iraq's throne, Khaz`al recovered his energy along this path, sending a theologian to Najaf with a huge sum of money estimated at 20,000 gold liras to distribute there for publicity for himself. He also sent Muzahim al-Pachachi to Baghdad for this purpose, too.

The theologian did not distribute anything of that money but kept it all to himself, and it is said that he hid it in the walls of his house and built on it, not opening it except shortly before the man's death. As for Muzahim al-Pachachi, his efforts in Baghdad failed, and he wrote Khaz`al a letter dated March 9, 1921, from which we would like to quote this excerpt:

The Honourable Master Chief,

> After receiving the honour of kissing your honourable fingers, I submit that I, according to your order, went to Baghdad and spoke with those who know, and I found them, just as I had predicted, seeing the circumstances quite differently: convincing anyone of what is desired is the

---

[1] Ghassan Atiyyah (op. cit.), p. 368

hardest matter, if not impossible. I examined the status very well and came to know its inner and outer conditions. My frankness with Your Highness forces me to say the same thing which I had said a month ago: the matter is settled, and there is not the least benefit in it, if not some harm. It is not far-fetched that this harm may afflict people, such as myself if he tries to change what has already been agreed upon out of his loyalty to the people who tie and untie. I remain the same sincere servant who is truthful to Your Highness, may Allah prolong your life, may He grant us the joy of your long life and make you a pride and a treasure for myself.

Sent by,
Muzahim al-Ameen al-Pachachi[1]

Khaz`al realized that publicity and money spending were useless in the face of the will of the hidden forces that worked behind the curtains; therefore, he preferred to withdraw at the appropriate time instead of being stubborn. On June 14, the *Al-Iraq* newspaper published a statement under the heading "About Iraq's Throne", which it started by saying, "We have received the following from a trusted source in Basra", and this is the text:

"The Holiest Chief, His Highness Sheikh Khaz`al, supreme emir of al-Muhammara, met with a group of dignitaries and seniors of Basra, including Their Excellencies Ahmed Pash al-Sani`, Abdul-Lateef Pash al-Mandeel, Abdul-Kareem Beg al-Sa`doun and Muzahim Beg al-Ameen al-Pachachi, and notified them frankly of the following: 'When I presented the case of Iraq's throne for discussion and saw that those who nominated themselves for that throne were less than myself in status, competence and ability and in all qualifications and attributes a king or an emir should be known for, I nominated myself for it. But now, it has come to my knowledge that His Highness Prince Faisal has been nominated for this throne;

---

[1]Khayri al-Omari (op. cit.), pp. 57-58.

therefore, I forfeit my own nomination because I see in the person of His Highness Prince Faisal all the attributes and merits that qualify him to undertake this throne, and I face the nomination of His Highness Prince Faisal with elation and fully support him. I request all my friends and citizens to support him with all their strength."

Thus, Sheikh Khaz`al proved that he was more astute than Sayyid Talib and more visionary of the realities of matters!

What About Mecca?

Ja`far Abu al-Timman (Courtesy: Al-Hayat newspaper of 9 August 2014.)

At the time when Baghdad was busy with its own affairs, Mecca was busy, too, with its own. It had in it quite a few men of the revolution who had fled Iraq and were now refugees under the care of King Hussain and in his hospitality. They were two groups: a group was Baghdadi: Ja`far Abu al-Timman [photo below], Ali al-Bazargan, Mahmoud Ramiz, Shakir al-Qaraghuli, Isma`eel Kannah, Ameen Zaki and Abdul-Razzaq al-Hashimi. As for the other group, it was comprised of the masters of the mid-Euphrates and chiefs of their tribes; they were: Noor al-Yasiri, Hadi al-Muqawtir, Alwan al-Yasiri, Muhsin Abu Tibeekh, then Marzouq al-Awwad, Salah al-Mawh, Mahdi al-Fādhil, Sha`lan al-Jabur and Rayih al-Atiyyah [al-Humaidawi].

Faisal reached Mecca on April 25, and the telegrams had already started coming one after the other from Iraq to [his father] King Hussain. Ali al-Bazargan narrates saying that one night he was at the meeting place of King Hussain on the rooftop of his Mecca mansion. The king stretched his hand under his bed and took out a sheet of paper, saying that it was a telegram from the people of Iraq. He handed it to al-Bazargan, saying, "Take it, Sheikh, and read it." This was the text of the telegram: "We wish you send your son, King Faisal, to Iraq so he may be a constitutional king. We await his auspicious coming." It was signed by Muhammed Mahdi al-Sadr, Nouri al-Sa`eed, Hamdi al-Pachachi, Muhyi ad-Deen al-Sahrurdi and Bahjat Zaynal. King Hussain asked about the identity of those who sent the telegram. Al-Bazargan answered him by praising them all. The king asked again, "The Iraqis had first asked for Prince Abdullah to be a constitutional king over them; so, what prompted them to change their mind?" Al-Bazargan answered him, saying, "They asked for Abdullah when Faisal was king in Syria, and they now are asking for Faisal because he has no job." The king said, "But I, Sheikh, fear lest the people of Iraq should treat Faisal as they had treated his grandfather [Imam] al-Hussain (as) before." Al-Bazargan answered him, saying, "Sir, time has changed, and the people of Iraq are not like their ancestors during the time of al-Hussain son of Ali ibn Abi Talib, peace be upon them, for they now are generous to the weak and serve their king." It was then that the king clasped his hands and shouted in his Hijazi accent: "Children! Call Faisal!"[1]

After this, the Iraqis who were in Mecca met with the king and notified him of the desire of the people of Iraq to coronate his son, Faisal, as their king. He, therefore, said to them, "I have dedicated myself and those who follow me to serve the Arab nation, and many letters and telegrams have come to me about this request, and among them are many scholars and leaders of the Arab cause in the Euphrates area. I have ordered Faisal to go to Iraq, and he is my trust among the Iraqis. Rise and go along with him, and I hope nothing will take place to him in Iraq as it took place in Syria." Muhsin Abu Tibeekh stood up and said, "Iraq is not Syria, and the Iraqis desire His Highness. Here I am the first to swear the oath of allegiance to Prince Faisal as King of Iraq." He stretched his hand to Faisal to swear the oath of allegiance to him, followed by the swearing [of allegiance] by the rest of the Iraqis.[2] It is said that King Hussain turned to Sayyid Noor al-Yasiri to address him in his capacity as the oldest of

---

[1]Ali al-Bazargan, *Al-Waqai` al-Haqeeqiyya* (true events), Baghdad, 1954, pp. 229-230.

[2]Gen. al-Mizhir Al Fir`awn (op. cit.), Vol. 2, pp. 524-525.

those present, saying, "Sayyid Noor, I consider you as my older brother, and I have given my son, Faisal, as a trust to our grandmother, Fatima al-Zahraa, peace be upon her, then I have entrusted him to you." Sayyid Noor answered him, saying, "We shall welcome Faisal, and he will be the object of our respect and love, and we shall sacrifice everything we have for his sake."[1]

Faisal Goes To Iraq

On May 30, 1921, a general amnesty statement was issued for all those who had participated in the 1920 Revolution while making an exception for certain individuals. This measure was intended for the Revolution men who had fled Iraq to be in the company of Faisal upon reaching Iraq. On June 1, the government in London sent a telegram to Faisal permitting him to move to Iraq.[2]

On June 3, Faisal sent a telegram to Muhammed al-Sadr, Yousuf al-Suweedi and Ali Jawdat al-Ayyubi, who were in Damascus, to go to Cairo and from there to Hijaz. On June 6, these three men travelled from Damascus in a truck. When they reached Cairo, they found in it Rustam Haidar, Ibrahim Kamal, Sabeeh Najeeb and Makki al-Sharbati, so they all travelled from Cairo to Jidda after Maj. Cornwallis had joined them. Faisal had asked Cornwallis to be his adviser and mediator with the high commissioner in Iraq.

The British government sent a military cruiser, Northbrook, to transport Faisal and his retinue to Iraq. On June 21, the cruiser sailed from Jidda carrying — in addition to those who had come from Cairo — all those men of the revolution with the exception of four: Ja`far Abul-Timman, Muhsin Abu Tibeekh, Marzouq al-Awwad and Rayih al-Atiyyah, who all refused to accompany Faisal, expressing their desire to perform the ritual of the pilgrimage the season of which was approaching. It is said that Abul-Timman said that he did not like to participate in that "wedding procession".

---

[1] Abd al-Shaheed al-Yasiri, *Al-Butoola fi Thawrat al-`Ishreen* (heroism in the 1920 Revolution), al-Najaf, Iraq, 1966, pp. 240-241.

[2] Graves (op. cit.), p. 293.

The first telegram that reached Baghdad about Faisal sailing from Jidda was sent by Ja`far Abul-Timman to some nationalists in Baghdad, and this is its text: "His Highness Sherif Faisal sailed today to Basra. Prepare a suitable welcome." A copy of this telegram reached the hands of the *naqeeb*. In his memoirs, Philby says the following about this subject:

> "One day, after a lengthy session of the council of ministers, the *naqeeb* sheikh asked me to stay because he wanted to talk to me personally. He then asked me, 'Do you know anything about this?' He put in my hand the telegram after everyone had left the room, the telegram which had come from Jidda and was signed by Ja`far Abul-Timman. I answered, 'No, I know nothing, but can I keep this telegram? I shall go immediately to meet Cox then return to let you know what he says.' Then I went immediately to the residency where I found Cox who was not busy and said to him, 'The marketplaces are full of rumours that Faisal had sailed from Jidda heading to Basra. Is this true?' He answered me, saying, 'I assure you, Philby, that I know nothing about it, for no such reports have reached me.' It was then that I took out the telegram saying, 'Then, perhaps you would be interested in reading this.' He repeated his previous assurances that he knew nothing about it, then I went out to let the *naqeeb* know about the outcome."[1]

On June 14, Churchill delivered a lengthy statement about Iraq in the British House of Commons in which he said,

> "There is no intention to force the people to accept a particular ruler, and they will be fully free to look and express their opinion, whether in electing a ruler or choosing a national assembly. The British government of His Majesty has informed Prince Faisal that it does not oppose his nomination. If he is elected, the British government will support him. He is now on his way to Basra, and there is no

---

[1] John Philby (op. cit.), p. 56.

doubt that if Faisal is elected, we will have reached a solution in which there is a successful and happy future."[1]

Al-Awqat al-Baghdadiyya [Baghdad Times] newspaper published Churchill's statement the next day, so Philby was very much disgusted with it, but he concealed his disgust because he was preparing for a lavish dinner and ball party on the evening of that day at the `Ilwiyya Club. The party was attended by a large number of invited people. Among them were Cox and his wife and Ms Bell. Philby first danced with Cox's wife, who was very cheerful. Then he danced with Ms Bell and others. Philby says in his memoirs that he drank too much in order to drown his grief and sadness. When he danced his last dance with Ms Bell, he was very drunk. During the dance, he held an intense discussion with her and did not realize what he had done due to being drunk, but his wife told him about it the next morning.[2]

Three days later, a telegram reached the *naqeeb* from King Hussain, the text of which was:

O Branch of the lofty Prophetic Tree, His Grace, the most honoured master, the honourable naqeeb. It is necessary that I notify you that my son, Faisal, is going to you based on the repeated requests of the public, and due to the intermixture of our family with yours; so, I need not discuss what your effort requires for the ease of the land, the doubling of the desire and the securing of everyone's future. This is what I expect of the resolve of your noble descent, religious and national sense, and may Allah grant us and your own selves success.

On behalf of Venerable Mecca on June 17, 1921 A.D.
Hussain

The *naqeeb* rushed to answer King Hussain with this telegram:

---

[1]Abdul-Razzaq al-Hassani (op. cit.), Vol. 1, p. 33.

[2]John Philby (op. cit.), pp. 57-48.

To the one who has the power and the greatness, His Majesty King Hussain, the sultan of Hijaz, may Allah support his power. With the hand of honours and regards have I held the telegram of Your Majesty which notifies us of His Highness the Prince, the man of the great destiny, Prince Faisal, may Allah safeguard him, coming to Iraq. We have been overwhelmed with pleasure at this glad tiding and supplicate for his safety. We are awaiting his coming one hour after another due to our eagerness to meet him. By the blessing of the Almighty, when His Highness comes, we shall perform our obligation to serve him since the union of descent and old lineage requires us to do so. As regarding the highly respected royal order to this sender to endeavour, all of us, to do whatever eases the land, it must be fulfilled at any rate due to the requirement of the national sentiment, and we plead to Allah for success.

On behalf of Baghdad, on June 19, 1921 A.D.

Signed: the *naqeeb* of Baghdad's nobility[1]

Welcoming Delegation

Telegrams kept reaching Baghdad about Faisal's approaching arrival and the need to get ready for it. Among those telegrams, one was sent by Sayyid Muhammed al-Sadr to his father, Sayyid Hassan, and another from Yousuf al-Suweedi to his son Naji. Naji al-Suweedi took an interest in the matter, so he sent invitation cards to Baghdad's dignitaries and men of opinion inviting them to a meeting at Cinema Royal in the morning of Friday, June 17, to look into the program of welcoming Prince Faisal. When the meeting was held at the appointed time, Naji stood up and thanked the attendants, informing them of the arrival of the telegrams

---

[1]Abdul-Razzaq al-Hassani (op. cit.), Vol. 1, pp. 33-34.

about the prince approaching. He said that he would be the Iraqis' guest and that they should do what they have to in accordance with their reputation as being generous and hospitable. Then he added, saying, "The government and municipality will do what they should, but this invitation is directed at you, citizens, for you are the ones who are the invitees and the invited, and the prince will reach Basra on the 23rd. Any one of you who wishes to participate in the public delegation to welcome him should write down his name. Some friends will go around to record the names of those willing to do so. The delegation will travel to Basra on the eve of this coming Sunday." Then Naji al-Suweedi explained that each member of the delegation would take care of his own travel expenses.[1]

The public delegation travelled by train on the eve of Sunday, June 19, as was scheduled. It was noticed that two ministers accompanied it: Philby, minister of the interior, and Ja`far al-`Askari, minister of defence. It can be said that the travelling of these two ministers was part of the plan which Cox had put in order to prove his neutrality to the public. Philby was exerting all his efforts to resist Faisal's nomination, as we have seen, whereas al-`Askari was to the contrary. This was one of the political games with which people were fooled!

It is worth mentioning in this regard that Philby demonstrated a strange activity in all the stations by which the train passed till its arrival at Basra. At every station, the area governor went to welcome him with a large crowd of people who asked him what they should do in welcoming Prince Faisal. Philby always answered them by saying that there were no official orders in this regard, that the prince came as a candidate, not as a king, and that they were free to do whatever they pleased towards him. Philby instructed provincial governors, each alone, to welcome the train that carries the prince without organizing a demonstration, for this is left to the people themselves and the reception even in Baghdad and Basra is organized in a non-official way.[2]

---

[1]-- *Al-Iraq* newspaper in its issue of June 18, 1921.

[2]John Philby (op. cit.), p. 60.

Faisal's Arrival

King Faisal circa 1919 (Courtesy: BBC Hulton Picture Library)

The cruiser carrying Faisal and his retinue reached the Basra sea port at 5:30 pm on June 23, and Basra had made preparations to welcome him, erecting triumphal arches at the main street, and some steamboats and riverine ships came out to the river bank decorated with Arab flags, and a large number of villagers assembled on the river banks repeating welcoming chants.[1]

As he was getting down the cruiser, Faisal was surprised when he read a board raised at the entrance of al-Ashar on which it was written "Long Live the Iraqi League!" and another at the Basra entrance saying "Long Live Basra Part of Iraq!" It became clear later that there was a petition bearing 4,500 signatures of Basra residents that was delivered shortly before then to the high commissioner requesting to separate Basra from Iraq, but it did not win the consent of all Basra residents; it was resisted by a large number of them[2], and the high commissioner strongly rejected it.[3]

Faisal stayed over at the house of Basra's administrative officer, Ahmed Pasha al-Sani`, and his retinue was distributed to houses of some Basra notables. The next morning, a party was held at the administrator's house and was attended by Basra's dignitaries and delegates. Welcoming speeches were delivered, and poems were recited by Muhammed Zaki al-Muhami (the attorney), Ata Ameen, Kadhim al-Dujaili, Abdul-Rahman Khdayyir, Muhammed Abdul-Hussain, Abdul-Hafiz Taha, Ahmed Hamdi

---

[1] Muhammed Abdul-Hussain, *Thikr Faisal al-Awwal* (mentioning Faisal I), Baghdad, 1933, pp. 15-17.

[2] Sulayman Faydhi (op. cit.), pp. 269-273.

[3] Philip Ireland (op. cit.), pp. 256 (footnote).

Mulla Hussain and Mahran Mahunian. Then Faisal delivered a lengthy extemporal speech from which we quote the following:

> "I tell you frankly, swearing by the Prophet and his Progeny, that I have no personal ambition, but I aspire to serve this land seeking to please Allah Almighty. I wish to see some others occupying high positions, those whom the consensus of the nation endorses, and I swear by my honour, by the soil of my grandfather and by the grave of our Grandfather the Prophet (P), that I am the first to swear the oath of allegiance to the man whom the entire nation accepts. So, if you wish that you permit someone to be in charge over you, I advise you to be honest in what you say, and if any of you speaks one word, he must not swerve from it."[1]

Faisal stayed in Basra for only one day, leaving it by train in the evening of the next day of his arrival going to Hilla. His reception at the stations between Basra and Hilla was very lukewarm due to the instructions which Philby had issued to the governors, and Faisal was very angry about it. In his memoirs, Philby says the following:

> "I and Cornwallis spent most of the time on the way in his (Faisal's) cabin discussing the situation, sipping whisky and soda. Faisal made it clear that he did not go to Iraq except after the British government had invited him to do so and that he expected the British officials to actively assist him in his nomination for the throne. I was fully frank with him: it was obvious that the British government wanted him to be Iraq's king, but the election must be free since instructions have been issued in this regard to all British officials in the country. I added to that saying that if he wanted to win the votes of the public in the country on the basis that he was a

---

[1] Gen. Mizhir Al Fir`awn (op. cit.), p. 528.

candidate of Great Britain, his hope for success would then be weak."[1]

Faisal became very angry at hearing such a talk, and it became obvious to him that the road before him would not be easy as he used to imagine. When the train reached Hilla, Faisal's resentment increased, for he found only two men at Hilla's station to welcome him. Ali Jawdat al-Ayyubi describes in his memoirs what happened, saying:

Jafar Pasha al-Askari (Muḥammad Jaʿfar Pasha bin Muṣṭafā bin ʿAbd ar-Raḥman al-ʿAskari) (Courtesy: Wikipedia Commons)

"When we reached Hilla, we found at the station only the assistant to the administrative inspector, Bertram Thomas, and the head of the municipality, Abdul-Razzaq Sherif. The late Jaʿfar al-ʿAskari [photo to the right] burst, remonstrating the head of the municipality for not paying attention to preparing the reception as it should have been. The head of the municipality, who received his orders from the British political governor, apologized, saying that Jaʿfar did not send him a telegram about Faisal's arrival, doing so only to the nationalists."[2]

The case did not stop at this limit: Bertram Thomas entered Faisal's cabin in the presence of al-Ayyubi and his companion, Sabeeh Najeeb, and very rudely asked him this question: "Why did your respectful self come to Iraq?" Faisal answered him with this question: "Why do you ask me?" Thomas said, "Because the people do not want you." Faisal responded to him thus: "Why do you want to interfere between myself and the people?" Thomas said, "So I may tell you." Faisal's last response to him was: "I do

---

[1]John Philby (op. cit.), p. 62.

[2]Ali Jawdat, *Thikrayat* (memories), Beirut, Lebanon, 1967, p. 144.

not need you to tell me, and you will see if they want me or not." It was then that Thomas left.[1]

In Najaf And Karbala

Faisal and his retinue left Hilla the next morning, riding in cars to Najaf. Philby and Cornwallis deliberately distanced themselves from him in Najaf. His appearance wearing the Arabian outfits and surrounded by men of the Revolution gave the public the impression that the goal which the Revolution demanded was now a reality.

The first thing which Faisal did in al-Najaf was to visit the Shrine of Imam Ali, and then he visited some theological scholars. Finally, he settled at the house of Sayyid Hadi al-Naqeeb where a large gathering assembled. Faisal delivered a statement of gratitude, thanking the Najafis and praising the Iraqi as well as the Hijazi revolutions. Then Baqir al-Shibeebi stood up and delivered a statement on behalf of the attendants in which he said, "We were eagerly looking forward to this auspicious visit by Iraq's great guest, Prince Faisal, to the homeland of the Revolution, the desired outcomes of which we hope will be perfected. We also hope that Allah will help the achievement of the goals of His Majesty King Hussain for the independence of the Arab lands, for the Arabs' unity and for the achievement of the goals of the Arab Revolution, the revolution of liberation and emancipation."

In the evening, Sayyid Abbas al-Kilidar threw a lavish dinner banquet in which Faisal delivered a speech in which he said that he would resolutely reform and mend the affairs of the country. He was followed by Baqir al-Shibeebi, who delivered a very enthusiastic speech saying, "The Iraqi Revolution was born to old liberation ideologies since the time of the Turks. We have sacrificed everything precious and not precious; so, we cannot deliver the fruit of our lengthy efforts and bitter labours except to hands that are sincere and keen about the independence of our homeland, interests, national and patriotic goals." It is said that Faisal

---

[1]*Ibid.*, pp. 144-145.

regarded this statement as having been directed against him and was angered by it.[1]

In the morning of June 27, Faisal and his retinue headed to Karbala. Karbala's administrative officer was at the time Hameed Khan. Graves says that Karbala's reception for Faisal was not enthusiastic because the administrator was not willing to welcome him, so he went to Baghdad hastily; therefore, the preparations for welcoming Faisal were done hastily.[2]

Faisal spent one day in Karbala, during which he visited the shrines of [Imāms] al-Hussain and al-Abbas, peace be upon them and spent his night in the hospitality of Khalil al-Asterbadi. In the morning of the next day, June 28, he left Karbala for TwoWayReach [Twaireej], where he stayed for five hours, hosted by Sayyid Hadi al-Qazwini[3]. Then he headed to Hilla.

What is noteworthy is that the Hilla reception this time was different from the way it was the first time. It seems that the people of Hilla realized their faulty behaviour towards Faisal and those in his company, men of the Revolution, so this time they went out to welcome him in large crowds in which women, youths and school students participated.[4] They kept chanting, "Allah greets King Faisal!" When Faisal reached Hilla, he stayed at the house of Muhammed Ali al-Qazwini. The people of Hilla rushed to greet him there, and a number of poets delivered poems in his praise, welcoming him.

His Arrival In Baghdad

A statement was announced in Baghdad that Prince Faisal would be arriving by train at 7:00 am on June 29. Baghdad's municipality had earmarked 50,000 rupees to spend on his reception; therefore, triumph arches were installed in several places in the city, and the streets were

---

[1]Abdul-Shaheed al-Yasiri (op. cit.), p. 350.

[2]Graves (op. cit.), p. 296.

[3]Ali Jawdat (op. cit.), p. 146.

[4]Appendix to *Dijla* newspaper dated June 29, 1921.

decorated with Arab flags and palm fronds. The streets' sidewalks and homes' balconies were crowded with onlookers. Welcoming people went to the train station in al-Karkh in the vanguard of whom were Cox, Gen. Holden, Ms Bell and the cabinet ministers.

As they were on the train, a telegram reached the above [welcoming party] that the rail tracks had suffered a malfunction and that the prince was coming by car hopefully at the set time. People kept waiting till eight o'clock. Then another telegram reached them saying that the tracks were repaired and that the prince was coming by train and would reach Baghdad in the afternoon. At this, Cox was of the view that the reception at noon would be hard due to the extreme heat, so he decided that the prince should remain on the train upon his arrival till 6:00 o'clock so the reception could take place in the evening. The welcoming crowds, therefore, returned home.[1] The municipality made a public statement saying that the prince's arrival would be at 10:00 o'clock according to the Arabian timing.[2]

We do not know whether this delay was deliberate or accidental. At any rate, it was useful for the Sherifi propaganda: people kept saying that the delay was caused by the British because they did not want the prince to receive such a great public welcome. Various rumours kept circulating among the public in this regard, leading to the status of Prince Faisal rising in the eyes of the people.

The reception took place at 6:00 o'clock, as Cox had decided, and the prince was received with extreme enthusiasm. The masses shouted his name in the streets where he passed by, and he greeted them with his hand, smiling, till he reached the house which was prepared for him inside the Qashla, which used to be the quarters of the wali [provincial governor] during the Ottoman period, and it is located on the bank of the Tigris River. Baghdadi newspapers kept calling it the "emirate house".

The prince was glad for the great reception which took place for him, but he was at the same time depressed due to the stance of Philby and the political governors towards him in the governorates. He was told that those governors could gather people to welcome him at the stations,

---

[1]Lady Bell, *Letters of Gertrude Bell,* London, U.K., 1947, p. 489.

[2]Appendix to the *Dijla* newspaper of June 29, 1921.

but they did not do it. He kept wondering whether the high commissioner stood by his side, and if that was the case, why did the political governors undertake a stance contrary to that of their chief?[1]

Ms Bell visited him at 7:00 am the next morning, so he welcomed her and thanked her for the efforts she exerted for his sake. She assured him during the talk that the high commissioner was absolutely biased toward him. When Ms Bell came out of the prince's place, crowds of well-wishers started coming to greet him. Among them was a delegation from the governorates. Poems were recited before him, the first of which was composed by [Jameel Sidqi] al-Zahawi. Ms Bell says that Ahmed al-Sheikh Dawood had undertaken a seat for him at the door and remained so in the next days: he used to stand up whenever a delegation came to congratulate him in order to show his allegiance to Prince Faisal as a representative of the people. He did that 50 times. Ms Bell comments about this, saying, "Ahmed al-Sheikh Dawood became the laughing stock of everyone because of the silly things which he was doing, while Faisal and the others did not pay him the least attention."[2]

Faisal was careful about visiting al-Kadhimiyya the next day following his arrival. At ten o'clock in the morning of that day, as the delegations were still coming to greet him at the Qashla, his convoy moved and headed to al-Kadhimiyya by way of al-Karkh. A great reception took place for him in al-Kadhimiyya, and sacrificial animals were slaughtered at his feet. Having performed the ceremonial visit of the sacred mausoleum there, he went to visit Sayyid Muhammed al-Sadr at his house, then went to visit Hajj Abdul-Hussain al-Chalabi. Poems were recited for him at both houses.[3]

In the morning of the next day, which was Friday, Faisal went to visit the mosque of Imam Abu Haneefah in al-A`dhamiyya. The reception held for him there was similar to that which took place in al-Kadhimiyya. After that, he went to visit the mosque of Sheikh Abdul-Qadir [al-Gailani] in Baghdad, where he performed the Friday prayers. The Bab al-Sheikh quarter was ready to receive it: animals were sacrificed, flowers were

---

[1]Lady Bell (op. cit.), p. 489.

[2]Burgoyne (op. cit.), Vol. 2, pp. 223-228.

[3]Dijla newspaper of July 2, 1921.

scattered, and rose water was sprinkled. Having finished the Friday prayers, he went to visit the *naqeeb*'s house, where he was welcomed by the *naqeeb*'s oldest son, Sayyid Mahmoud. The latter addressed him, saying, "The *naqeeb* family, Your Highness the Prince, is your right hand which you use wherever you wish for the interest of the country." Then a small pupil advanced and recited al-Farazdaq's famous poem[1], one of the lines of which says, "This is the one whose might the desert knows..., etc."[2]

Philby's Fate

When Philby was in the company of Prince Faisal on the Najaf-Karbala route, he fell seriously ill with malaria, so he was taken to Hilla where he was treated for a few days. His wife came to him from Baghdad to be his nurse. On the eve of July 3, when he recovered, he returned to Baghdad. On the next morning, Philby went to meet Cox. The following dialogue went on between both men:

---

[1]Al-Farazdaq ibn Ghalib is one of the greatest Arab poets. He was born in Basra in about 641 A.D. and died in about 732 A.D. His real name is Hammam ibn Ghalib ibn Mujashi al-Darmi at-Tamimi, and he was contemporary of another very famous poet, namely Jarir, with whom he had exchanged extensive literary criticism which lasted as long as he lived. The poem to which author al-Wardi refers here was composed by al-Farazdaq in praise of one of the Prophet's grandsons, namely Imam Ali ibn al-Hussain ibn Abi Talib, nicknamed "al-Sajjad," the one who frequently prostrates to his Lord. This poem is considered to be one of the best masterpieces of Arab poetry. Al-Farazdaq composed it instantaneously in the presence of then caliph Hisham ibn Abdul-Malik, the 10th Umayyad caliph who ruled from 723 – 743 A.D. Hisham asked him why he did not compose one like it in his own praise. Al-Farazdaq said, "Had your grandfather been like his grandfather, had your father been like his father, and had your mother been like his mother, I would have done so." Hisham was so angry that he ordered him jailed at Usfan, a place between Mecca and Medina, where al-Farazdaq nevertheless continued to compose poetry taunting and belittling Hisham who finally had to release him, hoping he would leave him alone and stop the barrage of critical poems. – Tr.

[2]*Al-Iraq* newspaper of July 4, 1921.

Cox said, "It seems you did not get along with Faisal very well. He is bitterly critical of your stance during the trip, and he said that he would not stay in Iraq if the stance of all British officials and their support for him is not effective."

Philby said, "I cannot understand how you expect me to look at the official orders, your orders, which remain unchanged, with regard to the freedom of election. I have for so long been assuring the *naqeeb* and others that we are determined to fulfil our promises to them that Faisal naturally realized that his success would be weak if the election went on freely, and I explained this to him honestly."

Cox said, "I know that you have said this to him, but you now know for sure what the British government wants."

Philby said, "I know it, of course, and I realized it for quite some time despite all the assurances which you made to me to the contrary. But what I cannot understand is: If the British government wants and is determined to let Faisal be king, why does it not appoint him in a direct way without twisting, instead of insisting on the elections mockery? At any rate, I feel that I am completely responsible for the assurances which I made to everyone so they may participate in dealing with the election matters."

Cox said, "I know this, but I cannot understand how you can compromise between this stance of yours and staying in your job."

Philby said, "If I am expected to manage the election affairs, I do not wish to remain in my job. And if you can appoint someone to succeed me, I shall leave and hand him over my position immediately."

Cox said, "Thank you, Philby. I am sorry, you cannot continue to cooperate with us."

Philby realized that Cox wanted him to resign, which he did. Cox chose another man to replace him, namely Thompson who was then adviser to the minister of finance.[1]

In the afternoon of July 5, Ms Bell went to visit Philby at his house. An angry dialogue went on between her and Philby's wife. Both Philby and Ms Bell have provided us with details of that dialogue, each differing from the other in some respects. Philby says in his memoirs that Ms Bell

---

[1] John Philby (op. cit.), pp. 63-65.

visited him when he was having tea with his wife and said to him, "Jack[1], I am sorry to hear the news." She meant the news about his resignation. His wife roughly responded as she was getting out of the room, passing by her, "No, you are not sorry." At this juncture, Philby advanced towards Ms Bell and served her a cup of tea, pacified her and talked to her about his pleasure in getting away from such an insinuation.[2]

As for Ms Bell, she narrates the story as follows:

> "On Tuesday, I went to visit Philby and his wife to express my regret for what happened, so a very painful dialogue took place: Philby's wife burst crying, and she accused me of being the reason for the firing of her husband, then she got out of the room. It was then that I reminded him of our long friendship and asked him to believe that I did all I could to convince him that any government official could not benefit from opposing his government's orders. His embracing the issue of Sayyid Talib, the cunning man, cannot be believed, but he made himself and Sayyid Talib one and the same person."[3]

After this, Philby kept touring Iran for three months. On his return to Baghdad, Cox offered him the post of British Commissioner in Trans-Jordan in place of Lawrence, which he accepted, and he travelled by air to Amman. But Philby did not change his habit, for we have seen how he differed in his opinion from the high commissioner in Palestine just as he had differed with the high commissioner in Iraq, and this led him to submit his final resignation from serving the British government.

Philby after that went to Jidda where he opened an agency for importing cars and other things and became a friend of King Abdul-Aziz ibn Saud and his personal adviser. In 1930, he declared his acceptance of

---

[1] In a footnote above, I have indicated that John Philby is also known as "Jack Philby", so do not be confused; Ms. Bell knew his name very well! – Tr.

[2] *Ibid.,* p. 65.

[3] Burgoyne (op. cit.), p. 224.

Islam and took the name "al-Hajj Abdullah Philby". But after the death of King Abdul-Aziz, he disputed with the latter's son, Saud, and left the Kingdom of Saudi Arabia almost as an expelled person. On October 1, 1960, Philby died in Beirut as an outcast of both the Saudi and British governments.

Philby did not leave any wealth despite his ability to make millions. Rather, he left books that are excellent in describing his great travels which he made in the Arabian Peninsula and the Empty Quarter, and it can be said that he had an odd personality that was not without genius. He wanted to compete with Lawrence in fame, so he surpassed him in many aspects.

Al-Naqeeb's Banquet

On the eve of July 7, the *naqeeb* threw a great banquet which was then regarded as a reconciliation banquet between himself and Prince Faisal. The banquet was held at the *naqeeb's* house, which faced the Sheikh Mosque. The mosque and the streets leading to it were lit with bright lights, and the masses crowded to welcome the prince and to chant for him. When the prince reached the house, the *naqeeb* welcomed him at the foot of the stairs leaning on the arm of his private doctor, so they embraced right and left according to the customary method, then walked hand in hand towards the centre of the hall where Faisal sat between the high commissioner and the *naqeeb*.

The most important event that went on in that banquet was a poem recited by Ma`ruf al-Rusafi comprised of four sections lauding the meeting between the *naqeeb* and the prince, of which we would like to quote the fourth section:

The naqeeb stretched to the prince the hand of support and of help,

So let every evil trouble-maker among the people be shamed,
And let our master, the naqeeb, live as our master the prince has.

After the recitation of this poem, al-Rusafi delivered a speech in which he said, "Yes, Gentlemen, what do the people want after the joining of both of these two great shining stars who have come out in harmony, embracing in Iraq's skies, shaking hands on the banks of the Two Rivers? I, Gentlemen, do not know any man more worthy than our master, the *naqeeb*, as representing in his actions all the people of Iraq. Why not, since he has killed time with his experiences, put on honour with his knowledge and good manners, rode the skies of loftiness and glory in his lineage and upbringing...? So, Prince, Your Royal Highness, when our master the *naqeeb* shakes your hand, it is as though all hands of the Iraqis do so. On this eve, in this populated house, it is as though all lands of Iraq hug you. As for you, O honoured *naqeeb*, the days shall recite for you thanks for what you have exerted in our interest of auspicious efforts to unite the people and to get the nation together. So, long live His Royal Highness the great Prince Faisal, long live our master, the great *naqeeb*, and long live the Iraqis and the Arabs!" Al-Rusafi's poem and speech were time and over interrupted with repeated enthusiastic applause.[1]

It is worth mentioning on this occasion that an order was issued to appoint al-Rusafi as head of the sciences advancement committee in the ministry of education four days before this banquet.

On July 11, when the council of ministers was in session, the *naqeeb* submitted a proposal asking for naming Faisal King of Iraq provided his government is parliamentary, democratic, constitutional, and restricted by the law and the council endorsed it.

Ms Bell wrote later describing the shift that took place in the *naqeeb*'s stance towards Faisal. He shifted his position from one who hated and was hostile to him to one who loved and supported him. She stated that she visited the *naqeeb* at his house and found him exuberant and very happy about the new stance toward Faisal. He talked to her, saying, "Khatoon, you are [like] my daughter, I want to tell you about what goes on in my mind. Since Sir Percy Cox arrived, I did not do anything against his advice or the wish of the British government. When I came to know that Faisal is good enough to be a king and that the great [British] government supports him, I decided to avoid all hearsays and rumors and personally declare him as king in the ministerial council. I asked myself: should I consult with Sir Percy Cox? My mind answered me that I had already made my decision, and if Sir Percy Cox differs from me, I cannot

---

[1] *Al-Iraq* newspaper of July 9, 1921.

change it, for I am an old man, and I am responsible only before Allah; therefore, I did not consult with anyone."[1]

What is noticed is that the *naqeeb* was not satisfied with changing his stance towards Faisal (only), but changed it towards democracy, too. He started calling for it after he used to alienate himself from it and hate it. Ms Bell pointed this out in a letter dated august 21. She said that the *naqeeb* those days was advocating democracy. She expressed her astonishment and wondered: "How can a basically aristocratic *naqeeb* call for democracy?!" Ms Bell then narrates on this occasion an interesting anecdote that involved the *naqeeb* in those days. Its summary is that a Shammar tribal chief visited the *naqeeb* at his house, so the *naqeeb* asked him, "Are you democratic [*deemoqrati* in Arabic]?" The sheikh answered, "No, by Allah, I am not *mughrati* [in the Bedouin jargon]." Then the sheikh wondered what the word meant, so the *naqeeb* said, "Well, then, I am the sheikh of *deemoqratiyya* (democracy)." The sheikh retracted his statement, thinking that he had given the wrong answer; he said, "I seek refuge with Allah! If you are the sheikh of *mughratiyya* (democracy), I am one of them; I am your servant, but what is it?" The *naqeeb* then explained to him what democracy is. He said, "It means equality among the people; nobody is small or big." This statement was not liked by the sheikh, for he realized that democracy meant the disappearance of the presidency over the tribe, so he said, "If this is the *mughratiyya*, Allah bears witness that I do not belong to it."[2]

Most Important Parties

The period which Faisal spent in Iraq before his coronation was two months, that is, from June 23 to August 23, during which many parties in his honor were made. We cannot detail them all, but we would like to state something about four of them due to their social and historical implications.

Among the first of those parties was one held by the Baghdad Municipality at the Maude Gardens in al-Salihiyya in the Karkh flank. It

---

[1]Burgoyne (op. cit.), Vol. 2, p. 231.

[2]Lady Bell (op. cit.), p. 499.

took place on the eve of June 30, that is, one day after the arrival of the prince at Baghdad, and it was attended by Cox and his wife, Gen. Holden, Ms Bell and many senior Iraqi and British dignitaries. It was noticed that most poems and speeches delivered included a reference to Prince Faisal as Iraq's king and saviour.

The party was opened by Abdul-Majeed al-Shawi with a welcoming statement, and then he sought the permission of the prince to present what the men of letters had prepared for this occasion: poetry and prose. Then Khalil Ameen al-Mufti stood up and delivered a poem which he concluded with this verse:

We have named you a king over us,
We shall not accept anyone else in your place.

Those present applauded this verse and three times asked it to be repeated. Voices rose from among them, saying, "We have sworn the oath of allegiance to you as the king."[1] After that, al-Zahawi stood up and recited his poem, the first lines of which said,

We greet you, so be safe, O King,
And we choose you for the throne:
The epicycle has willed it.

He was followed by Sheikh Mutlaq al-Qatifi, who delivered a poem that had a special impact on those invited, for he was one of the orators of the Hussaini pulpit and had a clear voice with a musical tone. Ms Bell described his poem by saying, "It was very long. I did not understand a word of it, yet it was great, for the man recited it with a tone, raising his hand from time to time. The dark that cast its shadows over the trees round the attendants affected them in a way similar to hypnosis."[2]

Then Muhammed Hassan Kubba delivered a poem and a speech in which he described Faisal as the "Napoleon of the offspring of Adnan"

---

[1]*Al-Iraq* newspaper of July 2, 1921.

[2]Lady Bell (op. cit.), p. 490.

and the "Bismarck of the offspring of Qahtan [Joctan]". He was followed by Muhammed Baqir al-Hilli, who recited a poem that started with this verse:

The people, the far and the near
With your coming well augur.

Finally, the prince delivered an extemporal speech in which he thanked the poets for their poems but criticized them for exaggerating in praising him and his father since his father did not revolt except only to carry out his obligation. He told them that from now on, he wished to hear only encouragement of science, literature and a renaissance of the arts. His speech, therefore, was met with shouts and applause as usual.

As for the second party that followed it in importance, it was the one held by the Ja`fari School on the morning of July 9 at its place in the Suq al-Ghazl quarter in which al-Zahawi, Kadhim al-Dujaili, Abdul-Hussain al-Azari, Baqir al-Shibeebi and Ibrahim Naji al-Muhami participated. The prince delivered at its conclusion a speech in which he thanked the attendants and repeated what he had said on past occasions. He said,

> "I say that by Allah, by Allah, by Allah, I did not move [out of Hijaz] hoping for a worldly objective or desiring a material thing, nor did I do it seeking pride, a status and a position. No, neither I nor my father, nor any of my family members, undertook any action of the renaissance out of the desire for something. Rather, we did what we did, seeking to please Allah, the Exalted One, and nothing else. I swear by my honour and by the soil of my grandfather that had it not been for the insistence of most of my friends and the consensus of the Iraqi nation, I would never have thought of going to Iraq."

It was then that Ahmed al-Sheikh Dawood stood up and addressed the prince, saying, "You are the chief for whom we sacrifice our lives and around whom the hearts rally, and we do not accept anyone else other than you." Then he turned to those who were standing and addressed them, saying, "Do you swear the oath of allegiance to anyone other than

His Highness the great prince?" They answered him loudly, "No, No! We have sworn the oath of allegiance to Faisal as the king, and we do not want anyone else." It was then that tens of shouts were made.[1]

It is worth mentioning that after the passage of two days since that party, *Dijla* newspaper came out satirizing the stance of Ahmed al-Sheikh Dawood. It said about him that he screamed at the attendants asking them: "Do you want anyone other than His Highness the prince as king over Iraq?" Then he turned to the prince, saying, "They have sworn the oath of allegiance to you."[2] The newspaper meant that the attendants did not give any answer to his question but that he was the one who answered it on his own. In the *Iraq* newspaper, Salman al-Sheikh Dawood published criticism of *Dijla* newspaper, saying that it violated the truth with regards to its reference to his father, and he asked it to be more insightful in what it published. *Al-Iraq* newspaper commented about that, saying that many resentful letters had reached it about that subject.[3]

As regards the third party, which was held by Baghdad's Jews, it was held on the morning of July 18. In it, the chief rabbi presented a gilt copy of the Torah to the prince. With it, there was a valuable tablet on which this statement from the Torah was written:

אלה גבם של ולרסק את מעשיו לקבל את, כוחו יברך את! אלוהים
לעלות לא יכולים לכך שהם ולהתנגד ששונאים אותו.

Lord! Bless his strength, accept his deeds and crush the backs
of those who resist and hate him so they may not rise.

The prince received the copy of the Torah, which he kissed, and thanked the person who presented it to him. Then Saleem Afandi, assistant to the chief rabbi, delivered a welcoming speech. After him, a youth called Anwar Shaul[4] delivered a poem, after which al-Zahawi stood

---

[1] *Al-Iraq* newspaper of July 11, 1921.

[2] *Dijla* newspaper of July 11, 1921.

[3] *Al-Iraq* newspaper of July 13, 1921.

[4] This young Iraqi Jew, who was born in Iraq in 1904 and died in Jerusalem in 1984, seems to have grown up to be a brilliant prose and poetry writer, according

up and delivered verses of his poetry and a philosophical statement about the need for unity among humans. Then the original Torah was taken out of its place, and it is not taken out except for kings and great men. In conclusion, the prince delivered an extemporal speech in which he said, "I do not wish to hear the word 'Muslim', Christian' or 'Israelite,' for Iraq is the homeland of ethnicity, and there is only one thing in it: it says 'Iraqis' only."[1]

Dijla did not keep silent about this statement which Faisal articulated, that is, there should be no discrimination between the Muslims and others, for it published it in a way that stirred public opinion against it. This led to some readers feeling resentful, just as had happened with the Ja`fari party. Apparently, this newspaper remained persistent in its way of abusing Prince Faisal and his supporters, waiting for any opportunity to do that by any possible means.

As for the fourth party, it was the one held by Ali al-Sulayman — chief sheikh of the Dulaim tribe — on July 25 on the right flank of the Euphrates between Falluja and Ramadi. This party carries a special connotation because it had a Bedouin stamp to a certain extent, and it is said that the British are the ones who managed it in order to prove to the prince that they are the link between him and the [Iraqi] tribes.[2]

Ms Bell provided us with a description of this party in one of her letters. She attended it in the company of Fakhri al-Jumail. She said that Ali al-Sulayman set up a large tent about 200 feet long and prepared a podium at one of its sides where a table and chairs were placed. The prince sat in his Arabian outfit on the chair behind the table while Fahd al-Hathal, chief sheikh of the Anza tribe, sat on his right side. Between 400-500 tribe members sat in tight lines on the ground. The prince addressed the attendants in his Hijazi accent. He told them that four years ago, he

---

to the "Association of Jewish Academics from Iraq" which lists to his credit the book titled *The Story of my life in Mesopotamia*, his memoirs which were published in Jerusalem in 1980, as well as a collection of poems titled *And a New Dawn Broke* which was published in Jerusalem in 1983 and was reprinted in the next year. – Tr.

[1]*Ibid*, July 16, 1921.

[2]Ameen al-Rayhani (op. cit.), pp. 91-93.

could not imagine himself as being in such a place or in such a company. Then he spoke about Iraq's future and how he would boost their efforts under his presidency. He asked them, "Arabs, are you peaceful among yourselves?" They answered him in a loud voice, "Yes, yes, we are peaceful." It was then that Faisal said, "Starting from this day," and he stopped for a moment to inquire about the date and the hour, and when an attendant answered him about the Hijri calendar and the hour according to the sunset timing, he resumed his statement saying, "Starting from this day, the 19th of Thil-Qi`da [Monday, July 12, 1921] and from this hour, 4:00 am, any man who raises his hand on [against] another man is accountable to me. I shall judge among you in *majalis* [meeting places] attended by your sheikhs, and this is my right upon you, being your *wali al-amr* [guardian]." Here he was interrupted by an old man from among them who said, "What about our rights? Do we not have rights?" Faisal answered him, saying, "Yes, you have rights as subjects, and it is my duty to safeguard them." Thus did Faisal continue his speech, and the attendants kept supporting him with "Yes, yes, we agree; Yes, by Allah!" When he finished his speech, Ali al-Sulayman and Fahd al-Hathal, each from one side, stood and said to him, "We swear the oath of allegiance to you because the British government has accepted you." Faisal was surprised by this statement and turned to Ms Bell smiling, then he said, "My relationship with the British is known, there is no doubt about it, but we shall see our affairs among us." Faisal turned to Ms Bell again, so she raised her hands as they were on each other as an indication of the unity between the Arabs and the British government.[1]

Competition In Throwing Banquets

Prince Faisal became — during the period he spent prior to his coronation — drowned in a tumultuous flood of praise and flattery which had no end. People flocked to him from every corner, each seeking a status with him on account of the sugar-coated discourse he articulated. Poets had the lion's share, as is their tradition on such occasions. I may not exaggerate if I say that had Sayyid Talib [al-Naqeeb] been the candidate for Iraq's

---

[1]Lady Bell (op. cit.), pp. 495-497.

throne instead of Faisal, people would have tried to get close to him the same way that they were now doing with Faisal.

One of the manifestations of this flood was holding special banquets by city dignitaries and chiefs of tribes. Each of them liked to earn prestige by inviting the prince to their homes, and the prince was puzzled, not knowing what he should do. If he accepted someone's invitation, others would be angry with him, and this was a problem that robbed him of sleep.

So that the reader may become familiar with a portrayal of this problem, I would like to narrate to him the story of one of those numerous banquets thrown for Faisal. It was the banquet of Sayyid Ja`far Itayfah, head of al-Kadhimiyya [City] Municipality. This man maintained a strong link with the British since the beginning of their occupation of Baghdad, and he used to keep himself surrounded by them, holding banquets for them and serving them whenever they went to al-Kadhimiyya. At the same time, he was in competition over the post of head of the municipality (mayoralty) with al-Hajj Abdul-Hussain al-Chalabi, and he would not relish the thought that Prince Faisal would go to Chalabi's house without going to his.

Ms Bell says in one of her letters that "Sayyid Ja`far Itayfah came once complaining to me. He said that his honour was broken because the prince visited al-Kadhimiyya twice without getting near his house. Ms Bell describes in her letter how Ja`far served the British, and kept standing by their side with courage, so much so that he became prone to the extremists' hostility; therefore, she said to him when he complained, "Never mind, go to Faisal and invite him to have tea at your house, and I shall invite the high commissioner and the commander-in-chief."[1]

Sayyid Ja`far made preparations for the invitation with everything he could do, and he was quite wealthy. It is said that he spent on it about 60,000 rupees, a huge amount of money in those days. He commissioned an Armenian man famous for making sweets in Baghdad to make sweets the like of which were never made before, and the amount he paid that Armenian man for doing so was 3,000 rupees. Ms Bell describes in her letter the table prepared on that day by saying that she

---

[1]Burgoyne (op. cit.), Vol. 2, p. 236.

had never seen in all her life a table containing such an abundance of sweets and fruits.[1]

The invitation took place in the afternoon of Tuesday, August 16[2], and when those invited finished having tea, Sayyid Ja`far gave the prince priceless presents. Among them were two [Persian] carpets, on one of which the picture of Ahmed Shah was painted. He also gave him an antique gilt watch having four pointers, a ring with a stone of rare chrysolite and two *jubbahs* (long outer cloaks) lined with precious fur. Sayyid Ja`far did not forget to give Cox, Holden and Ms Bell precious gifts, too. It was rumoured at the time that Sayyid Ja`far did all of that out of spite of Chalabi.

---

[1]*Ibid.*

[2]Yes, according to the calendar I have, the day of the week was, indeed, Tuesday, August 16, according to the Gregorian calendar, or August 3 according to the Julian Christian calendars of the year 1921. All Christian dates used in this book are Gregorian. The Islamic Hijri calendar shows the date to have been Thul-Hijja 11, 1339 A.H. – Tr.

Chapter Three

Faisal As King

Before Faisal had reached Iraq, the British did not know whether or not he would succeed in pleasing the Iraqis. They were like the father who sends his son to the test as he watches him closely to see if he passes or fails.

Only a few days passed since Faisal's arrival in Iraq when the British were sure that he would succeed. In a letter dated July 7, Ms Bell said, "Faisal's character has crossed three-quarters of the road."[1] Graves mentions the reasons that helped Faisal succeed saying, "He was handsome, polite and dignified, and his speeches won admiration in form and in context. Also, his achievements and norms of conduct in the war were indicative of his courage and strength of resolve."[2]

Actually, Faisal had the ability to attract people's hearts, and his accent when he spoke was Hijazi which is loved by the Iraqis. Whenever he spoke in a meeting, his speech was direct, without pedantry or affectation. Add to this, he used to talk to each group of people according to what suited it. Many Shi`as thought that he was one of them because of so many references in his speeches to the feats of the Imams from

---

[1]Lady Bell, *Letters of Gertrude Bell*, London, 1947, p. 491.

[2]Graves, *Sir Percy Cox*, London, 2nd edition, p. 299.

among the Ahl al-Bayt whom he described as his ancestors, swearing by their soil. Thomas Lyell narrates that he asked Abdul-Wahid al-Hajj Sikar how he, the religious Shi`a man that he was, could call for Faisal as king although he [Faisal] was Sunni, so Abdul-Wahid answered him, saying, "Deep inside his heart he is a Shi`a."[1]

It is narrated that a group of mid-Euphrates sheikhs were visiting Faisal when one of them asked him, "May Allah have mercy on your father, O Protected One; are you Shi`a or Sunni?" Faisal lowered his head for a short while, then kept feeling his beard with his hand. He then said, "Can one leave his mother and stick to his father's wife?"

Ameen al-Rayhani says, "Faisal used to use one statement to each group of people, one that is inspired by their traditions, and political, religious trends. He used to plead to the Shi`as for the unity of Islam and Islamic brotherhood, and he would recite to the Sunnis from the Abbasids' golden pages, reminding them of al-Rashid and al-Mamoon and the distinction which the Arabs had over the Europeans. And he used to shout and stress to the minorities that he was sticking to the principle of equality in rights and responsibilities among the subjects from various religious sects."[2]

Faisal And Al-Khalisi

The most important success that Faisal achieved along this path was securing the oath of allegiance of the senior *mujtahid,* namely Sheikh Mahdi al-Khalisi in al-Kadhimiyya. Sheikh Mahdi al-Khalisi used to hold the Hashemite family in contempt for standing in the war [World War I] on the side of the infidel British, and his eldest son, Sheikh Muhammed, held the Hashemite family in even greater contempt. When Faisal went to Iraq, he exerted his efforts to get close to Sheikh Mahdi and to win his heart, but Sheikh Muhammed was on his [father's] side, exerting his efforts to resist this proximity and endearment between Faisal and his father. Faisal was finally able to win the pleasure of Sheikh Mahdi and get

---

[1]Thomas Lyell, *Ins and Outs of Mesopotamia,* London, 1923, p. 206.

[2]Ameen al-Rayhani, *Faisal al-Awwal,* Beirut, Lebanon, 1958, p. 90.

his fealty. We quote here what Sheikh Muhammed wrote in his memoirs about this subject:

"Faisal knew that his fealty in Iraq could not have been concluded without securing my father's fealty. Anyone who knows Faisal knows that he is the maquette of deception and forgery for which he is neither envied nor praised. He undertook the religious appearance which is full of sincerity to Islam and Muslims and visited my father repeatedly in our school in al-Kadhimiyya while wearing the outfit of Hijazi Arabs and carrying a piece of the Ka`ba's curtain on which *ayat al-kursi* [verse of the throne] is inscribed in gold, [with the aim of] showing that he had no purpose but to spread the teachings of the Qur'an, supporting the Ka`ba, and ridding the Islamic lands of the foreigners' hegemony. He gave that piece to my father as a gift. In one of his visits, he [Faisal] was alone with him [father] and demonstrated to him that he had come to Iraq to save it from the British and that his job could not be accomplished except with my father's consent and fealty. If he would swear the oath of allegiance to him, it would be so; otherwise, Faisal would be forced to return from wherever he had come. My father said to him, 'It is possible that we grant you our fealty provided you become a king over Iraq independently and separately from any foreign power by any name so that nothing tarnishes Iraq's independence no matter what it may be. If this is done, you will stay in Iraq as a king; otherwise, you will leave and leave the Iraqis and the British until they [Iraqis] take their right and reach their goal." Faisal said to my father, "I take your fealty according to this condition." A [copy of the] Holy Qur'an was presented between them as means of auguring well and to receive its blessing, and Faisal took my father's fealty on the condition that my father would obey his order in saving the Iraqis from the British and achieving full and complete independence which is not tainted by anything no matter what it may be, [whether] in name or form. If he could not do that, he would leave Iraq at the first sign made by my father and would leave the Iraqis alone. Faisal accepted the fealty and invoked the testimony of Allah Almighty for it, and thus my father offered him his fealty on this condition. This remained their secret. When he [Faisal] wanted to leave, he took my hand and said, 'Come, let us work together and try to agree on saving Iraq and protecting its independence, and I am ready to do anything that benefits the country; so, what prevents you from agreeing?' I did not answer him at all because I did not like to surprise him while he was in our house with something which he would hate, and I did not want to agree with him while not feeling right about it. He left; I escorted him to the door of the school against my wish. Then I returned to my father and said, 'This man is the first to divide the Muslims and to assist their enemies against them, so how can he be accepted, and how can there be fealty to him to take charge? What means of assurance is there regarding this man despite his past bad deeds against the Muslims, even if he offers a 1,000 conditions, and how can we obligate him to fulfil the terms if he does not meet them after assuming power over Iraq?' One of his close friends (Mawlood Pasha Mukhlus) said that he [Faisal] was in Syria betraying the Syrians and trying to subjugate them to the French with all possible means, but the Syrians did not obey him, so the French came to know that he would be of no benefit to them in Syria, nor would he be able to have an impact on the Syrians and to silence them; therefore, they expelled him after losing hope of his use. And this man is of the making of the British, their employee, and their hired hand against the Muslims from the first day of the World War till this day; so, how can it be right to depend on him and to hand Iraq over to him?' When my father heard all of this, he recited this verse of the Holy Qur'an: *'Then the people of Pharaoh picked him [Moses] up (from the river): (It was intended) that (Moses) should be an adversary to them and a cause of sorrow'* **(Qur'an, 28:8).** He said that it is possible the British used the Sherif to serve their interests so Allah may turn the Sherifs into supporters of the Muslims and enemies of the British. I said to myself, 'What goes bad does not produce anything but trouble.' I would not dare to speak with my father more than that. When the meeting was over, my father called me to the house and said, 'Do you think that you know what I do not?! Faisal is more than what you mentioned, but I feared lest the people should swear the oath of allegiance to him collectively, and we have no strength to expel him, thus the right of the Iraqis will be lost by signing the slavery check, out of their ignorance even though Faisal's name is on it, so I wanted to show people how they should swear the oath of allegiance so that Iraq may remain safeguarded whenever the Iraqis demand it."[1]

Sheikh Muhammed adds [in his memoirs saying] that Fahmi al-Mudarris was sent to his father by Faisal to ask him to write his allegiance so that it could be circulated to the public. Sheikh Muhammed opposed the writing of the oath of allegiance, but his father insisted on it. Having finished it, Fahmi al-Mudarris took it, and it was published in the newspapers the next day and separately in a special circular. Below is the text of the oath or declaration of allegiance as published in the *Al-Iraq* newspaper:

In the Name of Allah, the most Gracious, the most Merciful, and in Him do I trust

Praise belongs to Allah Who spreads the banner of righteousness to His creation, supporting them with victory over which the one who has earned honour and pride presides, the obeyed king, the one whom we must follow, the esteemed king, our great king, Faisal I, may his power perpetuate, son of His Majesty King Hussain I, may his state perpetuate. Therefore, let your allegiance to him be firm, cosign obedience to him, shouting his name, submit to his rule, and we are among those who follow such tracks, who have sworn the oath of allegiance to him in secret and in

---

[1] Excerpted from the manuscript of the memoirs of Sheikh Muhammed al-Khalisi.

public provided he becomes a king over Iraq restricted by a parliamentary council, separated from others' authority, independent as he bids and forbids, and to Allah belongs the affair.

Thul-Qi`da 7, 1339 [July 13, 1921]

[Signed:] One who hopes for his Lord's forgiveness,
Muhammed Mahdi al-Kadhimi
May he be forgiven[1]

Allegiance Of The A`dhamiyya People

It is worth mentioning that the first recorded [oath of] allegiance announced in Iraq is the one by the (Sunni) people of al-A`dhamiyya City, and it took place on July 11, two days before that of al-Khalisi. *Al-Iraq* newspaper published its details, citing its offices in al-A`dhamiyya, under this headline: "The people of al-A`dhamiyya swear the oath of allegiance to His Highness Prince Faisal as King of Iraq – the First Allegiance."

The newspaper mentioned that a large meeting was held there for the allegiance at the mansion of Naji al-Khudhairi based on an invitation by the head of the municipality, Ali Zareef al-A`dhami. It was attended by dignitaries of the city and heads of the tribes that surround it, and they were: Banu Rikab, al-Sawakin, Albu Mufraj, Banu Omayr, Albu Mahallah, the Luhaib tribe, the Jala`ita and the Nidawis. The meeting began with a recitation of the Holy Qur'an, and then Abdul-Hadi al-A`dhami stood up and said that a race was going on among the people to swear the oath of allegiance to Faisal as the king and that the people of al-A`dhamiyya should be faster than others with regard to this allegiance. He concluded his speech by shouting for King Faisal I and for independence, and the attendants echoed his shouts. Then the head of the municipality stood and asked them about the allegiance, and the attendants responded to him by saying that they accepted it and that none of them would lag behind. He called on them saying, "Have you sworn the oath of allegiance?" They

---

[1] *Al-Iraq* newspaper of July 16, 1921.

answered him in unison: "Yes, we have." Then he called on them again: "Is there anyone among you who opposes?" They said, "No, No then No!" Those present decided to sign three transcripts for which they deputed the head of the municipality to go to Prince Faisal and to swear the oath of allegiance on their behalf. It was then that the person who recited the Holy Qur'an recited this verse:

> **Truly those who pledge their fealty to you do no less**
> **than pledging their fealty to Allah: God's hand is**
> **above their hands: Then anyone who violates his**
> **oath does so to the harm of his own soul, and**
> **anyone who fulfills what he has promised Allah,**
> **Allah will soon grant him a great reward.**
> *Qur'an, 48:10*

Mulla Nu`man al-A`dhami recited a supplication to Allah to support the nation with success from Him, the Independent One. Everyone shouted, "Long Live the sultan of Iraq, Faisal the Great! Long Live Independence!"

On the eve of the next day, the Jews who were residing in al-A`dhamiyya held a special meeting of their own at the mansion of Ya`qub [Jacob] al-Jawhari [the jeweller]. In the meeting, the same thing took place as it happened the evening before at the Muslims' meeting. They all called for swearing fealty to Prince Faisal, organized a transcript and deputed Ya`qub al-Jawhari and Nasim Yamin to go to the prince with the head of the municipality to swear the oath of allegiance on their behalf.[1]

The Sure Method

Some enthusiastic nationalists desired to declare Prince Faisal as king immediately without the need for a public referendum, but Faisal did not have such a desire, and Cox was not in its favour, either. Graves says, "Both Cox and Faisal opposed any attempt by the extremist nationalists to rush the coronation because each of them felt that Iraq's king must not owe it to an unconstitutional seizure by any particular party. Rather, his coronation must take place with the full will-power of the people and in

---

[1] *Al-Iraq* newspaper of July 13, 1921.

a constitutional way. Each of them felt that crowning a king through a particular party would make him prone to be a political prisoner of the party, which helped him win a speedy arrival. Cox felt, moreover, that the British government, which facilitated matters for Faisal, deserved to enjoy some fruits of its success."[1]

The prevailing trend of the time was that an elected founding assembly should nominate Faisal and that crowning him must take place as it took place in Syria. But this would take a long time; moreover, it is not guaranteed, and the experiment which took place is not encouraging due to the extremist public enthusiasm and haste.

Cox finally thought of the following suitable way: organizing "transcripts" signed by people. It is said that Naji al-Suweedi is the one who suggested it to him.[2] It is not unlikely that al-Suweedi's idea was inspired by the people of al-A`dhimiyya, who organized the first transcript in the allegiance process for Faisal, as we have indicated above.

The gist of this method is that the dignitaries and chiefs in every district or city of Iraq are to be invited to a meeting at a particular place. Once the meeting convened, someone in charge would rise to speak about the purpose behind the meeting and mention the merits of Prince Faisal and his being qualified to assume the position of a king. He would then ask the attendants, "Is there anyone among you who opposes?" They would answer him by saying, "No! No!" He would then ask them, "Do you consent?" They would say, "Yes! Yes!" It is then that he submits to them the sheet of the transcript, which is printed and prepared in advance, to sign. The meeting would end as desired. This would be regarded as the fealty of all residents to Prince Faisal as the king.

The process of organizing and signing the transcripts began in late July and ended on August 6. It mostly went on as was expected: heads and dignitaries in most areas of Iraq took to signing the transcripts which were presented to them without opposition, and only a few of them did not, as we will point out.

---

[1]Graves (op. cit.), pp. 299-300.

[2]Khayri al-Omari, *Hikayat Siyasiyya* (political anecdotes), Cairo, Egypt, 1969, p. 85.

In this regard, an interesting anecdote is narrated. The director of the Tawooq district in Kirkuk governorate received an order to organize a transcript for Faisal's fealty, but shortly after that, he heard that the British had changed their mind about nominating Faisal, so the director was confused. The means of communication via telegram and telephone connections were not available in those days, so he resorted to organizing two transcripts, one of which was about accepting Faisal and the other about rejecting him. The residents signed both transcripts, which the director took to the governor's adviser, Capt. Miller. When the adviser asked him, "Where is the transcript?" he answered him with, "Which one of them do you want?", presenting both transcripts which the adviser took.[1]

In fact, this story is not strange in the traditions of those days if you look at the way the dignitaries and chiefs in Iraq used to do anything which the governors wanted them to do. It is interesting to cite here what Graves mentioned about a group of Imara City sheikhs. When Cox asked them after the Cairo Conference about the type of government they wanted, they said, "Allah is our Master, Muhammed is our Prophet, and Cox is our ruler."[2]

The Opposition Makes A Move

The process of organizing transcripts in Iraq went on as desired, according to the way we have already pointed out, and nothing happened against what was desired except in Baghdad. Graves says that al-Khalisi's *fatwa* [binding religious edict] had some impact in stirring the spirit of opposition there.[3]

The Baghdad meeting took place at Cinema Royal on July 28. When the administrative officer of Baghdad, Rasheed al-Khoja, stood to ask the attendants to agree on naming Faisal as king, one of them said to him, "We consent and agree to name His Highness Prince Faisal as king

---

[1] Abdul-Razzaq al-Hassani, *Tarikh al-Wizarat al-Iraqiyya* (history of Iraqi administrations), Saida, Lebanon, 1965, Vol. 1, p. 43.

[2] Graves (op. cit.), p. 301.

[3] *Ibid.*, p. 300.

of Iraq, but we want to put some conditions." It is then that voices were raised throughout the hall saying, "Yes, Yes," and a loud applause filled the hall. After deliberations, it was decided to add some statements to the fixed form, which is: the government must be "independent and stripped of any condition and severed from others' authority" and that the first thing King Faisal should do would be to "put together and assemble the general assembly that will coin the laws and the constitution in three months' time from the date of holding the reins of matters".[1] It is said that these statements angered Cox and made him hate Rasheed al-Khoja, and this finally led to the latter being fired from his post.[2]

It is worth mentioning that Sayyid Muhammed al-Sadr tried to make this same move in al-Kadhimiyya, but Faisal prevented him. Al-Sadr had invited to his house on one evening a large number of dignitaries and clergymen in order to sign a transcript for swearing the oath of allegiance to Faisal with a text about rejecting the British mandate. As those invited were gathered at al-Sadr's house, a well-known man from among the residents of al-Kadhimiyya went to Faisal, woke him up, and told him that a plot was being hatched against him in al-Kadhimiyya. The king, therefore, sent one of his companions to al-Sadr to summon him. Here we leave Ms Bell to tell us what talk went on between them according to what she stated in her letter dated July 27. She said,

> "A group of extremists exerted a desperate effort to replace the official fealty format with another containing full rejection of the British mandate; therefore, Faisal summoned al-Sadr, who was at the heart of the notion, and gave him a clear warning. He said to him, 'I am now practically the king, and I do not tolerate any silly action. Anyone who disturbs public opinion will get what he deserves.'"[3]

---

[1] Hussain Jameel, "Minal Turath al-Deemuqrati fil Iraq" (from the democratic legacy in Iraq), *Al-Hilal* magazine of December 1966.

[2] Abdul-Razzaq al-Hassani (op. cit.), Vol. 1, p. 51.

[3] Burgoyne, *Gertrude Bell*, London, 1961, Vol. 2, p. 230.

This opposition movement, which went on in Baghdad and in al-Kadhimiyya, annoyed Cox, and it prompted him to issue instructions to the administrative officers to encourage the residents to add clauses to the transcripts demanding a British mandate. I found among the royal palace documents a personal letter dated Thul-Qi`da 25 [July 31st according to the Gregorian calendar or the 18th according to the Julian Christian calendar], which coincided with the 31st of July of 1921 A.D.[1], sent from Diwaniyya by a man named Abdul-Majeed Fuad Zadah to Yousuf al-Suweedi in which he said, "The nationalists in Diwaniyya want to follow the allegiance of Hujjatul-Islam al-Khalisi, but the British adviser and his cronies from among the dignitaries and chiefs are exerting their efforts to change the transcripts and to recondition the British mandate in these transcripts. The sender of the letter indicated the text of the allegiance that those people wanted to impose on the residents; it was: 'I swear the oath of allegiance to Prince Faisal to be the king of Iraq under the mandate of the British.'" He says that this clause must be written by everyone above his signature; otherwise, they will expel him.[2]

Transcripts' Results

On August 19, all governorates sent their signed transcripts to Baghdad with the exception of the Muntafiq governorate. The following is a summary of what the transcripts contained arranged by the governorate:

Baghdad: 157 transcripts were sent, all swearing the oath of allegiance to Prince Faisal, but 68 of them demanded that he should be independent of the authority of others and that the national assembly — which represents the people — should convene in three months.

---

[1]This statement by the author shows that the A.D. dates he uses in his book are Gregorian, not Julian; therefore, I, Translator of this volume, shall stick from now on to adding the Gregorian Christian dates to the Islamic Hijri ones wherever the first is missing. – Tr.

[2]Excerpted from the documents of the [Iraqi] royal palace, Transcript No. K/11, Document No. 165.

Basra: 47 transcripts were sent, all of which swearing the oath of allegiance to Faisal, but most of those who signed them refused from the start to sign unless they knew the fate of the cessation idea which they advocated prior and to make sure that the British mandate would continue.

Mosul: 68 transcripts were sent up until that point, all supportive of Faisal, but six of them insisted on protecting the rights of the Kurds and other minorities, and seven of them preconditioned the continuation of the British mandate in addition to protecting the rights of minorities; 10 of them mentioned other conditions relevant to the Kurdish language and other matters. There were other transcripts on the way.

Kirkuk: 20 transcripts were sent in support of Faisal, and 21 rejected him. All the supporting transcripts came from Irbil area, which was at that time administrated by the Kirkuk governorate. There are other transcripts that are yet to arrive.

Dulaim: 26 transcripts were sent, all supporting Faisal, but 16 of them imposed a condition on him to accept British supervision.

Hilla: 41 transcripts were sent, all of which swore the oath of allegiance to Faisal without any condition, but 13 of them openly declared that he is accepted on the condition that the British mandate continues.

Karbala: 28 transcripts were sent, all swearing the oath of allegiance to Faisal without any condition.

Diyala: 41 transcripts were sent, all swearing the oath of allegiance to Faisal unconditionally.[1]

---

[1]Atiyyah, *Iraq*, Beirut, Lebanon, 1973, p. 392.

Coronation

In mid-August, after Faisal had been reassured of the results of the transcripts and he had realized that his crowning would shortly take place, he rented a house as his own residence. He found a suitable house belonging to a Jew named Sha`shoo`[1] on the bank of the [Tigris] river in the middle of the way between Baghdad and al-A`dhamiyya, and it is the house which came to be known proverbially among the people as "the mansion of Sha`shoo`". Faisal, therefore, moved into it while keeping his official quarters in the Qashla.[2]

Ms Bell says that she visited Faisal in his new house at sunset on August 15 as he and his companions were sitting on the rooftop. The view of the river and orchard behind it was magnificent, so the king smiled to her and said, "You are Iraqi! You are Bedouin!"

Faisal's delight and contentment did not last long. A very short period later, a telegram from (Winston) Churchill arrived saying that Faisal must announce in the crowning speech that the final authority is in the hands of the [British] high commissioner. Faisal protested, stating that the agreement made with him in London did not include this condition, and that his dignity must be safeguarded and he should appear before the people as an independent king; otherwise, he would not be able to win to his side the extremist nationalists.[3] Cox demonstrated some hesitation towards this position, but Ms Bell convinced him, saying that it was not

---

[1] This Jews' house used to be the mansion of the Ottoman *wali* (provincial governor) during the Ottoman rule. It dates back to the Abbasid period. Sha`shoo` bought the house from the *wali* after the British had occupied Iraq and entered Baghdad in 1917, the year that marked the end of the Ottoman rule over Iraq. – Tr.

[2] These quarters collapsed in the next year when swept away by the river's torrent, so a new palace was built for the king in an orchard owned by the endowment administration in the middle of the way between Baghdad and al-A`dhamiyya near the mansion of Sha`shoo`, and it is still standing though not as magnificantly as it used to be, just ruins.

[3] Philip Ireland, *Iraq*, Beirut, Lebanon, 1949, p. 262.

important to seek authority which could not be forcefully imposed.[1] Cox, therefore, sent a telegram to Churchill pointing out the bad impact that the desired announcement at the coronation would cause. He also said that sufficient authority could be imposed on the country through less conspicuous methods[2]; therefore, Churchill consented to this view at the last moment.

It was decided that the coronation should take place on August 23. Faisal himself chose this date because it coincided with Thul-Hijja 18 according to the Hijri calendar, which is the day the Shi`as regard as a feast they call "Eidul-Ghadeer", believing that the Prophet appointed [his cousin and son-in-law] Ali as the caliph after him. By choosing this date, Faisal wanted to remind the Shi`as that he belonged to the lineage of Imam Ali and that his coronation would take place on the same day when his ancestor was appointed for the caliphate.

The coronation took place at the Qashla square near the Clock Tower, where a podium was set up for the king and his retinue. A special distinctive chair was placed for the king, who appeared to be high. Chairs were lined up facing the podium for those invited to sit. A number of British soldiers were brought to perform the salutation as the honour guards, and a band was there to play the royal anthem. At six o'clock in the morning, Faisal came out of his official quarters on the river bank surrounded by Sir Percy Cox and Gen. Holden and followed by Cornwallis, Hussain Afnan and two companions, namely Tahsin Qadri and Ameen al-Kisbani. They all went to the podium, walking on a carpet. Faisal sat on his special chair as Cox sat on his right side and Holden on the left. Sayyid Mahmoud al-Naqeeb sat on Holden's left. Ms Bell says, "Faisal looked dignified but very tense, for it was an exciting moment, and he kept looking at the first row, so he saw me, whereupon I signalled a small greeting[3] by way of encouragement."[4]

Cox started the party by handing over Hussain Afnan a declaration to read. Its gist was that Prince Faisal had been elected as king

---

[1]Burgoyne (op. cit.), Vol. 2, p. 238.

[2]Philip Ireland (op. cit.), p. 262.

[3]Lady Bell (op. cit.), p. 500.

[4]Burgoyne (op. cit.), Vol. 2, p. 239.

of Iraq by a 96% majority of the population. Then he shouted, "Long Live the King!" Mahmoud al-Naqeeb stood up and recited a supplication on occasion, and it was then that the Iraqi flag was hoisted, and the musical band played the British royal anthem because there was no Iraqi anthem yet. Then the cannons fired 21 shots.

The king then stood up and delivered a lengthy speech from which we would like to quote the following paragraphs:

> "I sincerely thank the good people of Iraq for having sworn the oath of allegiance to me, a free fealty that indicated their love for me and trust in me. Here, there is another duty which prompts me to express appreciation for the British nation which supported the Arabs during critical war times, spending its own funds and sacrificing its own sons for the sake of their liberation and independence. I have repeatedly stated that what we need for the progress of this land depends on the assistance of a nation that supplies us with its funds and men. Since the British nation is the closest of all nations to us and the most keen about our interests, we shall derive from it and seek assistance only from it in order to reach our anticipated goal as soon as possible. There is an awareness that if people follow their kings' way, the kings follow their people's way. According to the extent of solidarity, the rising will be. I shall spare no effort to seek help of the nation's men in their various abilities, classes and beliefs, for all are to me equal. The nation, as a whole, is my party; I have no other party. The first thing for me to do is to start the elections and to put together the founding assembly. Let us unite and solidify, have a forethought and insightfulness, knowledge and action, thus do I invite my nation, and Allah is the One Who grants success and assists."[1]

The party did not last long. Ms Bell says that at the end of the party, she went to her office, and the visitors started going to her, and they were mostly those who were invited to attend the party. Ali al-Sulayman was

---

[1] Abdul-Razzaq al-Hassani (op. cit.), Vol. 1, p. 47.

one of them. He kept talking to her about his impressions about the party. He said to her, "By Allah, Sir Percy Cox was like the moon among them, and his face was like Paradise."[1]

Sayyid Muhammed al-Sadr had sent the king a letter congratulating him for receiving the crown and suggesting to him to visit al-Kadhimiyya in order to seek the blessing of the Shrine of Imam al-Kadhim.[2] The king responded to this suggestion and was present in al-Kadhimiyya on the morning of August 25 where a party was held for him inside the sacred shrine. The party was opened by Muhammed Abdul-Hussain, then Sayyid Muhammed al-Sadr stood up and gave the king a sword in a gold scabbard and delivered an extemporal speech in which he solicited the achievement of the people's hopes. The king responded to him by saying that he would exert his effort toward that end. It was then that a surprise took the place of which the organizers of the party had no prior knowledge. Poet Rasheed al-Hashimi stood up and recited a poem that contained some irony about the king. Here are some of its verses:

O one wearing the crown in Baghdad,
May you be congratulated if you
For its independence came,
So decorate it with knowledge and overwhelming justice
And do not inlay it with pearls and sapphires.
Use wisdom and save a nation in agony
After rising, it installed a tyrant for its humiliation.
O leader of the people! Do not spoil its leadership,
So the rope of pledge may not be cut off,
And assault Sham[3] and plant at its head
Iraq's spear and let it neighbor Tikrit.
What shall I say to people among us
Who violated a pledge which we could see
In time of hardship firmly fixed?

---

[1]Burgoyne (op. cit.), Vol. 2, p. 239.

[2]Documents of the royal palace, Folder No. K/11, Document No. 308.

[3]At the time, "Sham" incorporated Syria, Jordan, Palestine and Lebanon, pieces of the cake which the victors of World War I divided among themselves. – Tr.

O nation that violated in Sham its pledge,
You sneeze, so shall I hear "Bless you"?![1]

Sami Khondah, who attended the said party, told me that he noticed how the king was very angry because of this poem, so Rasheed al-Hashimi was afraid he might be arrested by the police because of it; therefore, he came out with him before the party was over and went to the house of Sayyid Muhammed al-Sadr for his protection against arrest.

What is strange is that *Dijla* newspaper did not mention this poem the next day when it described the party but mentioned other poems in which there was a great deal of praise of the king.[2]

The New Administration

The king hardly finished problems associated with the coronation before starting to face state-related problems. The first of those problems was about forming a new administration. The *naqeeb*'s cabinet had resigned according to the formalities, and Cox wanted to assign the post of head of the administration to the same *naqeeb* once more, whereas the king wanted to assign it to a man who was not charged with cooperating with the British.

The king sent Abdul-Wahid al-Hajj Sikar to Najaf to ask the clergymen to cooperate with him in forming the cabinet. Abdul-Wahid went to Najaf, and after holding discussions with some theologians there, he sent the king a letter, the text of which is as follows:

In the Name of the most Exalted One

No remonstration, Your Majesty, our Great King

Your Majesty knows that I met in Najaf to serve its renowned scholars, Hujjatul-Islam mentor Sheikh Jawad Sahib al-

---

[1]Abdullah al-Jibouri, *Diwan Rasheed al-Hashimi* (a collection of poems by Rasheed al-Hashimi), Baghdad, 1964, pp. 69-70.

[2]*Dijla* newspaper of August 26, 1921.

Jawahir and mentor Sheikh Abdul-Kareem al-Jaza'iri and the rest of the great scholars. I explained to them your good Islamic intentions. Many of them seemed to be completely skeptical about Your Majesty. They ordered me to write to Your Majesty on their behalf their gratitude and good wishes to your respectful self on the occasion of ascending the throne of Iraq which is one of the most important borderlines of the Islamic world, and that you may live long. They also ordered me to submit to your respectful self that after they have entrusted you to be the king of Iraq, they both entrust you to appoint the ministers according to your high regards. Absolutely neither of them accepts to occupy any of these posts, this can never be. But they hope that Your Majesty will not assign these posts except to a patriotic Muslim who follows his creed, particularly the prime minister and [moreover] specifically the interior minister because on his ministry, after Allah, rest many important matters that are relevant to forming the assembly your honorable self is required to form quickly and completely. They both expect Your Majesty to quickly respond to the wishes that rest on Your Majesty. Meanwhile, they will be monitoring and expecting Your Majesty to fulfill your promise to them to improve the conditions and to attain the aspirations. Their most important wish is your speedy appointment of a pious minister of the interior, and to choose those because of whom the forming of the assembly will be good or bad, and surely Allah is the One Who grants success and Who assists.

On Thul-Hijja 25 [Tuesday, August 30], 1339 A.H. [1921 A.D.][1]

[sent by] Abdul-Wahid Hajj Sikar[2]

---

[1]The original Arabic text of some correspondences in this Volume refers a number of times to the year 1939 which apparently is a typographical error since the events discussed in this Volume, as we all know, took place in 1921 A.D. which coincided with the Hijri year 1339, not 1939. – Tr.

[2]From the royal palace's documents, Folder No. K/11, Document No. 264.

The king finally surrendered to Cox's will in assigning the post of head of administration to the *naqeeb*, but another problem faced him about who would take charge of the interior ministry. Ms Bell says the following in a letter dated September 4: "The past week, he was busy with the problem of forming the new administration. The king summoned me on Wednesday. When I went to him, he kept talking to me seriously about the administration, and the focal point of the problem was the interior ministry which had remained vacant since the expulsion of Sayyid Talib [al-Naqeeb]. The king thinks that this [interior] ministry is the criterion whereby people will judge him. If he appoints a man who is flunky and is known for being submissive to the British, people will judge the entire administration as being a farce, and they will judge the king as being a puppet in the hands of the British."[1]

The notion was finally to appoint Naji al-Suweedi for the interior ministry, but Cox did not endorse this appointment. Ms Bell comments about that, saying, "Cox is right because Naji al-Suweedi, although he is clever and well-intentioned, is not trustworthy. So, if he takes charge of the interior ministry, it will be our duty to watch him closely so that he may not swerve from the drawn path." She adds that she went with Cornwallis to Cox to convince him to agree to appoint al-Suweedi, but he insisted on his refusal.[2]

Cox chose Tawfiq al-Khalidi, but the king did not agree, for the king accused al-Khalidi of inclining towards the Turks. At the time, the Turks were spreading their rumours in Iraq against Faisal and the British, and they brought Ahmed al-Sanusi[3] near Iraq's northern borders in order to

---

[1]Burgoyne (op. cit.), Vol. 2, p. 242.

[2]*Ibid.*

[3]Ahmed al-Sherif al-Sanusi was a Libyan nationalist leader and a freedom fighter who protested the Italian invasion of Libya. He was born in 1873 and died in 1933. When World War I erupted, the warring parties competed with each other to win his support and that of his forces: Turkey and Germany on the one hand, and Britain and Egypt on the other. The first wanted al-Sanusi to lessen the pressure on Italy by agreeing to a truce and to open a new front against the British, whereas the others desired to assist al-Sanusi in order to crush the Italians, his main enemy, at the time. – Tr.

declare *jihad*. It was rumored that the French in Syria had sent al-Sanusi the sum of 20,000 pounds to help finance his *jihad* campaign.

Ja`far al-`Askari went to Ms Bell and said to her, "Appointing al-Khalidi in these circumstances is perilous because he supports those who incline towards the Turks in Iraq and hinder his work in the defence ministry. He, therefore, wishes to resign." Nouri al-Sa`eed went after that to Ms Bell and said the same to her, and he kept warning her against those who were inclining to the Turks and who were present in Iraq. Ms Bell protested to Nouri al-Sa`eed, saying, "The danger does not lie in only those who support the Turks, it also lies in the madness of his extremist fellows." Nouri answered her, saying, "The extremists are not dangerous to this extent so long as they bear Arab sentiment. My master, Faisal, knows how to deal with them, and they will disappear."[1]

The contention and argument in this regard went on for almost three weeks, and the king started threatening to go to London to put the issue before the officials there. Cornwallis went to him in the company of Col. Joyce, and Ms Bell went, too, and they all kept trying to convince him not to go to London then. They said to him that people would interpret his going there as a result of his dispute with Cox about putting the administration together, and this would harm both of them. Ms Bell says, "I think we were able to convince him, but we could not advance one step along the path of forming the administration."[2]

Finally, there was an agreement to let an unknown officer, namely the head of the military recruitment, al-Hajj Ramzi, to be in charge of the interior ministry. As for Naji al-Suweedi, he was appointed as minister of justice. A change was made to the ministry of education and health, which was split into two separate ministries. The ministry of education was placed in the hands of Sheikh Abdul-Kareem al-Jaza'iri. As for the health ministry, it was given to a Christian doctor from Mosul named Hanna Khayyat. Ms Bell says that she was the one who appointed Hanna Khayyat in the said ministry after introducing him to Cox and suggesting to him

---

[1]*Ibid.*, Vol. 2, p. 242.

[2]*Ibid.*, Vol. 2, p. 242.

to separate the health ministry from the ministry of education, and so it was.[1]

The forming of the new administration was announced on September 12, 1921. In it, al-Naqeeb was the prime minister, al-Hajj Ramzi was the minister of the interior, Naji al-Suweedi was the minister of justice, Ja`far al-`Askari was the defence minister, Izzat al-Kirkukli was the minister of labor and transport, Abdul-Lateef al-Mandeel was trade minister, Muhammed Ali Fadhil was minister of endowments, Hanna Khayyat was health minister, and Abdul-Kareem al-Jaza'iri was minister of education.

The announcement about forming the administration was hardly made when Abdul-Kareem al-Jaza'iri sent from Najaf his apologies for not participating in it. Here, discussions and arguments erupted anew about who would take charge of the ministry of education, provided he is a Shi`a. It was finally agreed to choose Sayyid Hibat ad-Deen al-Shahristani from Karbala, so he came to Baghdad to take charge of this ministry.

Shi`as And The School Of Law

After the king had finished solving the problem of forming the new administration, he started facing another problem: the necessity of hiring Shi`a youths for government positions. But he could not find Shi`as in enough numbers among those who had received a modern education and who were suitable to occupy these positions. After consulting with his advisers, especially his secretary, Rustum Haidar, his view settled on encouraging clever Shi`a youths from among those who received [the] old [form of] education to join the School of Law, which had been re-opened in the fall of last year.

Tawfiq al-Suweedi had appointed a headmaster for the School of Law in November of 1921 to succeed its former headmaster, Col. Bill. Al-Suweedi highlighted in his memoirs the problem which took place at that time about admitting Shi`a youths in the said school. He said the following:

---

[1] *Ibid.*, Vol. 2, p. 244.

"I remember what happened some day when some students seeking admissions and carrying sheets signed by Sheikh Shukur, headmaster of the Ja`fariyya School, testifying to the student bearing a sheet testifying that he is a graduate of the secondary [high] school despite my knowledge that the [Ja`fariyya] School did not reach the awarding of secondary degrees neither during the time of the Turks nor during the period of [the British] occupation. I explained to each applicant that he had to authenticate his certificate [of graduation] at the ministry of education or take a test to prove his secondary competency. He was followed by several youths who claimed that they were graduates of the Ja`fariyya School and were carrying the like of that strange sheet of paper. I remember some of their names: Abdul-Razzaq al-Azari, Abbas Mahdi, Muhammed Hassan Kubba, Ahmed Zaki al-Khayyat, Muhammed al-Shama`, Abdul-Hameed Mahdi, Abdul-Hadi al-Zahir, Sa`d Salih, Ja`far Hamandi and others. I refused to admit them and to depend on the sheets in their hands. It was then that they resorted to the government and to the palace. On that same day, the late Muhammed Rustam Haidar came to me and said, 'His Majesty the king wishes to help these [youths] and [wants them to be] accepted in the college!' I explained their legal situation to him. When Rustam insisted that I should exert my efforts to help them, saying that His Majesty the king emphatically wished that those men be admitted into the college, I answered him saying, 'The time for students to be admitted into high schools via royal wishes is gone, and these matters used to take place during the time of Sultan Abdul-Hameed; therefore, I am sorry I cannot do anything for them if they do not do what I have required them to do.' He went away angrily and never returned."[1]

The problem did not end there. The king was determined to get those youths admitted into the School of Law. Tawfiq al-Suweedi had to

---

[1]Tawfiq al-Suweedi, *My Memoirs*, Beirut, Lebanon, 1969, pp. 76-77.

finally admit them. Al-Suweedi claims that the king coerced Sati` al-Husari, who was then director of education, to authenticate their certificates, and then they went to him, so he admitted them into the school as he "surrendered his affairs to Allah."[1]

It is worth mentioning that what Tawfiq al-Suweedi states in his memoirs was not supported by Sati` al-Husari. Al-Husari has stated in his memoirs that he did not endorse the credentials of those Shi`a youths, but it was al-Suweedi who was lenient in accepting them. Al-Husari provides us with many details about this subject which tarnish al-Suweedi's image: he says that al-Suweedi took advantage of that opportunity and started being lenient in accepting the credentials of the Armenians and Jews in addition to those of the Shi`as, so much so that the matter reached the knowledge of the headmaster of Al-Ilyans School that he started awarding forged certificates to whoever wanted them in exchange for 50 rupees each. The same was done by Kidorian, headmaster of the Armenians' School in exchange for 30 rupees [per certificate]. As for Sheikh Shukur, he used to give each certificate away "seeking to please Allah". Al-Husari says that when he confronted al-Suweedi about this fact, al-Suweedi answered him, saying, "Mawlana [master], do you think that I did not know the truth?! The king has asked that we should be lenient in admitting the Ja`faris, and I have been lenient about admitting the Ja`faris and non-Ja`faris."[2]

Al-Husari adds that he talked to the king about this issue, explaining the harm that it could produce, so the king answered him by saying, "I never said to them to accept anyone, nor to accept forged certificates. The whole matter is that during my talk with the ministers, I told them that we are facing a problem: from their sect, the Ja`faris form a minority among the officials. You know that the original cause in this regard is the scarcity of those from among them who have certificates, and the government is forced to appoint individuals having incomplete study. Can they find a way to solve this problem while ensuring that the Ja`fari youths who could not complete their studies would be able to

---

[1] *Ibid.*, p. 77.

[2] Sati` al-Husari, *Muthakkarati fil Iraq* (my memoirs in Iraq), Beirut, Lebanon, Vol. 1, p. 408.

study?" Al-Husari suggested to the king to solve this problem by opening an evening secondary school where bread earners and government officials could study so they would be able that to join high institutions. The king liked this suggestion, and an evening secondary school was immediately opened.[1]

The King During Muharram

That year, the month of Muharram started on September 4[2], the month in which the Shi`as declared their mourning for the killing of al-Hussain ibn Ali. King Faisal took an interest in this month as the British had done after their occupation of Baghdad. He assisted the Hussaini processions with funds and gifted barrels of fuel for the torches of the evening processions. He also issued instructions to hold a mourning *majlis* [gathering] in his name and at his own personal expense in the courtyard of al-Kadhimiyya Shrine in the second 10 days of the month of Muharram. The king personally attended that mourning *majlis* more than once and sat in a compartment in the Shrine among the clergymen.

On the 10th of Muharram, the day during which a enactment was held inside the courtyard of al-Kadhimiyya Shrine, of how al-Hussain was killed. The king was present in the Shrine with his retinue. A large compartment had been prepared for him over the Qibla Gate in which he sat, and the processions kept passing before him. He ordered gifts to be given to those who were reciting eulogies in the processions and to those who performed the martyrdom enactment.

What caught people's eyes on that day was the presence of the new Iraqi flag with the four colours among the processions' flags, and this was the first time the Iraqi flag was raised in Hussaini processions. Apparently, some of those who were in charge of the processions were angry about the presence of that flag among other flags on that day, for it

---

[1]*Ibid.*, Vol. 1, p. 409.

[2]Yes, this date is quite accurate: September 4, 1921, according to the Gregorian Christian calendar, coincided on the first of the month of Muharram of the Hijri year 1340, and the day of the week was Sunday according to the calendar which I have been using for this and all my other translations. – Tr.

was, in their view, the flag which Sherif Hussain raised when he made an alliance with the infidel Britons against the Muslim Ottoman state as the *mujahidun* in Iraq were raising the flag of *jihad* in support of the Ottoman state; therefore, we found the bearer of the flag walking during the enactment beside the person who was playing the role of Omar ibn Sa`d and not beside the one who played the role of al-Hussain or his brother, al-Abbas, or other members of the Prophet's family (Ahl al-Bayt).

Sati` al-Husari was then sitting in the small compartment which was adjacent to that of the king, and this sight drew his attention, as he pointed out in his memoirs. He says in those memoirs that he noticed the Iraqi flag being carried beside the individual who was playing the role of Omar ibn Sa`d, commander of the Umayyad army, which fought al-Hussain. So, the flag was with him wherever he went, and people, especially women, cursed whenever the actor who was playing the role of Omar ibn Sa`d appeared. This meant that the Iraqi flag was in the procession of the commander who was being cursed by the public."

Al-Husari kept thinking of the serious repercussions that would result from this, so he turned behind him and saw among the companions Sabeeh Najeeb whom he knew since the Damascus days because he was a companion of Prince Zaid. He, therefore, told him that the man who was carrying the [Iraqi] flag must walk by the side of the man who plays the role of al-Hussain, not by the side of the one who plays the role of Omar ibn Sa`d. Sabeeh Najeeb descended from the compartment to issue the instructions to those who were in charge of organizing the function. The flag bearer obeyed this order and kept his distance from the actor representing Omar and went towards that who played the role of al-Hussain. But whenever he almost became close to the man who was playing the role of al-Hussain, the latter would roughly push him away. And whenever the flag bearer tried to walk beside him, he would again push him away and show signs of anger and reprimand. Sabeeh Najeeb went to al-Husari to ask him what should be done, so al-Husari said, "The best way now is that the flag bearer should withdraw from the field calmly without attracting people's attention. What is important is that he must not walk beside the horseman who represents Omar." Thus, the flag bearer withdrew from the sacred Shrine.

Al-Husari says that after returning to Baghdad, he narrated this incident to the king, who expressed his amazement and said, "My mind was busy listening to some explanations and following the movements of the processions and the voices of the masses; so, I paid no attention to the flag situation." The king thought that the way in which al-Husari dealt with that matter was quite sound.[1]

The Mayor Of Samarra

Sheikh Mahdi al-Khalisi wanted Samarra to have a mayor who would look after the Shi`a pilgrims and keep them out of harm's way, and he chose a man from among the people of al-Kadhimiyya bearing the Indian nationality named Agha Muhammed for it. He wrote a letter in this regard which he sent to King Faisal. When the king received al-Khalisi's letter, it so happened that Ali al-Bazargan entered. He [Faisal], therefore, complained to him about that request that al-Khalisi wanted and how difficult it would be to fulfil it. Ali al-Bazargan says the following:

"I went one day to visit His Majesty King Faisal I in the Sha`shoo` Mansion, and I used to see him without seeking prior permission, so I saw him in his room drinking tea. When he saw me, he said to me, 'Look at this, Ali.' He handed me a letter from imam Sheikh Mahdi al-Khalisi to King Faisal I asking him to appoint Mirza Muhammed, the Indian man who was assistant to the political governor of al-Kadhimiyya, for the Samarra county due to his services to the Muslims. His Majesty commented about that letter saying, 'What will people say about me if I appoint an Indian in this post? Did you carry out your revolution against the British so I may appoint the Indians for you in state posts?! Is there nobody in Iraq who fits to occupy these posts?' I said to him, 'Master, I shall do something that will please you with regard to this problem.' His Majesty smiled and said to me, 'If you can

---

[1]*Ibid.*, Vol. 1, pp. 88-89.

discourage Sheikh Mahdi al-Khalisi from appointing this Indian man, I shall be grateful to you.'"[1]

Al-Bazargan kept trying to convince al-Khalisi to change his mind. First, he went to meet al-Hajj Kadhim Abu al-Timman in the market area. They both went to al-Kadhimiyya to meet Sheikh Mahdi al-Khalisi. When they both talked to al-Khalisi about this subject, he said to them, "Yes, I am the one who asked King Faisal I to appoint Mirza Muhammed because he [the latter] is righteous." Al-Bazargan said to him, "Is Iraq now without the righteous and the sincere men, so you would ask for Indians to be appointed?" Al-Khalisi said, "I do not know anyone who is good for this post other than this man." Al-Bazargan then said, "I know someone, and I think that you think well of him." When al-Khalisi inquired about who that man was, al-Bazargan answered that it was Jalal Baban.

On the next day, Ali al-Bazargan went to al-Khalisi accompanied by Jalal Baban in order to introduce the latter to al-Khalisi, whereupon al-Khalisi ordered his son, Sheikh Muhammed, to write a letter to the king asking him to appoint Jalal Baban instead of Agha Muhammed. Al-Bazargan rushed to take the letter to the king. When the king received the letter, he addressed al-Bazargan thus: "May Allah bless you, Ali, you have saved me!" Then the king took a pen and referred the letter to the interior minister, writing on it, "I am awaiting the decision according to the contents of this letter." Al-Bazargan took the letter to the interior minister, and when the latter read it, he said, "Ali, you have not only saved His Majesty the king from this problem but saved all of us!"[2]

On December 4, 1921, Jalal Baban started his job in Samarra.[3] He kept exerting his efforts to look after the pilgrims and keep harm away from them.

---

[1]Ali al-Bazargan *Al-Waqai` al-Haqeeqiyya* (the true incidents), Baghdad, Iraq, 1954, p. 177.

[2]*Ibid.*, pp. 177-179.

[3]Younus Ibrahim al-Samarrai, *Tarikh Madinat Samarra* (history of Samarra city), Baghdad, Iraq, 1973, Vol. 3, p. 82.

Al-Ikhwan's Raid

When the king was trying to get close to the Shi`as in order to win their hearts, as we have stated, an incident took place, which was like a bomb that shook Iraqi society and was the reason for the king getting even closer to the Shi`as.

On March 11, 1922, when some Iraqi tribesmen were letting their cattle graze in a place south of Nasiriyya, 30 miles from the rail tracks, a large force of the Wahhabi Ikhwan [*al-Ikhwan al-Muslimoon*, the Muslim Brotherhood] of Ibn Saud staged a raid led by Faisal al-Duweesh that went to extremes in terms of killing and looting. Iraqi references estimated the number of those killed at about 700, estimating the loot at 130 horses, 2,530 camels, 3,811 donkeys, 43,010 she-camels and the destruction of 781 homes.[1]

This incident stirred great panic in Iraq, especially among the mid and central Euphrates tribes, and many people thought that it was the prelude for a sweeping Wahhabi attack on Iraq and that the Ikhwan would slaughter humans as they slaughter cattle and demolish the holy shrines, violate the privacies of women and destroy everything. It is worth mentioning that Iraq had before then suffered from Wahhabi raids and witnessed the looting and bloodshed in those raids. Moreover, the Iraqi tribes received exaggerated reports about the fierceness of the Ikhwan and their excessive desire to loot and shed blood. This led to the spread of a wave of panic among the public.

We must not forget the old hostility between the Hashemites and the Saudi families. When the Ikhwan raid took place, King Faisal suffered painfully, and his pain intensified when he saw how Cox was lukewarm and reluctant to undertake deterrent measures against those Ikhwan.

The fact is that the British had sent a reconnaissance plane to the site of the raid as soon as they heard about it, so the Ikhwan fired at the plane and hit it, prompting the British to send four other planes to them that dropped several bombs at them and sprayed them with machinegun bullets. One of those planes was hit and downed, but the pilot and his assistant were safe and were able to reach the rail tracks after walking for

---

[1]Abdul-Razzaq al-Hassani (op. cit.), Vol. 1, p. 59.

25 miles. On the morning of the next day, the British sent four other planes that chased the Ikhwan and rained on them bombs and bullets. Two of those planes were hit but were able to return safely to their bases.

It was common knowledge in Iraq at the time that the Ikhwan's raid went on in lieu of instigation from the British, or at least with their consent, on the basis that the friendship between Cox and Ibn Saud was very strong, and it made no sense that Ibn Saud would do anything to anger his friend, Cox. Cox tried to avoid this charge against him, so he wrote the king a letter telling him about the measures which the British Air Force undertook against the Ikhwan. The king, therefore, sent him a reply expressing his appreciation of what the British planes had done, but he expressed his opinion that it was necessary to undertake tougher measures. He pointed out that the Iraqi government had neither the authority nor the sufficient [fire] power to defend the country's borders, and that the tribes were now certain that the government was unable to protect them, and this would lead to the most serious harm to the fledgling Iraqi state.[1]

The king wanted Cox to be like him in his enthusiasm to discipline the Ikhwan, but Cox looked at the matter differently. Cox kept apologizing that he was waiting for the arrival of instructions from London and that he was waiting for the answer of Ibn Saud to a telegram that he had sent him. Ms Bell says that Ibn Saud's answer was several days late because Ibn Saud would usually send his telegrams on camel back to Bahrain so they would be transmitted from there to Baghdad, and this needed time.[2]

Administrative Crisis

When the king lost hope that Cox would help him defend Iraq against the Ikhwan, he kept thinking of another plan: mobilizing the Iraqi tribes and supplying them with weapons on the one hand while strengthening the Iraqi army on the other. But this plan did not win Cox's approval. Perhaps [Cox] was afraid of it since he believed that supplying the tribes with

---

[1]From royal palace documents, Folder No. t/4/a5, Document No. 45.

[2]Burgoyne (op. cit.), Vol. 2, p. 260.

weapons —especially those that carried out the 1920 Revolution — meant encouraging them to revolt again.

It is worth mentioning in this regard that the king at that time was surrounded by a number of chiefs of tribes who had participated in the 1920 Revolution, such as Abdul-Wahid al-Hajj Sikar, Sha`lan Abul-Joon, Muhsin Abu Tibeekh, Alwan al-Yasiri and Qati` al-Awwadi. These men used to stress to the king that the Iraqi tribes were able to fight the Ikhwan and overpower them if only they had enough weapons, and they were encouraging the king to stand firmly towards Cox and declare *jihad* on the Ikhwan.

The king sent on March 27 a request to the council of ministers asking for its endorsement of increasing the share of the defence ministry's budget in order to strengthen the means of defending Iraq against the attacks of those who followed Ibn Saud. When this request was presented to the council, Naji al-Suweedi stood to oppose it, pointing out that the Ikhwan's raid was the result of the traditional hostility between both Hashemite and Saudi families and that Iraq's defence was the responsibility of Britain since it is the one that undertook on its shoulders [the responsibility of] safeguarding domestic security in Iraq, in addition to repelling the dangers that threaten it from the outside. Ja`far al-`Askari responded to al-Suweedi and said that the agreement had been made before between the king and the high commissioner that the British government would be responsible for defending the left side of the Tigris as well as Imara and Basra and that the Iraqi government would be responsible for the eastern side of the Tigris and for both right and left sides of the Euphrates, provided it is supported by the British Air Force. Thereupon, defending Iraq's borders against the Ikhwan fell on the shoulders of the Iraqi government.

The opposition by Naji al-Suweedi was an unpleasant surprise to the king. Naji was regarded as a supporter and helper of the king; so what prompted him to change his stance now? What increased the king's resentment is that four ministers supported Naji al-Suweedi in his opposition; these were: Izzat al-Kirkukli, Hanna Khayyat, Abdul-Lateef al-Mandeel and al-Hajj Sirri, and the prime minister discreetly supported them. Also, Sasson Hisqail said something which was akin to supporting them.[1]

The king summoned the ministers who opposed him and announced to them that he had lost his confidence in them and that they should resign. Cox and Cornwallis went to the king in an attempt to pacify him but to no avail.[2] After that, the king's secretary sent to the prime minister a strongly worded letter. We provide the following excerpt from it here:

"It was the hope of His Majesty that the respected council [of ministers] in its session of March 27, 1922, would issue a clear resolution, acting upon which ensures the protection of Iraq's borders and citizens against attacks by [Saudi] desert tribes. He regretted the opinion of the minister of justice and those who followed him in like from among the respectful ministers after the defence minister had explained to them how critical the situation in the Euphrates valley was and that the responsibility of defending it fell on the shoulders of the Iraqi government. For this purpose, police stations and guard installations must be set up in certain places in order to monitor the hostile tribes and repel their attacks from any direction they come. Based on the above, I have been ordered to express to your excellencies the regret of His Majesty for the views expressed by the minister of justice and those of some of his fellows."[3]

Ibn Saud's answer reached Cox on March 29 in which Ibn Saud expressed his regret for what had happened. He said that Faisal al-Duweesh had done what he had done without his permission and that the culprit would receive his punishment. Cox presented this answer to the king and to the prime minister, and he issued instructions to publish it in the newspapers in order to pacify public opinion. But the people were not

---

[1]Abdul-Razzaq al-Hassani (op. cit.), Vol. 1, pp. 61-64.

[2]Burgoyne (op. cit.), Vol. 2, p. 266.

[3]From royal palace documents, Folder No. t/4/a5, Document No. 60.

pacified; rather, their agitation intensified. Graves says, "Although Ibn Saud expressed his regret, the country was angry and outraged. The rumour saying that the British were responsible for the incident had been circulated among ignorant people; therefore, those who instigated it used it to stir sentiments against the British. Shi`a *ulema* took the opportunity to bargain for political power under the claim of patriotism."[1]

Crisis Intensifies

The ministerial council had decided on March 18 to send a committee to Nasiriyya to investigate the Ikhwan's raid. The committee was comprised of Nouri al-Sa`eed representing the interior ministry, Dawood al-Haidari representing the ministry of justice, and the first head al-Hajj Ramadhan representing the defence ministry provided Maj. Yates, adviser to the Muntafiq governor, would join them later. On the 29th of the same month, the committee returned to Baghdad and submitted its report to the ministerial council. The report contained an estimate of the horrific losses inflicted on the Iraqi tribes as a result of the Ikhwan's raid. The report also pointed out that the Iraqi government was responsible for the incident because the office of al-Muntafiq's administrative officer had sensed the approaching danger at the time and sought the government's help, but the government did not help it.[2]

On the next morning, the 30th of March, the *Iraq* newspaper carried on its front page an editorial under the heading "About the Ikhwan's Attack on al-Muntafiq Tribes", in which it pointed out that the owner of the newspaper met Nouri al-Sa`eed after his return with his fellow committee members from Nasiriyya and asked him several questions. The newspaper published Nouri's answers, and in them, there was a strong attack on the Wahhabis and a scathing criticism of the ministers who refused to strengthen the Iraqi army. Nouri al-Sa`eed frankly said that on his return, he found senior government officials unwilling to expand the army's budget under the pretext of insufficient financial resources, declaring that this was regretful, and that the cause

---

[1]Graves (op. cit.), p. 310.

[2]Abdul-Razzaq al-Hassani (op. cit.), Vol. 1, pp. 60-61.

behind it was that they did not familiarize themselves with how critical the situation was, and that had they indeed done so, they would have changed their mind.[1]

On the same day, the *Istiqlal* newspaper published on its front page a very violent editorial signed by "al-Alawi" under the heading "Defence! Defence!", underneath which is a line of poetry:

If one does not defend his territory
With his own weapon,
It shall be demolished,
And if one does not shun
Taunting, he shall be taunted by everyone.

The article violently assaulted Ibn Saud and his followers and those who supported him in Iraq, giving Ibn Saud the title of "leader of the Peninsula's Bolsheviks" and "Najd's Lenin"! It said that there are persons who have nothing to do with this country and who spread rumours saying that the Ikhwan's raid was simple in order to keep the nation inattentive; thus it would be taken by surprise, knowing that the raid was a big attack in which much blood was spilled, women, widows and children displaced; so, does the Iraqi nation, which is known for its self-esteem and pride, accept all of this?[2]

Both of these articles, in their implicit attack on the opposing ministers, had a strong impact on the ministerial council which convened that day. When the council's secretary finished reciting the committee's report, Naji al-Suweedi quickly submitted his resignation, followed by al-Hajj Ramzi, Abdul-Lateef al-Mandeel, Izzat al-Kirkukli and Hanna Khayyat. The king quickly issued his decree the next day, accepting their resignation and appointing Tawfiq al-Khalidi as minister of the interior, while Sabeeh Nash'at became the minister of labour and transport. Sasson Hisqail had also submitted his resignation in solidarity with the five ministers who resigned, but the prime minister rejected his resignation upon Cox's instructions.

---

[1] *Al-Iraq* newspaper of March 30, 1922.

[2] *Al-Istiqlal* newspaper in its issue dated March 30, 1922.

Cox was angry with the king because he did not consult with him about accepting the resignation of those five ministers, and he was angry with Nouri al-Sa`eed and with the *Istiqlal* newspaper. Cox sent a letter to the prime minister to draw his attention to the statements which Nouri al-Sa`eed had made to the *Al-Iraq* newspaper which he regarded as a serious breach of the official etiquette, for how could a government official criticize the ministers in such a way? Cox asked the prime minister to put in place rules which would prevent such a thing in the future.[1] Cox also sent another letter to the prime minister in which he said that *Al-Istiqlal*'s article was very serious and led to confusing the government and halting its businesses due to the moderate tone in Ibn Saud's answer. Cox said that *Al-Istiqlal* newspaper should publish an article announcing its regret for its previous article and highlight the peaceful stance of Ibn Saud towards Iraq. Cox sent a copy of each of these letters to the king.[2]

On April 1, Cox sent Churchill in London a telegram complaining about King Faisal's behaviour. In it, he said the following:

> "This reckless measure which he undertook in a storm of agitation, without consulting me or anyone else, was very regretful, especially with regards to al-Mandeel where Basra's [public] opinion will be negatively affected because of being forced to resign. At the time when I very much regretted the king's reckless behaviour, I advised him, when I heard what had happened, that it would be more suitable under the current circumstances that the *naqeeb* should submit the resignation of the entire administration and immediately call for the formation of a new one. But the king preferred to demand the resignation of five ministers involved in the case. It is unfortunate that this was followed by Sasson's resignation, which was not accepted anyway."

Churchill responded to Cox, saying, "I am surprised about Faisal expelling four ministers without consulting you. Surely this conduct was

---

[1] From the royal palace's documents, Folder No. t/4/a5, Document No. 66.

[2] *Ibid.*, Document No. 63.

not in agreement with the spirit of his personal pledges to follow your advice in important matters. I shall be very regretful if Sasson Afandi insists on resigning. You could, if you would tell him that I personally sent a telegram about him."

Apparently, the king realized the necessity of being moderate in his stance vis-à-vis Cox, so he started allaying his toughness. We notice this in the telegram that Cox sent to Churchill, by which he answers the latter's previous telegram; he said the following:

"It seems now that Faisal realizes that he was very reckless, and he [now] tends to find means to enable one or two [resigning ministers] to return after a short while if he can do that without losing his dignity. I think it is better that your letter to him about this issue will be personal, expressing your disappointment for his having chosen this troubling path without consulting with me or with his usual advisers. I am of the view that it is neither the policy of the British government of His Majesty nor my own personal inclination that his status as a king be undermined or that he is forced to surrender by forcing him to nullify reckless or ill-advised behaviours which he had done without consultation. But if he shows an extremist trend in that direction, my treatment is to ask to let him be excused, and the cause of it must be made public."[1]

Call For The Karbala Conference

When the crisis in Baghdad was at its peak, the mid-Euphrates was about to produce a strong movement to gather all tribes and mobilize them to defend Iraq in the face of the Ikhwans' attacks. Some chiefs of tribes were behind it, such as Abdul-Wahid al-Hajj Sikar, Alwan al-Yasiri and Qati` al-Awwadi.

---

[1] Salih Jawad Kadhim, *Muhawalat Istijlaa Jadeeda* (a new vacating attempt), *Al-Muthaqqaf al-Arabi* magazine of June 1974.

Al-Najaf's scholars, headed by Sayyid Abul-Hassan al-Isfahani [1861 – 1946 A.D.] and Mirza Hussain Naeeni [1857 – 1936 A.D.], held meetings to discuss this subject. They finally decided to hold a conference in Karbala to be attended by chiefs of tribes and city dignitaries in order to discuss putting a plan to defend the country. Then they sent the following telegram, which ends with the signature of Sayyid Abul-Hassan and Mirza Hussain, to Sheikh Mahdi al-Khalisi in al-Kadhimiyya City:

> "Respectful Hujjatul-Islam Muhammed Mahdi al-Khalisi, may his blessings continue. There should be no reliance on the promise of the British authority to repel the evil of the Khariji Ikhwan against the Muslims; thereupon, we hope you will be present in Karbala a few days before the Ziyara and that you order the chiefs of tribes, such as Noor [al-Yasiri], the emir of Rabi`ah, and all other chiefs, after conveying our greetings to them, to attend. On our part, we shall bring to the meeting the chiefs in order to discuss their affairs by the will of Allah."[1]

It was decided to hold the conference from the 10th to the 15th of Sha`ban, coinciding with 6 to 11 April. This timing was chosen to coincide with the "mihya"[2] which falls on mid-Sha`ban. Sheikh Mahdi al-Khalisi sent his son, Sheikh Muhammed, to the king to invite him to attend the said conference. The king responded to the invitation and said that he would go to Karbala on the 14th of Sha`ban. Also, al-Khalisi sent the following telegram to 150 chiefs of tribes:

> "On the occasion of the Ikhwan's attack on Iraq's borders, it has been decided that the scholars and all chiefs of tribes should be present on the tenth day of the revered month of

---

[1]Muhammed Mahdi al-Baseer, *Tarikh al-Qadhiyya al-Iraqiyya* (history of the Iraqi issue), Baghdad, 1923, Vol. 2, pp. 391-392.

[2]This "mihya" is a tradition followed by Shi`a Muslims to celebrate the birth anniversary of the 12th Imam, Muhammed ibn al-Hassan al-`Askari al-Mahdi, also known as "al-Qaim". – Tr.

Sha`ban; therefore, you must be present on that day in Karbala."

In early April, on instructions from Sheikh Mahdi al-Khalisi, a committee was formed to oversee the conference and organize the travel to it. Its members were: Noor al-Yasiri, Kadhim Abu al-Timman, Qati` al-Awwadi, Alwan al-Yasiri, Baqir al-Shibeebi and Abdul-Hussain al-Chalabi. The committee met and devised a program of 13 articles which it printed at one of Baghdad's presses. The most important item in the program was selecting four sub-committees which were as follows:

The First Committee: it was comprised of Muhammed al-Khalisi, Abdul-Hussain al-Chalabi and Abu Talib al-Isfahani, and its task was to spread advice about the need to maintain full comfort and tranquility during the meetings. This committee was to travel to Karbala via the Hilla-Najaf route.

The Second Committee: It was comprised of Sadiq al-Asterbadi, Hamdi al-Pachachi, Abdul-Rasool Kubba, Idris al-Kadhimi and Abdul-Hadi al-Chalabi. Kadhim Abu al-Timman would be in charge of it and be responsible for administering its affairs, and its task was to make preparations for the trip of Sheikh Mahdi al-Khalisi and those in his company from among the people of al-Kadhimiyya and Baghdad first to Hilla then to Karbala.

The Third Committee: It was to be formed in Karbala and be comprised of Muhammed Hassan Abul-Mahasin, Isa al-Bazzaz, Khalil al-Asterbadi, Hashim Shah, Muhammed al-Kashmiri, Muhammed Ridha Nasr-Allah, Omar al-Alwan and Abdul-Kareem Awwad, and its task was to organize the meetings in Karbala.

The Fourth Committee: It was to be comprised of chiefs and caretakers of the holy shrines in Karbala, and its task was to identify the oncomers, assign a place for their stay, and facilitate getting them to attend the meetings.

On the morning of April 5, the members of the first committee left al-Kadhimiyya as scheduled. They were: Muhammed al-Khalisi, Abdul-Hussain al-Chalabi and Abu Talib al-Isfahani. They went to Najaf, where they contacted Sayyid Abul-Hassan al-Isfahani and Mirza Hussain al-Naeeni in order to speed up their trip to Karbala. Al-Isfahani responded to their request immediately. As for al-Naeeni, he refused to travel. Sheikh Muhammed al-Khalisi tells us in his memoirs about al-Naeeni's refusal:

> "I met Mirza Naeeni, and he apologized for being unable to attend because it reached his knowledge that we organized a program for this meeting, and he did not agree because the program was the doing of the advocates of *al-mashrootiyya*, Conditionalism[1], according to him. So, I was very surprised because Mirza Naeeni was one of the toughest advocates of Conditionalism, and he is the one who wrote the book *Tanbeeh al-Umma* (attracting the nation's attention) in which he advocates Conditionalism, the basic canon, and *tajaddud*, or renewalism, whereas we have been rejecting it, and we continue to do so in the sense which al-Naeeni meant, but the program has nothing to do with Conditionalism at all. This strict man was pretending not to know, feigning naivety, so I kept debating with him as he kept insisting, so much so that

---

[1]Conditionalism, which was advocated by Hamilton, quoting Kant, defines what is conditional as "the one whose both existence and concept depend on something else. It is conditional to that thing, and its canon is that thinking of things necessitates knowledge of their conditions," according to *Al-Mu`jam al-Shamil li Mustalahat al-Falsafa* (The Comprehensive Glossary of Philosophical Terms). Also, the Christian Evangelical Alliance defines Conditionalism as a concept of special salvation in which the gift of immortality is attached to (i.e. conditional on) belief in Jesus Christ. The Oxford English Dictionary (OED) traces this concept to the 17th Century, providing the following definition of a conditionalist: "[He is] one who held that the grace of God is dependent on conditions, or moralists." Since the *Tanbeeh al-Umma* book is unavailable, it is difficult to conclude whether Conditionalism has had any roots in Islamic theological philosophy, or if it is an imported concept that crept into the beliefs of some Muslims who apparently were influenced by Kant and other such philosophers. – Tr.

I said to him, 'You are the one who sent the telegram; so, how do you explain your refusal, and how do you answer people if they ask about the reason for your absence? What is your excuse?' But this did not affect him, and he kept insisting not to participate in the meeting and not to go to Karbala. When I lost hope, I parted with him, resenting his manners and deeds." Sheikh Muhammed [al-Khalisi] started thereafter speaking ill of Mirza Naeeni in an ugly way for which there is no room here.[1]

On the late morning of Friday, April 7, the motorcade of Sheikh Mahdi al-Khalisi moved from al-Kadhimiyya. The people of al-Kadhimiyya went out to bid him farewell. The Dirwaza Gate yard was full of people who were loudly invoking the Almighty to bless Muhammed and the Progeny of Muhammed. The motorcade went towards the Karkh side, where many Baghdadi folks joined it. When he reached Hilla, a huge welcome was awaiting him, and markets were shut down for the occasion. Al-Khalisi spent one night in Hilla at the house of Sheikh Muhammed Sammakah, then he left in the morning for Karbala, where the city's chiefs had come out to welcome him up to Twaireej in a convoy of 14 cars. Among them, there were people from Najaf, such as Sheikh Abdul-Kareem al-Jaza'iri, Sheikh Abdul-Ridha al-Sheikh Radhi and Sheikh Baqir al-Shibeebi. Also, 400 horsemen from the tribe of Al Mas`ud and others went out to welcome him. When he arrived at Karbala, he performed the *ziyara* then stayed at the house of the late Mirza Muhammed-Taqi al-Shirazi.[2]

Sunnis' Participation

Sheikh Abdul-Wahhab al-Naib had invited a number of Sunni scholars in Baghdad to attend a meeting in the Khaldiyya *takya* [Sufi gathering place] in order to discuss the Ikhwan issue and whether it was [religiously] permissible to fight them. On the morning of April 5, the meeting was

---

[1]Quoted from the manuscript of memoirs of Sheikh Muhammed al-Khalisi.

[2]*Al-Rafidain* newspaper of April 12, 1922.

held, and it was attended by most of those who were invited, whereas some others did not attend it. Among those who did not attend it were: Mahmoud Shukri al-Alusi, Abdul-Haleem al-Hafati [1], Yousuf al-Ata, Hamdi al-A`dhami, Sulayman al-Sanawi and Qasim al-Mufti.

Abdul-Wahhab al-Naib opened the meeting, and he kept bringing to memory the horrible things which the Wahhabis did to Iraqi Muslims. Then he raised this question: "What do you say about this group called the Ikhwan? Do you see that fighting them and repelling their likes from staging these attacks is permissible since they violated the Muslims' sanctities, shed their blood, and confiscated their wealth while having committed no crime and without any explanation being given?" Then he cited [from Islamic history] what Abu Bakr had done to the people who reneged from Islam and what Imam Ali did to the Kharijites who prayed and fasted more than these folks. He suggested that a chapter about the Wahhabis in the book by [the Hanafi Sunni *faqih* Muhammed Ameen ibn Omar] Ibn Abidin [2] should be read. An attendant read a paragraph of that book saying that anyone who sheds the blood of Muslims is *kafir* (apostate), and fighting him becomes permissible. Those present, thereupon, agreed on it and were unanimous about the obligation of defending the public. Then Ahmed al-Sheikh Dawood stood up and made

---

[1] This is what the Arabic text reads, but I could not find any information about this "Hafati" which is quite likely a typographical error for "Haqani," and surely Allah knows best. – Tr.

[2] The full name of Ibn Ameen's book is رد المحتار على الدر المختار, that is, the answer of the puzzled one to *Al-Durr Al-Mukhtar* (the selected pearls) which was published in Beirut, Lebanon, by Dar al-Kutub al-`Ilmiyya. I could not find the year of birth of Ibn Ameen, but he died in 1252 A.H./1836 A.D. I, Translator of this book, wrote a 480-page book about the founder of Wahhabism, namely Muhammed ibn Abdul-Wahhab. He was born in `Uyayna, a small Najd town, in 1115 A.H./1703 A.D. and died in 1206 A.H./1791-92 A.D. Abdul-Wahhab belonged to the Tamim tribe, and he was very much influenced by the philosophy of extremist Ibn Taymiyya, namely Ahmed ibn Abdul-Halim ibn Abdul-Salam ibn Abdullah al-Khidhr, "Taqiyy ad-Din," who was born in Harran, ancient Carrhae, a town built by Harran brother of prophet Ibrahim (Abraham), peace be upon him, from whom (Harran) derived its name. Harran at the time was part of Iraq, but it is now within Turkey's borders. Ibn Taymiyya was born in 661 A.H./1263 A.D. and died inside a Damascus, Syria, prison in 728 A.H./1328 A.D. – Tr.

a statement supporting the above. Also, a juristic dialogue went on between Abdul-Wahhab al-Naib and Ahmed al-Sheikh Dawood in this regard. Al-Naib asked, "What do you call these folks, oppressors or Kharijites?" Ahmed said, "They certainly are Kharijites." Al-Naib pointed to what Imam Ali did to the Kharijites, and he was the cousin of the Chosen Prophet. Those present said, "A great role model is he." Ahmed stated how they [Wahhabis] took women captive and had sexual intercourse with them even though they were Muslim women. Amjad al-Zahawi said, "They must be disciplined by all means." It was then that al-Naib said, "Our Ja`fari [Shi`a] brothers are determined to meet and issue a resolution in this regard. Since we have no contention between ourselves and their own selves about anything, our word is one and the same." The attendants said, "There is no doubt about that."

The attendants settled their view to elect a delegation from among them to attend the Karbala Conference. Al-Naib was chosen to be the delegation's head, and Ahmed al-Sheikh Dawood, Ibrahim al-Rawi and Abdul-Jaleel al-Jameel were to be its members. They started writing a *fatwa* [binding religious edict], the text of which was: "What is the edict of the renowned Muslim scholars regarding those who claim to follow Islam while regarding everyone else who is different in their belief than them, from among the Muslim groups, as being *mushrik* (polytheist), deeming it *halal* [permissible according to Islam] to fight them, to shed their blood, to take their wealth and to take their children captive without reason, and they have already attacked the lands of the Muslims as an act of hostility and initiated the attack, so should they be fought and repelled or not? Please issue your edict for us, may Allah grant you His rewards!" The answer, and surely Allah knows best, is: "Yes, they must be fought in such a case." This edict was signed by Abdul-Wahhab al-Naib, Abdul-Malik al-Shawaf, Ibrahim al-Rawi, Khdhayyir al-Qadhi, Muneer al-Qadhi, Abdul-Jaleel al-Jameel, Taha al-Rawi, Nu`man al-A`dhami, Ali al-Qaradaghi, Amjad al-Zahawi, Muhammed Rasheed al-Sheikh Dawood, Khalil Hassan al-Naqi, Baha ad-Din al-Naqshabandi, Ahmed al-Rawi and Muhammed Rauf.[1]

At eight o'clock in the morning of April 10, the procession of Sunni scholars came out of the Fadhl Mosque in Baghdad. In their

---

[1] *Al-Istiqlal* newspaper in its issue dated April 6, 1922.

vanguard was Abdul-Wahhab al-Naib, Ibrahim al-Rawi, Ahmed al-Sheikh Dawood and Abdul-Jaleel al-Jameel. With them were many educated youths. The public came out to bid them farewell with their flags and drums. They reached the bridge which they crossed in the direction of the train station in al-Karkh. From there, they rode in cars and headed to Karbala, which they reached at 4:00 pm. After meeting with al-Khalisi at al-Shirazi's house, they went to the house of Qasim al-Rashdi, who hosted them.

In the evening of the same day, Mosul's delegation reached Karbala and was comprised of Mawlud Mukhlus, Sa`eed al-Hajj Thabit, Ayyub Abdul-Wahid, Abdullah al-Ni`mah, Thabit Abdul-Noor, Abdullah from the descendants of the head of scholars, Ajeel al-Yawir, and Muhammed Agha, chief of the Gargaris. They stayed at the house of Omar al-Alwan.

A telegram reached al-Khalisi from the people of Tikrit and Shirqat, stating that they delegated Mawlud Mukhlus to represent them in the conference and that they were ready to implement any decision issued by him with their wealth and lives.[1] Then al-Khalisi received from Tikrit a transcription with this meaning bearing the signatures of the following: Naqeeb al-Sayyid Ahmed, a head of a Tikrit tribe; Muhammed Arab, a head of a Tikrit tribe[2], Mustafa al-Hajj Hassan, a head of a Begat tribe, Ahmed al-Khattab, a head of a Begat tribe, Nida al-Hussain, a head of a Tikrit tribe, Zaidan al-Khalaf, a resident head of the Hadithis' tribe, and Salman al-Hajj Hameed, a head of the Hadithis' tribe.[3]

Some people could not relish this sectarian solidarity in Karbala, so they started talking against it, spreading bad rumours. The *Istiqlal* newspaper made a reference to it, saying, "Some interest-seekers were appalled by the nation's solidarity which they saw, i.e. it's standing in one rank against the Wahhabis, so they started spewing their venom. They

---

[1]*Dijla* newspaper of April 13, 1922.

[2] Are there many heads or chiefs or chieftains of one and the same tribe? Yes, there are. I, Translator of this book, belong to a tribe and I know the tribal system. There are many heads or chiefs or chieftains within one and the same tribe, each is a chief in his own community.

[3]*Al-Rafidan* newspaper of April 11, 1922.

have spread false rumours and created probabilities which no rational man can think of."[1] The interior ministry could not tolerate this talk, so it issued an order to shut down the *Istiqlal* newspaper for three weeks under the charge that it was publishing confusing reports.[2]

The Conference Convenes

The king apologized for not attending the conference under pressure from Cox, and he agreed to be represented in it by Tawfiq al-Khalidi, the interior minister.[3] The king was not comfortable with al-Khalidi, as we have seen; therefore, he sent to Karbala Nouri al-Sa`eed to personally represent him. When Nouri reached Karbala, he took off his official uniform, wore sandals and kept contacting nationalists such as Othman al-Alwan and his brother Omar, Qati` al-Awwadi and Qasim al-Rashdi. He was assisted in so doing by the police commissioner of Karbala, Hashim al-Alawi.[4]

Those who went to Karbala for the *ziyara* numbered at the time at about 200,000, and Karbala had never witnessed such a crowd in the "mihya" *ziyara*. The government sent to Karbala an army of 200 infantry and 300 cavalier soldiers led by Muhyi ad-Din al-Sahrawardi to safeguard the governorate's security. Sheikh Muhammed al-Khalisi went to visit the soldiers at their quarters, accompanied by Muhammed Hassan Abul-Mahasin. He delivered a speech to them in which he pointed out to Iraq's demands and warned them against being deceived by the British who wanted them to use their weapons against their Muslim brethren. An officer responded to him with an enthusiastic statement which made him realize that the army would stand by the side of the nationalists if a war erupted between them and the British.[5]

---

[1] *Istiqlal* newspaper of April 6, 1922.

[2] *Istiqlal* newspaper of April 5, 1922.

[3] From documents of the Public Records Office in London No. FO 7770 – 371.

[4] Salih Jawad Kadhim (op. cit.), p. 178.

[5] Excerpted from the manuscript of the memoirs of Sheikh Muhammed al-Khalisi.

On the morning of April 9, the conference was opened with a preliminary meeting attended by Sheikh Mahdi al-Khalisi, Sayyid Abul-Hassan al-Isfahani, Tawfiq al-Khalidi and invited senior guests. It was decided in that meeting to organize transcripts signed by chiefs and dignitaries containing the people's principles and basic objectives with reference to the issue of the Ikhwan. In meetings that were held in the days that followed, the transcripts were organized and signed, and this is a portrayal of one of them:

In the Name of Allah, the most Gracious, the most Merciful

We the undersigned, heads, leaders and chiefs of Iraq's tribes, on behalf of our own selves and representing the members of our tribes, in response to the call of Hujaj al-Islam[1], may their blessings continue, whom we are obligated to obey, an obligation imposed by our religion round our necks at every time and period, have come to Honored Karbala on the 12th day of the month of Sha`ban of 1340 [Monday, April 10, 1922], being guided by the chief scholars of the faith. Based on what has been inflicted by the Kharijite Ikhwan on our Muslim brethren, their savage killing, looting and pillaging, we have made a pledge among ourselves, contracted, and are of the consensus, so much so that none of us would do anything against what is dictated by the interest of our homeland, and to safeguard the holy shrines and the gravesites of walis [the righteous, friends of Allah], so we have decided to repel the Kharijite Ikhwan and to fight them with support from the regular army of our king with everything we can and within our power, and to undertake the necessary measures. Based on our attachment to the throne of His Majesty, our great King Faisal I, may his power last, the matter of how to repel the Kharijite Ikhwan, how to fight them, the number of defending tribes, their weapons, rations, places, times, and organizations are all up to the will

---

[1]"Hujaj" is plural of "hujja," proof, evidence, sign, of the Grace of the Almighty, a religious title granted to a higher class of the heirarchy of the Shi`a clergy. – Tr.

of His Majesty our king and his wise management. Yet we ask for our looted wealth to be retrieved, that blood money be paid to those of us who have been killed, those whose blood has been shed unjustly and aggressively. We have, for this purpose, organized two copies, one of which we have submitted so that it may be presented to the thresholds of His Majesty, and the second remains under the supervision of the flagpost scholars, and surely help comes from Allah."[1]

On the morning of April 13, which coincided with the middle of Sha`ban, the final meeting was held at al-Shirazi's house, and it was a large public meeting. It was opened by Ja`far Abul-Timman, who read a telegram that arrived from the king thanking those who organized the conference, whereupon all those present stood up out of respect for it. Then Abul-Timman delivered a speech in which he praised the theology scholars for their concern about the safety of the country. He detailed the horrible things which the Ikhwan committed in Hijaz and Iraq, concluding his speech by supplicating for the king and for the theology scholars, praising the conferees. Then the conference concluded before noon.[2]

What attracts one's attention is that during the time when the conference was in session, the *Al-Iraq* newspaper published a report saying that Ja`far Abul-Timman was a candidate for the post of minister of trade.[3] On April 15, a royal decree was actually issued assigning the post of minister of trade to Abul-Timman. Graves comments about this, saying, "The appointment of Abul-Timman was akin to an appeasement by the *naqeeb* of the extremists."[4]

But we must not forget in this regard that Abul-Timman joining the administration was followed nine days later by another man who is regarded as having a political stance that was the opposite of that of Abul-Timman. He is Abdul-Muhsin al-Sa`doun, to whom the ministry of justice

---

[1]*Al-Iraq* newspaper of April 15, 1922.

[2]Muhammed al-Mahdi al-Baseer (op. cit.), Vol. 2, pp. 396-398.

[3]Al-Iraq newspaper of April 12, 1922.

[4]Graves (op. cit.), p. 310.

was assigned. This man played later very important roles in Iraqi politics, which was supportive of the British, as we will detail in the next part.

Splinter Chiefs

The Karbala Conference was outwardly quiet, but in reality, it was not what it seemed to be, for a split took place among the chiefs of tribes during that conference. Some of them refused to sign the transcripts, and they were headed by Addai al-Jaryan, chief of the Abu Sultan tribe, Rasheed al-Unayzan, chief of the Yasar tribe, Omran al-Zanboor, chief of the Banu Ajeel tribe, Shamran al-Challoub, chief of the Fatlah-Hindiyya tribe, and Murad al-Khalil, chief of the Jibours [or Jibouris].[1]

These splinters met in Hilla after the conclusion of the Karbala Conference and decided to organize a transcript that contradicted those who organized the conference in which they protest the interference of the religious scholars in political affairs and declared their upholding of the British mandate. Three of them contacted Ali al-Sulayman, chief of the Dulaim [tribe], who told them that he would go to Baghdad to meet Cox and to get his opinion about this subject, asking them to meet him in Baghdad.

On April 19, Ali al-Sulayman reached Baghdad and met Cox to ask him about his opinion regarding the organizing of the opposing petition. Cox advised him not to do it, telling him that a transcript that they would issue following their consultation with him would be regarded by the public as a British setup and would then be useless. Cox was of the opinion that it would be better for them to go to meet the king to explain to him the dangers towards which the extremists were leading him and leading the country with him.

On April 23, Ali al-Sulayman, accompanied by 40 tribal chiefs, went to meet the king. They talked to him about what Cox had recommended to them, stating to him in clear words that they did not swear the oath of allegiance to him except with the condition that he should listen to the British advice. On the next day, they all went to meet the *naqeeb*. The naqeeb told them that he liked the transcript idea,

---

[1]*Al-Iraq* newspaper of April 17, 1922.

encouraging them to do it, so they decided to implement his suggestion. They organized a lengthy transcript which they filled with taunts against the conference and those who organized it. This is what it read:

"We had been invited to the meeting in Holy Karbala the date for which was from the 11th to the 14th of Sha`ban, 1340, so we responded to the invitation. Having met with Hujjatul-Islam Sheikh Mahdi al-Khalisi and become familiar with the sheet which was to be signed, we found out that those demands listed in it were of no benefit to the government and the country, and we noticed from behind the curtains that the intentions of those who signed that sheet are harmful to the interests of the Iraqi government and that they bring woes and calamities to this land as we had in the past experience. Since we, from the beginning, had sworn the oath of allegiance to our master, the one for whom we sacrifice our lives, His Majesty King Faisal I, in a well-known way and conditions which forever remain firm, we, therefore, refuse to participate in signing that sheet in order to safeguard this land and the honour of the Iraqi government from the disturbance and chaos which lead to desolation and destruction. We, the undersigned chiefs of Iraq's tribes, have met and discussed among ourselves what pleases this homeland, supports the pillars of its government and brings goodness, prosperity and comfort to the people of the land and of the desert from among its population. We see this to be confined to the following items:

Since our Iraqi government is now in the preliminary phase and is in need of everyone who can help it with matter and with manner, till it reaches the degree of perfection and independence of others, the British government, which is commissioned by the League of Nations to be in charge of a mandate over Iraq, must be requested for all the needed aids on which the firming of the corners of the government of Iraq hinges, such as safeguarding order, firming the security, building the country..., and it must be relied on as a friend who is sincere to the country and to its people.

Since most men of the board of the present government are not from among the staunch Arabs who form the sweeping majority of Iraq, and they have neither experience nor knowledge of the affairs of the land and the conditions of the servants of Allah, they rather are comprised of a band of different elements whom the tribes cannot trust nor on whom can they depend, they, therefore, must be replaced by the well-known men of the country who can be trusted and relied on and to whom this country can assign special social centres among the tribes.

If the board of the Iraqi government is formed of those described in Article Two [above], an Iraqi assembly must be formed that determines the form of government and the type of administration in this land.

Thereupon, we plead for the speedy implementation of these three articles so the minds may calm down and the hearts may be at ease, and Allah is the One Who enables others to affect reform."[1]

After organizing this transcript, they presented it to Cox, who advised them not to submit it based on their stance is well known and it has already achieved its anticipated impact. Cox feared the submission of this transcript would lead to the organizing of contradictory transcripts by their opponents. In fact, what Cox feared did actually take place. Members of some tribes who were affiliated with those who organized the said transcript started organizing transcripts in which they declared that they did not recognize their present chiefs and that they wanted to choose

---

[1] I found this sheet among the royal palace documents, and it is written on a single piece of paper without a date or signatures. Apparently, it is not the original transcript but a copy of it which was written to be preserved among the palace's documents at the time.

chiefs other than them. Those individuals sent their transcripts to al-Khalisi in duplicate so he could keep a copy of them and submit the others to the government.[1]

At the same time, Sayyid Ja`far Abu Tibeekh reached Hilla accompanied by a number of chiefs of the Khaz`al tribesmen in order to sign the first transcript opposing the conference. Sayyid Ja`far stated that all Shamiyya tribes stood behind them with the exception of Sayyid Noor al-Yasiri, his cousin Sayyid Alwan and Abdul-Wahid al-Hajj Sikar, and that Salim al-Khayyun and Khayyun al-Obaid, as well as some chiefs of the Muntafiq, supported them, too. Then they held a big meeting in Hilla, which was attended by the

Major-General Sir Percy Zachariah Cox (Courtesy: Getty images)

governorate adviser, whom they notified that all the Euphrates [basin area] strictly stood to resist any interference against the British mandate.[2]

Cox And Faisal

Confidential documents which could later be obtained clearly indicate that a heated conflict took place between Cox and King Faisal about the Karbala Conference. The king supported the conference, as we have noticed, whereas Cox was sceptical about it and regarded it as a scheme from the "Bolsheviks and Turks" to stir the Iraqis against the British: on April 4, five days before the conference, Cox [photo right] wrote the king's secretary a long confidential letter in which he said the following:

"The military authorities have specified information that the Bolsheviks and Kamalis [followers of Mustafa Kamal

---

[1]Muhammed Mahdi al-Baseer (op. cit.), Vol. 2, p. 398.

[2]Salih Jawad Kadhim (op. cit.), p. 183.

Ataturk] coordinate their plans in order to create problems for the Iraqi government and for British policy in Iraq. A few days ago, I received from the British Commissioned Officer in Tehran a copy of an appeal directed from al-Najaf on Rabi I 15/November 1921 to the Russian commissioned minister containing an assault on the British policy in Iraq and on King Faisal. The Turkish Bolshevik plans, as His Majesty the King knows, continue, and they go on at the same time when a movement has set out of al-Najaf as a result of the Ikhwan's raid on the Iraqi tribes which has taken advantage of the public's complaint about that raid. Reports have reached me from a source which I believe to be well informed saying that the defence against the Ikhwan's attacks was only an outward pretext and not the real reason for the meeting which will be attended by sheikhs and scholars in Karbala. It is believed that this movement is in reality, the result of what went on in informed circles about the stumbling in the treaty negotiations about the mandated subject and that there is the notion to entice the king to attend the meeting in Karbala so they would force him to ask for full and immediate independence from the British government. In case this demand is not met, the extremists in Baghdad, supported by the Euphrates sheikhs who participated in the 1920 Revolution, will gather a national assembly for the British government to do what they wanted. In order to reach their goals, they will first try to get weapons from the British authorities under the pretext of defending themselves against the Ikhwan." Cox concludes his letter by saying, "The information which this letter contains, in addition to the general trend of the military intelligence, may have given His Majesty the King and his government something for serious active contemplation, especially due to what the newspapers have mentioned, i.e. pressure was applied on His Majesty the King to get him to attend the conference which will be held in Karbala under the auspices of Sheikh Mahdi al-Khalisi." Then Cox says, "The purpose of this letter and its contents must be dealt with confidentially, but I nevertheless do not object if it reaches, in its confidential form to the administration beside His Excellency the Prime Minister."

Two days after the writing of this letter, Cox sent a telegram to London and repeated what he had stated in that letter, that is, the conference was managed by the Bolsheviks and Turks, but he added to that what indicated that he was grumbling about the king's conduct; he said:

"All the information that I have in this regard, and the (information) that the headquarters has, I have submitted to the king and the *naqeeb*, but the king remained insisting on his view that the goals of the conference are not harmful and that he can control it. As for the *naqeeb*, he is no less seriously confused about the possibility that the king would fall into the hands of the extremists and Shi`as. I and Cornwallis have exerted our efforts to convince the king that his attending the conference would be a serious mistake, so he promised that he would monitor the developments in the coming few days before making his final decision. There is a real concern among the moderates about the developments. Many people attribute the whole movement to the king himself since he takes advantage of the fear of the Ikhwan (which is being utilized to the extreme) to first gain public support for his stance vis-à-vis the mandate, and second to force his ministers to agree to expand the army and provide the funds it needs. The king admitted the *mujtahids* issuing calls to Iraq's sheikhs. He did not consult me, nor did he consult Cornwallis, let alone the *naqeeb*, before aiding the movement, and I think that he did that without realizing the repercussions of the move or its full probabilities."

On April 19, Cox sent another telegram to London. This is its text:

"The meeting in Karbala is now over, and the pilgrims returned home. We informed you before of the conference's political outcomes, but it is obvious that the conference contained, in addition to its formal meetings, many intense discussions. I have sufficient information about these discussions with regard to the nature of the two parties involved. The extremists and the *ulema* feel disappointed and angry about their failure to create the upheaval which they wanted due to the sensitivity demonstrated by the sheikhs and the official restrictions that the authority imposed. On the other hand, there was a meeting representing the sheikhs who hated to be dragged again by the *ulema* into politics. Add to this the fact that there are many sheikhs who were strong to the degree that they were able to express their opinion strongly in this regard and refuse to participate in it. A large portion of the 'hot air' reaches us now from both parties and it will not disappear except after some time. The extremists' newspapers claim that the conference greatly backed the king's position in his negotiations with the British about the treaty on the basis of rejecting the mandate and protection and obtaining full independence. In fact, this is what the extremists were hoping for but did not get. On the other hand, there are signs indicating that one of the results of the Karbala Conference was the decline of the reputation of the king and his supporters in the eyes of those who wanted to keep the mandate." Cox ended his telegram by saying, "Several theories have surfaced explaining with precision the goal of the Karbala Conference and how its idea came about. Its motives have been rendered to the Bolsheviks or King Hussein or Mustafa Kamal [Ataturk] or others, but it is not wise to feel comfortable with any of these theories except after the situation calms down and stabilizes."

It seems that the king did not want to continue his feud with Cox. Perhaps he was afraid of its consequences; therefore, he started to show some [signs of] retreat towards Cox. On April 25, Cox wrote a telegram to London as follows:

"Faisal, I believe, has been influenced by the trend of the public opinion which surfaced since the Karbala Conference and the stance of a number of sheikhs who met here, so he summoned me hastily to discuss the general situation, and Cornwallis was present. He spoke in great detail, saying that his relationship with us in the past month was permeated with doubts, and that the resulting situation is worrisome and unpleasant, and that he felt it was necessary to clear the air, stressing his attachment to Britain, which is inseparable. He added saying that he realized that perhaps he made some mistakes, but he did not do what he did except out of his belief that he was trying to win success for the policy for which he came to Iraq [to pursue after being] invited by us. He said that he had to always remember that we expressed our inability to assist him with funds and forces outside the scope of the austerity program and that he has to rely on his own efforts as much as possible."

On April 29, Cox sent another telegram to London saying,

"Undoubtedly, the recent events have had an excellent impact on the moderates and in disciplining Faisal as well. The king came today to see me hoping that the British government of His Majesty will not get the impression that he was working against it or in any way opposing its policy, that if he found out that he had undertaken on his shoulders a task in which he could not succeed, he would retire in Britain, but he would not lose our friendship. He now is realising the strength of the moderate elements, and this is great progress. I think that I should notify you of it without any delay."[1]

---

[1]We have quoted this telegram and the documents before it from the Public Records Office in London No. FO.7770.371.

An Agreement With Ibn Saud

*Abdulaziz bin Abdul
Rahman Al Saud (Ibn Saud)-
Official portait 1940s
(Courtesy: Wikipedia)*

The Karbala Conference is generally regarded as a failure, yet it was not without some benefits for Iraq. One of those benefits is that it made Cox exert his effort to settle the dispute between Iraq and Ibn Saud in a way that, to a good extent, served Iraq's interests.

In May of 1922, that is, half a month after the Karbala Conference, a conference was held in Muhammara organized by Cox. It was attended by Sabeeh Nash'at, minister of transport and labour, delegated by Iraq, and by Ahmed bin Thanyan, delegated by Ibn Saud. It was also attended by Maj. Bordillon, secretary of Cox, who represented the latter. On May 5, a treaty was signed that defined the borders between both countries, Saudi Arabia and Iraq, known as the Muhammara Treaty.

Ibn Saud hardly examined the Muhammara Treaty before bursting in outrage, declaring that he refused to sign it on the pretext that his deputy in the Muhammara Conference was lenient and got out of the scope of his [Ibn Saud's] instructions. Ibn Saud kept declaring his annoyance with the British, with the claim that they now tilted toward the Hashemite family against him.

The famous Lebanese writer Ameen al-Rayhani visited Ibn Saud in those days. Ibn Saud kept talking to him about the British and his relationship with them. He said,

"People think that we receive a lot of money from the British. The fact is that they did not pay us except a little of what we deserved for what we did during the war and after it. We do not renege in our promise to them unless they do so. Between us and themselves there is a pledge which we keep even if ourselves and our interests are harmed. The British owe us, you see the truth Professor, and we do not make demands on them. It is a shame that we should make claims on them, but what is their policy now? You see them spinning and spinning. You see them weaving schemes against me, their friend Ibn Saud! They have surrounded me with enemies, setting up small states around me, installing kings from among my enemies whom they always help with money and political support: the Sherif in Hijaz, his son Abdullah in Trans-Jordan, and his son Faisal in Iraq. What is the purpose of all of these actions? What is the need for them? I, Ibn Saud, am a friend of the British, while they are in their Sherifi (Sherifian) policy treating me like an enemy. Who is Ibn Saud in the eyes of the Sherif and his sons? He is the Kharijite apostate ruffian; you see the truth, Professor. They have said it. Actually, they have said even more than that, and they despite that want me to attack the French in Syria in order to get them out. You see the truth." When Ibn Saud reached in his statement this point, he called on one of his scribes, ordering him to bring in some issues of the *Qibla* newspaper which King Hussein used to publish in Mecca at the time, and it contained articles attacking Ibn Saud and describing him as the "Kharijite ruffian". Then Ibn Saud resumed his talk saying, "We do not surrender an iota of our rights, but we do not say about our enemies what they say about us, and we do not demand save what was for our fathers and grandfathers before. Let the British know that. Let the Sherif and his sons know it, too."[1]

Cox asked Ibn Saud to meet with him to look anew into the Muhammara Treaty, and it was decided to hold the meeting in the Aqeer, a customs post on the Arab Gulf coast facing Bahrain. Cox arrived there on November 27, 1922, accompanied by his retinue, which was comprised of Sabeeh Nash'at, minister of transport and labour, Fahd al-Hathal, chief of the Anza tribe, Maj. Moore, the British Consul in Kuwait, and Maj. Dixon, the British political deputy in Bahrain.

---

[1] Ameen al-Rayhani, *Mulook al-Arab* (Arabs' kings), Beirut, Lebanon, 1951, Vol. 1, pp. 61-62.

The negotiations started the next day and went on for six days. Ibn Saud kept insisting that his borders should reach the Euphrates River, whereas Sabeeh Nash'at wanted those borders to be 200 miles to the south of the Euphrates. Cox tried to compromise both demands, but Ibn Saud was rigid in his position, inflexible. On the last day of the negotiations, Cox ran out of patience with Ibn Saud's inflexibility, and anger became visible on his face. When Ibn Saud saw that, he suddenly changed his stance and agreed to what Cox wanted him to do. Maj. Dixon narrates what went on during the last day of the negotiations saying:

> "As a result, when the last meeting took place, only Cox, Ibn Saud, Maj. Moore and I were present. Cox's anger with Ibn Saud intensified, and he described the latter's stance as being childish. We, therefore, witnessed an amazing scene from Ibn Saud when Cox rebuked him: Ibn Saud almost collapsed, and he began talking in a pitiful way, saying that Cox was the one who made him what he was, raising him to the status which he occupied and that he would surrender half of his kingdom if Cox ordered it. It was then that an agreement was made about the borders as they now exist which were actually drawn by Sir Percy Cox himself."[1]

The borders about which they agreed include a spot that was defined in a certain way as if it were a lozenge or a baklava piece covering a little bit more than 7,000 square miles, and it came to be known globally as the "baklava". It is said that Sabeeh Nash'at is the one who called it as such. It is a spot of great significance for Iraqi and Najdi tribes because it contains good water wells. An agreement was reached about them that they should be neutral: tribes from both sides could go there.[2] Thus, the "baklava piece" was for all, according to the expression of Ameen al-

---

[1]Graves (op. cit.), pp. 322-323.

[2] Sadiq Hassan al-Sudani, "Al-Alaqat al-Iraqiyya-al-Saudiyya" (Iraqi-Saudi Relations), an unpublished university thesis, p. 125.

Rayhani.[1] This was a solution found for what was regarded as one of the most important issues that resulted in border disputes between both countries.

It is narrated that defining the borders via that method left a bitter feeling in Ibn Saud's heart, so he asked to meet with Cox in person. Cox went to him with Dixon, and Ibn Saud kept addressing him in a sombre tone saying, "I trusted you, but you deprived me of half of my kingdom, and it is better you take it all and let me go into exile." As Ibn Saud spoke, tears almost burst out of his eyes, so Cox was impressed by that sight. He held Ibn Saud's hand and said to him, "I realize the extent of the impact on you; therefore, I have given you [additionally] two-thirds of the area of Kuwait, and I do not know how Ibn Sabah will receive this shock."[2]

This means that Cox took from Ibn Saud in order to give Iraq, and then he took from Kuwait to give to Ibn Saud. It is said that the emir of Kuwait remonstrated with Cox thereafter for what he had done with him; therefore, Cox answered, "On that bad occasion, the sword was stronger than the pen. Had I not given those lands to Ibn Saud, he would most certainly have taken them and perhaps more by force. I have pleased your strong neighbour and planted in his soul a friendly feeling towards Kuwait." The emir of Kuwait then said to him, "If the matter is as such, and if Ibn Saud one day dies and I became strong, like my grandfather Mubarak, will the British government object if I rejected this unfair border line and recovered the lands that I lost?" Cox laughed and said, "No, and may God bless your efforts!"[3]

---

[1] Ameen al-Rayhani, *Najd al-Hadith wa Mulhaqatih* (modern Najd and attachments), Beirut, Lebanon, 1954, p. 313.

[2] Hussein Khalaf al-Sheikh Khaz`al, *Tarikh al-Kuwait al-Siyasi* (the political history of Kuwait), Beirut, Lebanon, 1970, Vol. 5, p. 144.

[3] *Ibid.*, Vol. 5, p. 146.

Chapter Four

The Conflict Between Cox and Faisal

We saw in the previous section some aspects of the conflict between Cox and King Faisal about forming the administration, the Ikhwan's raid, and the Karbala Conference. Actually, the conflict between both men did not start at a particular time but used to cool off and then flare up again, and there were several reasons that stirred it anew whenever it tended to wind down.

This conflict was clearly noticed in the mid-Euphrates area. This area had special importance for the king and for the British at the same time. It is the home of the 1920 Revolution, and its tribes were divided into two contending groups. Some were loyal to the British, and others opposed them. The king used to court the tribes that opposed to them, bringing their chiefs closer to him and making them his advisers and aides. This used to anger Cox and cause him to continuously grumble about the king.

The king was keen on appointing government officials from the mid-Euphrates who went along with his plan of courting and assisting the opposing tribes. In mid-October of 1921, he was able to appoint Ali Jawdat al-Ayyubi as the administrative officer of Hilla. This man was one of the officers who had fought together with Faisal in Hijaz and Syria. When he received his post in Hilla, he kept administering it in a way that pleased the king and outraged the British.[1] He used to woo the chiefs who had participated in the 1920 Revolution, and he appointed in the counties under his administration mayors who went along with his plan. In his memoirs, al-Ayyubi stated that Sheikh Mahdi al-Khalisi was pleased with him and with the way he administered the governorate, so much so that he wrote him a letter to thank him. Al-Ayyubi published in his memoirs a zincographic picture of al-Khalisi's letter to prove that he at that time was one of the nationalists.[2]

The king tried to appoint an administrative officer for Karbala of the same type like that of al-Ayyubi, but he did not succeed, for Hameed Khan was then Karbala's administrative officer, a man whom the British liked, so the king fired him and appointed a man in his place from among his aides named al-Hajj Saleem. But this man hardly reached Karbala before a man sent by Cox had caught up with him and sent him back to Baghdad. This created a great deal of tension between the king and Cox. The *naqeeb* mediated between them and suggested a compromise which was: Abdul-Aziz al-Qassab was to be appointed in Karbala instead of Hameed Khan or al-Hajj Saleem.[3] Al-Qassab was then an administrative officer in Kut, so he moved to Karbala, which he reached in early February of 1922. He adopted a neutral way which was said to have neither pleased the king nor angered the high commissioner.

The Treaty Problem

The treaty was the greatest cause behind the conflict between Faisal and Cox, and it can be said that it was behind all manifestations of conflict between both men in one way or another.

Cox pointed out in a memorandum, which was published later, to the treaty problem and how the dispute about it started between him and the king. He says that he is the one who suggested to the British

---

[1] Yousuf Karkush al-Hilli, *Tarikh al-Hilla* (the history of Hilla), al-Najaf, Iraq, 1965, Vol. 1, p. 180.

[2] Ali Jawdat, *Thikrayat* (memories), Beirut, Lebanon, 1967, p. 155.

[3] Abdul-Aziz al-Qassab, *Min Thikrayati* (from my memories), Beirut, Lebanon, 1962, p. 217.

government to establish the relationship between itself and Iraq on the basis of a treaty instead of the [existing] mandate. He mentioned the reason that prompted him to do it: he found the Iraqis loathing the idea of the mandate and interpreting it as "obedience to the mandating authority". The British government endorsed his view, but it wanted a treaty within the limits of what is meant by mandate, whereas King Faisal wanted to end the mandate completely and replace it with a simple alliance treaty.[1]

As for the king, he explained his position towards the treaty in a talk with Ameen al-Rayhani at a later time. He said to him:

"Mr Churchill made two promises to me: to abolish the mandate and to recognize Iraq's independence. He now brought us a treaty full of references to the mandate and to the League of Nations. If there is a mandate, what is the use of the treaty, and what purpose does it serve? And if there is a treaty, what is the need for the mandate? Needless to say, one of the checks is not needed; it is not useful. We insist on what Mr Churchill promised us, which is what the Iraqis, the moderates and the extremists, demand. I still think and hope that he will fulfil his promise; otherwise, the situation is very critical, brother, very critical."[2]

Negotiations about the treaty began on September 29, 1921, that is, 38 days after the crowning of the king, when Cox submitted to the king a draft of a treaty which he described as "only a draft", not final, a "mere experimental attempt" to begin the negotiations. On October 15, Maj. Young, the one who was later known as Sir Herbert Young, reached Baghdad; he was sent by the British government to help Cox negotiate. The treaty draft since then kept moving between the British Probation House, the ministerial council, and the palace, and the king was trying every time to amend the draft, returning it to the ministerial council so it would again be returned to the Probation House and so on.

---

[1]Cox and [Sir Henry Robert Conway] Dobbs, *The Making of Iraq*, translated by Bashir Farjo, Mosul, pp. 56-58.

[2]Ameen al-Rayhani, *Faisal al-Awwal* (Faisal I), Beirut, Lebanon, 1958, p. 126.

Negotiations went on discreetly without the public knowing anything about them until late in May of 1922. On the 23rd of the month, Churchill announced in the British House of Commons, answering a question directed at him, that "King Faisal and his government did not inform Britain of the Iraqi people's rejection of the mandate." When this statement was published in Baghdad's newspapers, a great uproar took place within public opinion, and the opposition started mobilizing for action.

It was then late in the month of Ramadhan, and the opposition was waiting for Eid. On the morning of May 28, the first day of Eid al-Fitr, a general meeting was held in the Wazir Mosque facing the Qashla, where enthusiastic speeches were delivered protesting Churchill's statement. Then it was decided that a large meeting be held in the Haidar-Khana Mosque in the afternoon. The *Istiqlal* newspaper issued a call to the masses to attend the meeting. At the set time, i.e. on the afternoon of that day, the meeting was held. Muhammed Baqir al-Hilli, Ahmed al-Sheikh Dawood and Mahdi al-Baseer delivered speeches during it. Once the speakers finished delivering their statements, six individuals were deputed to represent the people in protesting Churchill's statement. They were: Muhammed al-Sadr, [Sheikh] Muhammed al-Khalisi, Ahmed al-Sheikh Dawood, Mahdi al-Baseer, Hamdi al-Pachachi and Yasin al-Hashimi.

The six delegates came out of the Haidar-Khana Mosque in the direction of the Qashla in order to meet the king, and the masses rallied behind them. When they reached the Qashla, they did not find the king in his official quarters. The interior minister met them in a nice way with a smiling face, then contacted the king in the Sha`shoo` mansion, asking for an appointment to meet with the delegates. The king's secretary answered him saying that the king would be ready to meet them at his mansion the next day.[1]

The delegates held a preliminary meeting on the morning of the next day at the house of Ahmed al-Sheikh Dawood, and none of them were absent except Yasin al-Hashimi, who sent them a small memo in which he said that he fully regretted informing his fellows that he could

____

[1] Al-Istiqlal announcement of Shawal 4 [1359 A.H.]/November 5], 1940.

not participate in their discussions and all such efforts, but he did not oppose their opinions and views.[1]

It is worth mentioning that al-Hashimi, at the time, was about to return to Syria after having reached Baghdad on the 9th of the same month, and he was before then prohibited from returning and was not allowed to do so except after the British consulate in Damascus had required him to give assurances that he would be trustworthy and sincere.[2] He, therefore, did not want to get involved in any problem with the British. He perhaps preferred to keep a distance from political activity temporarily till the situation cleared.

On the set date, the delegates, now numbering five, set out to meet the king with whom they had a long talk about which we do not know much other than what two of [the delegates had] mentioned: Mahdi al-Baseer and Muhammed al-Khalisi. According to al-Baseer, the king said that he wanted the people to know that up until then, nothing had happened that would harm Iraq's interests and that he kept vigilant in safeguarding the country's interests; therefore, he wanted the people to be assured.[3] As for Muhammed al-Khalisi, he says, "We asked the king to state that Iraq is independent and free of foreign interference under any label, so he kept tricking us as he is accustomed to doing in a skill that exceeds the limit, but it did not affect us due to our knowledge of his tricks. Following our insistence, he agreed that we should declare our rejection of the mandate and notify the League of Nations of the same via a telegram.[4]

Upon the departure of the delegates from the king, they issued a statement which *Al-Istiqlal* newspaper published, in which they said that the king did not oppose what the people wanted, that he was vigilant over the country's interests, that things were going on very well, and that they would start sending telegrams rejecting the mandate to free circles

---

[1]Muhammed al-Mahdi al-Baseer, *Tarikh al-Qadhiyya al-Iraqiyya* (history of the Iraqi issue), Baghdad, 1923, Vol. 2, p. 462.

[2]Sami Abdul-Hafiz al-Qaisi, "Yasin al-Hashimi", an unpublished university thesis, pp. 87-91.

[3]Muhammed Mahdi al-Baseer (op. cit.), Vol. 2, p. 463.

[4]From the manuscript of the memoirs of Sheikh Muhammed al-Khalisi.

throughout the modern world.[1] Then the delegates drafted the telegram as follows:

> "The Iraqis have proven their sure desire for full independence and categorical rejection of any mandate. Their serious movement [Revolution] in the year 1920 is the greatest testimony. On the occasion of the statement which Mr Churchill made in the British parliament about the matter of the mandate in Iraq, the Iraqi people held a peaceful demonstration, commissioning us to announce before your revered council and to other parliaments its view of rejecting the mandate; thereupon, we reject any mandate and protest any decision that opposes Iraq's full independence." Signed: Muhammed al-Khalisi, Sayyid Ahmed al-Dawood, Sayyid Muhammed al-Sadr, Hamdi Beg al-Pachachi and Muhammed al-Mahdi al-Baseer.[2]

The delegates carried this telegram and went to the telegraph office to send it to the League of Nations and to parliamentary councils in the United States, Britain, France and Italy, paying 1,500 rupees to transmit them. But the censorship delayed the sending of the telegrams and contacted the king, asking him if he permitted their transmission or not. Here, the king felt that he had entered into a critical situation and did not know how to get out of it: should he permit the sending of the telegrams and thus anger the British, or should he prevent it and thus anger the nationalists?

Ms Bell wrote on June 6, saying that the telegrams remained asleep in the telegram office as the king was trying to hold dialogue with the delegates about them. Then she comments, saying, "Ah, the king, the king! I wish he had been more strict and tough! He now is losing the opportunity of a lifetime, but what can one do?" Then she wrote two days later saying, "I now feel very pleased, for the king agreed to prevent those telegrams [from going out] for good. When the five donkeys—meaning

---

[1]*Al-Istiqlal* newspaper of Shawwal 4 [1359 A.H./November 5] 1940.

[2]Muhammed al-Mahdi al-Baseer (op. cit.), Vol. 2, p. 464.

the delegates—rented a car to send the telegrams to Iran so they could be transmitted from there, the king told them that their action would lead to the most serious harm, so they stopped."[1]

The Muntafiq Problem

At the time when the feud surrounding the treaty was intensifying, the Muntafiq, now Thi-Qar Governorate, was in an intense status of chaos and confusion, and this was an additional factor in intensifying the dispute between Faisal and Cox.

The British report which was submitted to the League of Nations described the status of the Muntafiq governorate, saying, "Its tribes used to keep the weapons which they had held, exerting their efforts, moreover, to get more of them, so much so that this governorate is now probably more armed than other Iraqi areas. For this reason, the tribes started feeling that they could defy the government, something for which these tribes were famous of during the Ottoman era. Also, the tribes became convinced that the new Arab government could be neutralized without any danger arising as a result. During the occupation period, the government used to follow a method of civil administration for quelling the chaos inherited from the Ottoman era, which was: restoring authority to the tribal sheikhs and supporting it with British influence in order to carry out the orders of the high authority. But the 1920 Revolution demolished the structure which was successfully erected, and the tribes returned to the status of chaos anew."[2]

The Muntafiq tribes, as is the case with the mid-Euphrates ones, were divided into two groups: either loyal to the British or opposing them. But the loyal group was the larger one.[3] There was a very strict and irritable British adviser, namely Major Yates. This adviser used to rule the governorate as he pleased, and there was no strong administrative officer to stand in his face; therefore, most people used to resort to him to solve their problems and did not care about the administrative officer, so much

---

[1] Burgoyne, *Gertrude Bell*, London, 1961, Vol. 2, pp. 273-274.

[2] Report on the Administration of Iraq – 1920, p. 18.

[3] Abdul-Aziz al-Qassab (op. cit.), p. 231.

so that it was rumoured among the people that the promise which the administrative officer gave anyone might not materialize; as for the adviser's promise, it was a sure thing and a must to implement and was not subjected to any rejection.[1]

Maj. Yates was of the habit of gathering all tribal sheikhs who supported him and urging them to sign a petition asking for the British mandate to continue.[2] On June 22, the *Istiqlal* newspaper published an editorial about the Muntafiq governorate signed by "Abdul-Razzaq A" in which it stated that Maj. Yates gathered the sheikhs of tribes and told them that Britain insisted on upholding the mandate over Iraq. It said that the doctor had to force the patient to drink the medicine even if the patient refused. The writer of the article said that the chiefs of tribes responded to him in a way that indicated their loyalty went to the king and obedience to the scholars of religion. They thus proved to him that they were a nation with a living conscience, refusing to surrender to any force which wanted to harm the nation's full independence. On the 25th of the same month, the *Istiqlal* newspaper published another article signed by "An Informed Muntafiq Man", in which he pointed out national conferences convening in some areas of al-Muntafiq in order to rebut the claims of advocates of colonialism and to support the Iraqi issue by demanding full independence and rejecting the mandate. The writer said that the authority arrested some of those who held those conferences while expelling the others.

Those who were grumbling about Maj. Yates started resorting to the king, pleading to him to save them. Telegrams and petitions started going to the king complaining; therefore, the king contacted Cox to request him to transfer Yates from the Muntafiq governorate. But Cox was pleased with Yates and regarded him as the suitable man who could control the governorate and restore security to it. The opposition newspaper started attacking Yates violently, perhaps due to instigation by the king, and this angered Cox.

The king decided to appoint Yasin al-Hashimi as the administrative officer of the Muntafiq governorate due to his faith that he

---

[1] Sami Abdul-Hafiz al-Qaisi (op. cit.), p. 101.

[2] Muhammed al-Mahdi al-Baseer (op. cit.), Vol. 2, p. 466.

could stand in the face of Yates. Al-Hashimi reached Nasiriyya on June 19, so those who were grumbling felt stronger through him and kept escalating their activity in opposition and defiance of Yates, just as we conclude from a personal letter sent by Muhammed Hassan Haidar to the king's secretary. Here is its text:

"The Most Respectful Chief,

"Our tribes are now in the best status of staging peaceful demonstrations and Islamic protests when the Muntafiq's adviser and his aide, Kuchnik, and their licentious companions reached Suq al-Shuyukh several times. Despite what Suq al-Shuyukh has, the chiefs paid no attention to people's hearsay or threats. All they wanted them to do was to sign for what the souls of those mean ones inclined. The chiefs insist on refusing to surrender to their wishes and orders, although the time is very tense and volatile, for the matters are in their hands. Moreover, the present mayor has notified them officially that he would not interfere in the tribes' affairs, so they confined him in his own house, rendering him neither tying nor untying. A total of 21 telegrams, all signed by senior leaders and openly rejecting the mandate, have been sent, some of them to your own excellency, and I sent them a few days ago to Baghdad. Had it not been for the kindness of His Majesty our King, for whom we sacrifice ourselves, who sent the brave hero, Sayyid Yasin Pasha al-Hashimi, as our administrative officer, we would have all perished. We, therefore, plead to Allah to enable us to please him and to please the scholars, to obey our king and master, may his power continue.

"The most insignificant Muhammed Hassan al-Sheikh Haidar[1]."

Al-Hashimi could not stay in the Muntafiq governorate for long. The tribes loyal to the British, especially the Azairij and al-Husainiyya,

---

[1]From the royal palace's documents, Folder No. K/11, Document 167.

started secretly and publicly cursing him, demanding he leaves the governorate and return to Baghdad. Al-Hashimi was forced to leave Nasiriyya at night after entrusting the governorate's matters to the mayor of Suq al-Shuyookh, Rauf al-Kubaisi.[1]

After al-Hashimi's departure from the Muntafiq governorate, Maj, Yates sent planes to strafe some opposing tribes. He also ordered that Abdul-Mahdi al-Muntafiqi and Baqir al-Shibeebi be arrested, accusing both of them of staging the demonstrations against his policy. Both men stayed in prison for several days, during which they managed to send several telegrams to Baghdad newspapers protesting their arrest; therefore, the interior ministry issued an order to release them.[2]

The matter did not stop there; rather, the dispute intensified anew between Maj. Yates and Rauf al-Kubaisi, causing the government to summon al-Kubaisi to Baghdad and fire him from his job.[3] The king's patience ran out because of the conditions in the Muntafiq, so he sent to London Jibrail (Gabriel) Haddad Pasha to complain to the British government about Maj. Yates and also about the Kurdish issue.[4]

Ms Bell Speaks Out

In early June 1922, Ms Bell wrote her father a lengthy 18-page letter informing him of the situation in Iraq and of the king's stance towards it. This letter bears great historical importance because it represents the British viewpoint of King Faisal at the time. This letter revealed the extent of severe pain which Ms Bell felt about King Faisal. After having loved and assisted him so he could ascend Iraq's throne, she finally found him supporting the opposition leaders who, according to her expression, were "the meanest of all extremists". In her letter, Ms Bell likened King Faisal to a great snow statue melting before her eyes. Below we convey the gist of a portion of that important letter in which she says the following:

---

[1] Abdul-Aziz al-Qassab (op. cit.), pp. 231-232.

[2] Muhammed Mahdi al-Baseer (op. cit.), Vol. 2, pp. 466-467.

[3] *Ibid.*, Vol. 2, p. 467.

[4] Graves, *Sir Percy Cox*, London, 2nd edition, p. 312.

"At 4.30 [p.m.], I went to have tea with the king, and I was determined to disclose to him for the last time what went on in my mind towards him. I started talking with him by asking him whether he was confident of my sincerity and extreme love for him, whereupon he answered, saying that he had no doubt about that because he knew what I had done for him last year. I, therefore, said to him that I could speak to him at full liberty and that I felt very miserable, for I had formed a beautiful snow statue which I granted my loyalty, and then I saw the statue melting before my eyes. After its noble features had disappeared, I preferred to go, for 'Despite my love for the Arab nation and sense of responsibility about its future, I cannot tolerate seeing my dreams evaporate, the dreams that guided me day after day,' for I think that he was walking in the guidance of the loftiest of principles, but I saw him becoming a victim of various types of vicious rumours. He listens to what is said by people who, during the war, betrayed the Arabs and who cooperated with the British, and if the Turks return to Iraq tomorrow, they will betray those who cooperated with Faisal. I brought him the matter of Nasiriyya as an example and said to him that he was wrong in judging that matter from beginning to end: Maj. Yates was one of three men who stood by my side against Wilson when I supported the Arab cause. I expressed my prediction to the king that Maj. Yates would resign from his office as a result of the bad suspicions with which the king surrounded him, and that I will resign on the same day because I will not wait for the villains whom the king trusted to tarnish my reputation in his eyes. The dialogue between myself and himself about this matter became heated, and he kept kissing my hand time and over again, causing me a great deal of embarrassment. Then he said that his duty obligated him to assure the extremist nationalists 'whom you refused to recognize time and over again.' I answered him, saying that this was not true, for we did not reject except those who were serving their own interests. As for those from among them who were sincerely working for the national government, we accepted and also welcomed them. 'Take, for example, Ja`far Abul-Timman, who was one of the leaders of the 1920 Revolution and now is a cabinet minister. We, in general, and I, in particular, maintain a friendly tie with him. It is not reasonable that we will not find a way to work with them provided King Faisal supported us in so doing.' At the conclusion of the meeting, I obtained his permission to publish an official denial of the reports that the newspapers were publishing. And when I wanted to get out, I tried to kiss his hand, so he [instead] hugged me warmly."[1]

Ms Bell concludes her letter by saying, "King Faisal is the one who, of all people, is loved the most, but he lacks the strength of demeanour in an amazing way, for deep down, he trusts us despite many deviations which derail him."[2]

What is noteworthy is that at the time when Ms Bell felt disappointed with King Faisal, many national opposition leaders felt disappointed with him, too. Ameen al-Rayhani says the following in this regard: "People misunderstood King Faisal's position in those days; therefore, neither the British nor the Iraqis were fair to him. The British said about him that he turned against them after his coronation, and the extremist nationalists said that he was serving the interests of the British and carrying out their orders. In reality, King Faisal was neither this nor that, for he wanted to safeguard his throne on the one hand, and he, on the other, wanted to get the British to fulfill their promise without being hostile to them."[3]

The Ministers And The Treaty

On the eve of June 22, the final treaty draft was submitted to the council

---

[1] I have placed the quotation marks in this excerpt per my discretion; the original Arabic text contains none. – Tr.

[2] Burgoyne (op. cit.), Vol. 2, pp. 272-273.

[3] Ameen al-Rayhani (op. cit.), p. 125.

of ministers for its endorsement. A sharp discussion and argument about it went on, and the session ended shortly before 8:00 pm without a decision about it having been reached. The secretary of the council, Hussain Afnan, hurried to Ms Bell in her Sinak Quarter home to inform her of what went on during the session. Ms Bell recorded in one of her letters what Hussain Afnan had told her. Below we quote what the letter contained about that session:

The first to speak in the session was Abdul-Muhsin al-Sa'doun, who urged the endorsement of the treaty, whereupon Tawfiq al-Khalidi opposed him by saying that 95% of the Iraqi people do not accept a treaty that contains the mandate principle. The prime minister asked Ja'far al-'Askari a question about whether or not the army was able to control the disturbances in the country if they happened, so al-'Askari answered him by saying that no Arab individual fought against another. Ja'far Abul-Timman was meanwhile silent but was watching his fellow ministers so he could report them to his chiefs, the Shi'a *ulema*; therefore, each minister kept looking stealthily at him for fear of him, with the exception of Abdul Muhsin al-Sa'doun and Sasson Hisqail. Abul-Timman spoke at last. He said that the ministerial council could not look into the treaty since it was an issue in the founding assembly should look into and that all the holy masters and leaders of the Muslims opposed the treaty. He was opposed by Sasson Hisqail, who said that the electing of the members of the founding assembly needed several months, suggesting that the council of ministers should accept the treaty, which should thereafter be submitted to the founding assembly to endorse it. The discussion on this point went on for two hours, and then it was decided that the session be adjourned till the 24th of June. Mr Hussain Afnan says that the prime minister, al-Naqeeb, was unable to make any decision since he was mentally paralyzed.[1]

The 24th of June was a noisy day in Baghdad. It was rumoured among the public that the treaty was about to be ratified without any mention in it of abolishing the mandate; therefore, the marketplaces were shut down, and delegates were formed representing various professions such as cloth merchants, blacksmiths, coppersmiths, shopkeepers and

---

[1] Burgoyne (op. cit.), Vol. 2, p. 276.

others.[1] They went out in a demonstration in al-Rashid Street in the direction of the *naqeeb*'s house on the bank of the [Tigris] River near al-Bab al-Sharqi [Baghdad's Eastern Gate]. The British report pointed out that the whole demonstration was masterminded by Sheikh Mahdi al-Khalisi.[2]

When the delegates of craftsmen reached the *naqeeb*'s home, some of them asked to meet him, so he granted them permission. They kept talking to him to show their protest against the treaty. Apparently, he could not tolerate seeing a group of commoners such as these interfering in matters of politics and government. This is something that he was not used to seeing, and he could not imagine that it would one day take place. He, therefore, asked them, "In whose name are you protesting?" They answered him: "In the name of the country." It is then that the *naqeeb* lost his patience, so he rose from his seat and shook his cane in their faces angrily, rebuking them. He said to them, "Who are you to protest in the name of the country? I am the man of this homeland, and I know more than you of the needs and purposes of the country. Go back to your homes and businesses," so they silently went out.[3]

At noon, a special delegation sent by Sheikh Mahdi al-Khalisi reached the *naqeeb*'s house, and it was comprised of [his son Sheikh] Muhammed al-Khalisi, Abdul-Hussein al-Chalabi and two other men. The *naqeeb* asked them to sit, and he kept chatting with them nicely. Muhammed al-Khalisi spoke with him about the treaty and kept warning him of its dire consequences as if he was warning of the torment of the Judgment Day, whereupon the *naqeeb* answered him, saying, "My foot has already stepped into my grave; I am about to die, and no part of my body enjoys any [form of] pleasure any longer due to the intensity of its weakness. Far it is from me to lose my Hereafter for the sake of a few days which I live in this life without enjoying anything in it; so, let your father the Sheikh be assured, and let everyone know that I do not scheme against

---

[1] *Al-Istiqlal* newspaper of June 25, 1922.

[2] Report on the Administration of Iraq, 1922 – 1923, p. 13.

[3] Ameen al-Rayhani (op. cit.), p. 138; also Ameen al-Rayhani, *Mulook al-Arab* (the Arabs' kings), Beirut, 1951, Vol. 2, p. 385.

Islam, nor do I plot against it." After that, he invited them to eat lunch with him.

In his memoirs, Muhammed al-Khalisi says that when they ate at al-Naqeeb's table, they noticed that the *naqeeb*, despite his old age, ate more than all of the four of them combined and that when apples were brought after the meal, he ate more than the four men could have eaten even if they were very hungry. Muhammed al-Khalisi comments about this saying, "I came to know that the man was lying in his statements, for one who eats like that is diverted from Islam and from serving it."[1]

Anyhow, the council of ministers ratified the treaty in its session of June 25. It is fair to state that the *naqeeb* included in the text of the treaty a statement obligating its endorsement by the founding assembly. Cox tried to dissuade the *naqeeb* from including that statement in the treaty, but the *naqeeb* insisted on it and addressed Cox as thus: "This is my opinion and the opinion of my homeland in the matter, for there is nothing between myself and yourselves other than friendship along the path of duty; therefore, I have accepted to bear the responsibility in my [old] age. So, if you insist on your viewpoint, I shall leave and enter there," pointing to a private room, the door of which led to the library, "and nobody will see me after that."[2]

Ja`far Abul-Timman was absent from the session during which the treaty was ratified, then he came the next day and expressed his opposition to the treaty's preamble and some of its articles because they contain what implies the mandate principle. Then he submitted his resignation and left. The king tried after that to convince the *naqeeb* to postpone his acceptance of the resignation, but the *naqeeb* insisted on accepting it. On June 29, the *naqeeb* sent Hussein Afnan to Abul-Timman carrying a brief letter to him in which he said that he had accepted his resignation.

---

[1] This is excerpted from the manuscript of memoirs of Sheikh Muhammed [Mahdi] al-Khalisi.

[2] Khayri Ameen al-Omari, *Shakhsiyyat Iraqiyya* (Iraqi personalities), Baghdad, 1955, Vol. 1, p. 20.

Tension Intensifies

On June 26, the day when Abul-Timman submitted his resignation, a large number of chiefs of tribes and leaders of the opposition met with Sheikh Mahdi al-Khalisi in al-Kadhimiyya. Al-Khalisi announced in the meeting, according to what Ms Bell narrated in one of her letters, saying, "Your allegiance to King Faisal is now nil because he violated the terms which he pledged during the allegiance and which state the safeguarding of the country's independence."[1]

On the next day, the situation in Baghdad and al-Kadhimiyya became tense, and Cox came to know that the leaders of the opposition were determined to stage a large demonstration. This prompted him to send a telegram to Bushahr [Iran] asking about building a prison on Hungam Island[2] and whether it would be ready to house prisoners. Cox deliberately made the report about the telegram public so people could hear about it, and thus, fear would be instilled in their hearts.[3]

No demonstration took place that day. This made Cox think that his telegram scared people. But the opposition's newspapers intensified their campaigns and kept publishing petitions hostile to the mandate. Reports reached the British that King Faisal was supporting those newspapers and that four of his aides went to Najaf to collect signatures against the mandate. Moreover, the king refused to ratify the treaty and demanded some amendments in its Arabic version, and he kept contacting the ministers secretly, urging them to have it amended.

Ms Bell says in letters she wrote during that period that her blood boiled because of the double-standard behaviour of King Faisal, that Cox was also angry and felt very disappointed with the king. Ms Bell could no longer be patient, so she decided to sever her ties with the king for good, and she informed Nouri al-Sa`eed of it. Nouri conveyed the report to the

---

[1]Burgoyne (op. cit.), Vol. 2, pp. 275-277.

[2]Hungam is an Iranian island located south of Qeshm Island in the Gulf. It is 36.6 km wide with a truncated cone shape and is generally calcareous and low lying. The highest point on the island is Nakas Mountain which is about 106 meters high. – Tr.

[3]*Ibid.*, Vol. 2, p. 277.

king, who sent her an invitation to have tea with him, but Ms Bell refused it, and then she finally accepted after a great deal of insistence by Cornwallis. When she arrived, the king received her warmly and kept talking to her and trying to convince her of how critical his position was, but she confronted him by saying that she did not believe a word of what he was saying. The conversation went on between them for two hours, which the king concluded by very warmly hugging her, as she described. She said she came out of his place, agreeing with him emotionally but differing with him politically. Then she finally said, "If he does not undertake the right course in the future, he will lose his throne for the second time [after having lost it in Syria], and I do not know where he can find a third throne."[1]

The situation calmed down relatively during the month of July, but tension resumed late that month. On the 30th of the month, Ms Bell wrote saying:

"The king was this week very tiresome to us. The propaganda opposing the mandate, which was going on in the Hilla governorate with the king's implicit endorsement, made the mid-Euphrates [area] come close to the extreme limit. A sheikh who is loyal to us was killed there for political reasons. When Mr Cornwallis wanted to undertake the necessary measures to arrest the killer, the king accused him in the presence of Sir Percy Cox that he always stood by the side of his enemies. Sir Percy expressed his amazement at this statement, for how could Faisal, who is a constitutional king, interfere in administrative matters such as arresting killers? The king was rebutted, so he angrily responded by saying that he would leave the *diwan* (office) and go home, but he did not do so but stayed in the *diwan* and continued to receive all the villains and abusers. This behaviour brought about a reaction among the sheikhs who supported the mandate and who came to my office, filling it, and Ali al-Sulayman was one of them. They kept swearing oaths that the king was

---

[1]*Ibid.*, Vol. 2, pp. 276-280.

discrediting them. The king was also interfering in the police appointments to the degree that almost led to the resignation of their senior officers, Arabs and British alike, and these came to my office to join the grumbling tribal sheikhs."

Ms Bell adds to this something about Nouri al-Sa`eed. She says, "It seems that Nouri al-Sa`eed was behind the recent police appointments; therefore, I invited him to have lunch with me and asked him for an explanation for what went on. Nouri was able to clear himself of the matter, so I told him about the king's conduct which was exacerbating us. I said to him that if the king kept doing so, no British officer would accept to serve under his command. Nouri said that he was ready to leave Iraq the next day if that would help. Nouri knows that Iraq cannot be a state without our help, and if he himself is not worthy of it, his son or grandson would see the work done. This is the hope that gives him assurance." Ms Bell then says, "I do not like from among all Iraqi men, starting from the king downwards, as much as I like Nouri. He is the son of an Iraqi government employee; so, how could he gain this amazing foresight? He can understand from half a word. He realized our viewpoint and sentiments about truth and honour and kept them before his eyes as a goal and a final example, something which may be impossible to realize in the East. His absolute trust in our straightforwardness and wisdom makes me always blush."[1]

The Najaf Meeting

The mid-Euphrates area was very sensitive about what went on in Baghdad i.e. the feud between the British and the opposition. Every event that took place in Baghdad somehow found an echo in that area.

In the month of August, when the conflict reached its peak, the chiefs of the mid-Euphrates [tribes] who had participated in the 1920

---

[1]*Ibid.*, Vol. 2, pp. 285-286.

Revolution kept preparing themselves for the opportunity to stage another revolution. Cox says, "The mid-Euphrates area is about to carry out a revolution, the features of which indicate that it will not be less serious than the one which these same extremist elements had stirred in the year 1920."[1]

August 12 coincided with the Ghadeer *ziyara* in al-Najaf. Apparently, the tribal chiefs wanted to take advantage of this *ziyara*, for it was noticed that the crowds of pilgrims in Najaf at the time reached a limit that the city had never seen before, so much so that many pilgrims were forced to sleep inside the holy shrine, in roads and public parks, and it is said that the number of pilgrims at the time reached 300,000.[2]

The interior ministry had felt the seriousness of the matter, so it mobilized in al-Najaf, a large police force. It also instructed Abdul-Aziz al-Qassab, the administrative officer of Karbala, to go to al-Najaf in person to monitor the situation. The administrative officer went to al-Najaf three days before the *ziyara* and stayed at the municipality house at the town's entrance. On the next day, Ali Jawdat al-Ayyubi, Hilla's administrative officer, reached al-Najaf accompanied by Shamiyya's mayor, Abu Skhair's mayor, some Hilla government officials and tribal chiefs. It became clear later that the king had instructed him to do so. Al-Ayyubi stayed at the house of Abdul-Muhsin Shalash.

The people of al-Najaf hardly heard about al-Ayyubi's arrival when they rushed to welcome him. The Ghari School board decided to hold an honouring party for him. Karbala's administrative officer opposed the holding of that party for fear a gathering could take place that would threaten security, but then he finally agreed. The party was held at the appointed time. Speeches and enthusiastic poems were delivered in it against the mandate, demanding full and complete independence. At the conclusion of the party, al-Ayyubi delivered a fiery speech. A few hours after the end of the party, a telegram reached al-Ayyubi from the interior ministry, ordering him to return to Hilla immediately.[3]

---

[1]Cox and Dobbs (op. cit.), p. 59.

[2]Abdul-Aziz al-Qassab (op. cit.), p. 221.

[3]Ali Jawdat (op. cit.), pp. 156-157.

On the eve of Ghadeer Day, i.e. the night of August 11, a large number of tribal chiefs gathered at the house of Sayyid Abul-Hassan al-Isfahani. Among them were: Abdul-Wahid al-Hajj Sikar, Muhsin Abu Tibeekh, Abadi al-Hussain, Alwan al-Yasiri, Sha`lan Abul-Joon and Qati` al-Awwadi. Al-Isfahani sent a message to Karbala's administrative officer requesting him to come to his [al-Isfahani's] house. When the administrative officer arrived, he found them sitting on the rooftop. Al-Isfahani spoke, saying, "Sayyid Muhsin Abu Tibeekh has some matters which he would like to submit to you." Then Abu Tibeekh spoke, saying,

"I was in Baghdad, and I met Cornwallis, adviser to the interior ministry, to whom I mentioned what the British advisers in the governorates are doing, they're pressuring the people, arrogance and abuse, and I asked him to remove them. After a long talk with him, he promised me to remove these advisers from their positions. A period of time has passed by, but he is yet to fulfil his promise. I, therefore, requested the administrative officer to ask the interior ministry to carry out this order immediately. If this does not materialize, we are not to be held responsible for what happens in the country."

When Abu Tibeekh finished his statement, al-Isfahani turned to the administrative officer [governor] to ask him: "What do you say about this request?" The administrator answered, "I do not know about such a promise, but I have to do one thing: ask the administration about this subject and notify you of its answer." The attendants asked the answer to come the next day and that they were awaiting it in a hurry so they would do what would be required. Here, the administrator turned to al-Isfahani to explain the seriousness of the situation in Najaf due to the large number of the pilgrims on the one hand, and to the large number of policemen on the other. He expressed his concern that a friction could take place that would lead to bloodshed; therefore, he requested al-Isfahani to issue a *fatwa* [binding religious edict] prohibiting the assembling [of people] in the town during the *ziyara*. When al-Isfahani heard this statement, he turned to Sheikh Abdul-Kareem al-Jaza'iri, who was sitting beside him and started talking to him in Persian. Then al-Isfahani declared his consent to the administrator's opinion and instructed al-Jaza'iri to write the *fatwa*. Once its writing was completed, al-Isfahani put his signature on it and handed it over to the administrator, who took it and left the meeting quickly to announce the *fatwa* to the people through the local criers. The *fatwa* produced its effect immediately: No assembly detrimental to security took place in Najaf after that.

The administrator sent a telegram to the interior ministry inquiring about what Muhsin Abu Tibeekh had said about the advisers. The answer came to him from the ministry and from Cornwallis. Both denied any promise about withdrawing the advisers. The ministry asked the administrator to immediately issue a statement that such a report was not true.

The administrator found himself in a very precarious situation: he was afraid the falsifying of that report would lead to public agitation, to speeches and exciting poems being delivered, and he saw that it would be wise to wait. When some chiefs went to see him at the municipality to ask about the answer, he told them that he would notify them of the answer soon, so they left. But as soon as they came out of his office, it was rumoured that the administrator was determined to arrest them. They, therefore, hurried to leave Najaf and go to Abu Skhair, where they sent a telegram to the interior ministry, complaining about the administrator and accusing him of wanting to arrest them although they did nothing to jeopardize security.[1] Then they mentioned in their telegram that they were absolutely determined to boycott the government if it did not meet their demands immediately.[2]

Abdul-Aziz al-Qassab says the following in his memoirs: "He actually did not mean to arrest them, as they imagined; rather, he intended to visit them to clarify the matter for them. He sent a servant to find out where they lived so he could visit them, but when they heard that the servant was asking about them, they mistakenly thought that it was for

---

[1]Abdul-Aziz al-Qassab (op. cit.), p. 226.

[2] Abdul-Razzaq al-Hassani, *Tarikh al-Wazarat al-Iraqiyya* (history of Iraqi administrations), Saida, Lebanon, 1965, Vol. 1, p. 68.

the purpose of arresting them; therefore, they drove their cars and rode their horses, leaving Najaf in a hurry.[1]

The Cabinet Resigns

Unrest spread in some parts of the mid-Euphrates, especially in the Abu Skhair and Shamiyya areas, and Tawifq al-Khalidi, the interior minister, felt unable to deal with the situation as long as the king supported those who were behind it. On August 3, al-Khalidi submitted his resignation from the cabinet. When the council of ministers (cabinet) met on August 9, al-Khalidi spoke to explain why he resigned. He said, "Unrest has overwhelmed the country for the past 10 days, and this has led to the extremists being unruly and the movement against the government's policy aggravating." Then al-Khalidi presented to the council a telegram from Karbala's administrator and a letter from the mayor of Abu Skhair, both containing a description of the disorder and unrest that went on in Najaf and among the Shamiyya tribes, which led to the weakening of the kingdom.[2] Then al-Khalidi stated that the extremists claimed that the king supported them in attacking the government.[3] He, therefore, sees that the king must announce to the public his support for the administration and trust in it. The prime minister spoke in support of al-Khalidi's viewpoint. After the discussion, the ministerial council decided unanimously to submit the following request to the king:

> "Based on the rumours which some extremists in the capital and governorates have circulated which have caused concern and confusion in some places, and due to concerns about the matter worsening if the situation remains as it is now, the council of ministers requests His Majesty the Great King to support his hard-working government in managing the affairs as His Majesty desires and wishes, so it may become

---

[1]Abdul-Aziz al-Qassab (op. cit.), pp. 225-226.

[2]Abdul-Razzaq al-Hassani (op. cit.), vol. 1, p. 87.

[3]Graves (op. cit.), p. 315.

obvious to the people that the government of His Majesty relies on the support of His Majesty."[1]

On August 12, the king sent his answer to the council's request, saying that he did not find any justification for changing his present plan. This answer proved that the king personally desired the fallout of the administration, contrary to the wish of Sir Percy Cox.[2] When the king's answer was read in the ministerial council, the ministers felt that they had to submit their resignations, which they all did with the exception of one of them, namely minister of endowments Muhammed Ali Fadhil.

The *naqeeb* wrote to the king that he refused to accept the ministers' resignation and hoped that he would support his stance and announce his confidence in him and in them. Cox hurried to the king to urge him to support the *naqeeb's* stance in rejecting the ministers' resignation. The king first agreed to what Cox had requested, but he shortly thereafter changed his mind and asked for the *naqeeb* to resign, claiming that his stay in the government was unconstitutional after the resignation of most of his ministers.[3] Thus, the *naqeeb* had to submit his resignation.

The situation became quite critical. What worsened it is that the king sent Cox a personal letter containing something like a threat. He said in it that due to the present instability and the responsibility between him and the high commissioner being undefined in domestic administrative affairs, he had to explain to the high commissioner and to the British government that in case a revolution erupted in the country, a reality which is expected to happen according to his confidential information—according to his expression—he would not be held responsible for what might result from it. The king asked in his letter that the high commissioner should undertake the government on his shoulders or make room for him [king] to administer the affairs of the country the way he saw fit.

This was more than Cox could tolerate; therefore, he drafted a strongly worded answer to the king in which he blamed the king for the

---

[1]Abdul-Razzaq al-Hassani (op. cit.), Vol. 1, p. 87.

[2]Philip Ireland, *Iraq*, translated by Ja`far al-Khayyat, Beirut, 1949, p. 280.

[3]Graves (op. cit.), p. 315.

current unrest. But Cox did not send this answer to the king, halting it so it would not bear a negative impact on the approaching celebration of Coronation Day.[1]

Ms Bell says that Nouri al-Sa`eed went to the king and informed him that the British had lost faith in him and that he was heading towards annihilation, but the king maintained his course heedlessly, playing the role of the unruly child who cannot be convinced.[2]

Parties Founded

On June 25, 1922, the council of ministers issued a law permitting the formation of political parties and putting strict penalties on any assembly for which an official permit was not issued. It is believed that there were three reasons that prompted the government to issue such a law:

FIRST: The government feared the situation in the summer of 1922 would develop similarly to the developments in the summer of 1920 when political demonstrations were held in the name of celebrating the birth anniversary of the Prophet or during the Hussaini mourning gatherings, so it wanted to prevent it through this law.

SECOND: The government believed that its supporters in Iraq were more than its opponents, but they were not organized, and once the law was issued, they would be able to form a party or more of their own through which they would win the upper hand or rebut their opponents.

THIRD: The finance minister, Sasson Hisqail, had expressed this opinion in the council of ministers: If the government prevents people from establishing political parties, they would resort to forming them underground. Apparently, the ministers, supported by the British, were convinced of the soundness of this view, especially since it came from Sasson who was trusted and admired by the British.

---

[1]Philip Ireland (op. cit.), p. 280.

[2]Burgoyne (op. cit.), Vol. 2, p. 291.

Anyhow, three political parties were founded in August of 1922, two of which were opposition parties, namely the Nahdha (renaissance) Party and the Watani (nationalist) Party, while the third was supportive of the authority, which was the Hurr (free) Party.

The Renaissance Party was founded in al-Kadhimiyya on August 2, and the members of its executive committee were: Ameen al-Charchafchi, Ahmad al-Zahir, Abdul-Rasool Kubba, Asif Qasim Agha, Abdul-Razzaq al-Azari, Mahdi al-Beer and Muhammed Hassan Kubba. As for the Watani [nationalist] Party, it was founded in Baghdad on the 19th of the same month, and the members of its executive committee were: Ja`far Abul-Timman, Ahmad al-Sheikh Dawood, Hamdi al-Pachachi, Mawlud Mukhlus, Abdul-Ghafoor al-Badri, Mahdi al-Baseer and Bahjat Zainal. It was noticed at the time that the Renaissance Party was supported by Sayyid Muhammed al-Sadr, whereas the **Nationalist Party** was supported by Sheikh Mahdi al-Khalisi.[1] It is said that the traditional competition between the Sadr and Khalisi clans had an impact on the formation of both parties; otherwise, they would have been one and the same.

As for **the Free Party**, it was founded in Baghdad with support from the *naqeeb*. His oldest son, Sayyid Mahmoud, was its head, while members of its executive committee were: Jameel Sidqi al-Zahawi, Abdul-Majeed al-Shawi, Fakhri al-Jameel, Hassan Ghaseebah and Dawood al-Naqeeb. Ms Bell wrote on August 15 saying, "The *naqeeb*'s son, Sayyid Mahmoud, has become head of a relatively moderate party after a great deal of persuasion and encouragement. As for the true force that moves it, it is Sheikh Ali al-Sulayman. The extremists have also formed a party of their own, but according to what I have heard, it did not make any significant progress. Ali al-Sulayman came to me accompanied by all senior tribal sheikhs whom he urged to sign an affiliation with Sayyid Mahmoud's party. They filled my office yesterday beyond its capacity and explained to me that they were ready to organize the whole country along the path of supporting mandate relations with Great Britain. It is wonderful to see such spontaneous excitement in the governorates for us,

---

[1] Muhammed al-Mahdi al-Baseer (op. cit.), Vol. 2, pp. 450-451.

but there is the opposition party that can cause a clear abuse, and it may produce a revolution unless we urge the king to tightly control it." Ms Bell added the next day to the above, saying, "The chiefs of tribes returned to their areas to organize party branches in the governorates, and I shall send Ali al-Sulayman by air to Ramadi. The good men of the Air Force have prepared a special plane for this purpose, and I mentioned to them that this would increase his prestige and would serve our interest. The extremists exert all their effort to agitate the mid-Euphrates."[1]

Exciting Incident

When the ministers submitted their resignation on August 14, the nationalists regarded it as a victory for them, and they kept telling people that a nationalist administration would succeed the Naqeebi one soon over which Muhammed al-Sadr would preside and that Ja`far Abul-Timman, Hamdi al-Pachachi and Mawlud Mukhlus would join it. On August 19, the *Al-Mufid* newspaper published a statement by Muhammed al-Sadr, urging people to persist in their demand for full independence and to reject the mandate by all legitimate means.

On August 20, both opposition parties held a joint meeting over which Mahmoud al-Sadr presided, followed by another session the next day. Both opposition parties decided to organize a public demonstration on the coronation anniversary and submit a petition to the king containing the people's demands for full independence and for forming a nationalist administration comprised of sincere, competent individuals.

On August 23, the anniversary of the coronation coincided, so it was celebrated at the king's quarters which overlook the [Tigris] River in the Qashla where the king received well-wishers. It was then that the demonstration—which was masterminded by both opposition parties—came, and it was a large one. The number of those who participated in it was estimated at 10,000. They filled the Qashla Square, and they kept shouting for the fall of the mandate and of colonialism. Then Mahdi al-Baseer stood on the platform that overlooked the square and delivered an enthusiastic speech in the name of the Nationalist Party. He was followed

---

[1]Burgoyne (op. cit.), Vol. 2, pp. 289-290.

by Muhammed Hassan Kubba, who delivered another speech in the name of the Renaissance Party.

As al-Baseer was delivering his speech, Cox arrived accompanied by Ms Bell and his retinue, and when Cox began to ascend the ladder steps that lead to the king's reception hall, a man from among the demonstrators named Hassoun Abul-Jibin[1] shouted, "Down with Britain! Down with Colonialism!" The demonstrators repeated this statement; therefore, signs of embarrassment appeared on Cox's face and on those of his retinue, but they went on ascending the stairs. They performed the congratulatory ceremonies as they should be, then returned from wherever they had come from.

Cox regarded this incident as a harsh insult directed at him and his country, and he thought that it did not take place by accident but was masterminded by the king's trustees, especially their head, Fahmi al-Mudarris. In his report to London, Cox says the following about this incident: "The king's trustees have deliberately set a date for the leaders of the opposition to be present at the time that the king was congratulated prior to my arrival, and they deliberately prolonged their stay there as Mahdi al-Baseer, who was one of the agitators of the 1920 Revolution, was delivering a fiery speech in which he insulted the British. He did that with directions from, or permission of, Fahmi al-Mudarris."[2]

It is worth mentioning that Ameen al-Rayhani narrated the incident differently. He says about it the following: "On the morning of the 23rd of august, a delegation from both said parties came with a crowd of supporters who gathered in the mansion's courtyard. The leaders asked the king to order someone to represent his majesty to hear the speeches delivered there. His Majesty ordered the head of trustees to represent him. The blind poet, Sheikh Mahdi al-Baseer, the Nationalist Party's speaker, addressed the assembly, exciting sorrow in the head trustee, so he stood

---

[1]This man had a [cheese] shop in the Sarai Market, and he was famous for his enthusiasm for demonstrations. It is said that he sometimes would put on shrouds as is done by people who carry out *tatbeer* [self-flagellation] with a sharp object during the Hussaini processions. He did so in order to indicate that he was ready to sacrifice his life for the sake of the homeland.

[2]Elie Kedourie, *The Chatham House Version*, London, U.K., 1970, p. 243.

to speak, and he had the right to speak since the king had delegated him, and it was right, too, to prove the enthusiasm—some said foolishness—in him which made him forget that he was an office holder in the mansion, and that the high commissioner of Great Britain was coming at that time to congratulate His Majesty the king on the anniversary of his coronation, and that it was his duty to receive and welcome him. It so coincided that when the gentleman head of the trustees was speaking against the mandate, the high commissioner, Sir Percy Cox, and men from the British Agency came to congratulate. It was then that everyone confronted them with the shouts of 'Down with the mandate! Down with the British!'"[1]

Actually, this narrative by al-Rayhani is not supported by British and Iraqi documents, and it was falsified by Mahdi al-Baseer himself.[2] Whatever the case may be, the secretary of the high commissioner sent on the morning of the next day a strongly worded letter to the king as follows:

"Your Excellency, the Head of the Royal Office:

"We wish you inform His Majesty the King that His Magnificence the [High] Commissioner strongly protests the treatment with which he was meted at the time when His Magnificence represents the government of the King of Great Britain, as he was passing by the reception room to perform the congratulatory ceremonies, and that His Magnificence has notified London of this incident and is asking for an apology, and that Fahmi Afandi al-Mudarris must be fired because he was officially in charge. His Magnificence also asks for a statement of the measures which His Majesty the King intends to undertake against both speakers who demeaned the status of the King by delivering exciting speeches.

---

[1]Ameen al-Rayhani, *Mulook al-Arab* (Arabs' kings), Vol. 2, pp. 297-298.

[2]Khairi al-Omari, *Fahmi al-Mudarris,* in "Al-Aqlam" magazine of December of 1964, p. 79.

"24 August 1922 A.D., Signed: Janine Percy."[1]

When this letter reached the king, he immediately ordered the firing of Fahmi al-Mudarris from his job. He also ordered his secretary, Rustum Haidar, to write an answer to the high commissioner expressing his great regret for what had happened and pledging to do what was needed according to the wishes of the high commissioner, requesting him not to keep any traces of the incident in his memory.

Some evidence indicates that Fahmi al-Mudarris was since starting his job at the palace secretly supporting the opposition, and the British became aware of it. This is why we saw Cox taking advantage of the demonstration and what happened during it to get rid of him. Fahmi al-Mudarris, on his part, used to believe that Rustam Haidar was hiding behind this maneuver, and this feeling kept controlling him for a period of time.[2]

Amazing Encounter

On the morning of August 24, i.e. the day that followed the coronation anniversary, the king suffered from severe stomach pain, so he summoned some doctors to examine him, including Ameen Ma'luf, [Harry] Sinderson and Saib Shawkat, who differed among themselves in diagnosing his ailment. In his memoirs, [Dr. Harry] Sinderson says that he diagnosed the sickness as an ulcer, whereas Ameen Ma'luf diagnosed it as a simple ailment that would soon abate.[3] Saib Shawkat told me that he was the one who diagnosed the sickness as an ulcer, whereas Sinderson diagnosed it as malaria.

After laboratory tests had been done, the sickness was diagnosed as an ulcer, and it was decided to conduct surgery for the king at his mansion at eight o'clock the next morning, provided it would be done by Dr. Abraham, the senior surgeon at the Royal Hospital. When Cox came

---

[1]Abdul-Razzaq al-Hassani (op. cit.), Vol. 1, p. 95.

[2]Khairi al-Omari (op. cit.), p. 79.

[3][Harry] Sinderson, *Ten Thousand and One Nights: Memories of Iraq's Sherifian Dynasty*, London, U.K., 1973, pp. 66-67.

to know about the decision to conduct the surgery for the king, he asked Sinderson, "I have to see the king before the surgery. Please inform him that I will be in the mansion at 7:30 am."

On the early morning of the next day, Abraham came to the mansion accompanied by a younger surgeon named Woodman to assist him in performing the surgery. Sinderson was commissioned to administer the anesthesia. Then Hanna al-Khayyat, public health director, came to oversee the surgery as a representative of the Iraqi government. Some Iraqi doctors also came to witness the operation. Sinderson says that six of the king's armed slaves were standing on the balcony overlooking the river [Tigris]. Then he comments, saying, "If anything happened to the king, our chance to save our lives would be quite remote."[1]

At 7:30 am, Cox arrived accompanied by Cornwallis. He entered to see the king, so the three British doctors left the room and stood on the balcony waiting. Here, an important question faces us: what was Cox's objective behind meeting the king at that critical hour, and what happened during it?

We have two accounts about that encounter. One of them was narrated by Ameen al-Rayhani, who quoted the king himself. The other was narrated by Graves, the British historian, who quoted Cornwallis. Here we cite both accounts so the reader may be able to compare:

Al-Rayhani says, "On the morning that followed the seating anniversary when King Faisal was surrounded by doctors and nurses who had prepared the incision knives and surgery tools, high commissioner Sir Percy Cox arrived. He greeted and took out of his pocket an order which he passed on to the king to sign. The order was to arrest and banish seven nationalist leaders out of Iraq. The king read it as he was suppressing his outrage, shaking his head [perhaps in resentment]. Sir Percy Cox, therefore, explained the purpose, thereby justifying what he did; the king did not respond with a word. But one of the British doctors advanced and addressed him, saying, "This is not the time, Commissioner, for these matters." Sir Percy Cox, therefore, said, "The issue is necessary to safeguard security. The country is in danger." The doctor said, "Postpone it till the surgery is done, which is more important for the life of His Majesty the King; we have to start it immediately." As he was holding the

---

[1]*Ibid.*, p. 68.

order in his hand, the king addressed Sir Percy, saying, "A few minutes later, I will be in the hands of these doctors, and I may never return to life from my coma; so, are you asking me, Sir Percy, to let this order be the last thing I do in life? Do you expect me to banish these people, residents of this land, from their homeland before my death? No, by Allah, it is not possible, it is not possible." Having said so, he passed the order back to the high commissioner, who tucked it in his pocket and left the hall without saying a single word."[1]

As for Grave's narrative, here is its text: "On 25 August, Faisal was bedridden due to a severe ulcer, so the doctors decided to conduct surgery on him the same day. Shortly before the operation, he was visited by Cox—who was accompanied by Cornwallis—after seeking permission from his doctors. They both explained the critical situation to him and that they had reached the crossroad with him. Cox urged him to abandon the extremists and to take the side of the British; otherwise, he would have to face the consequences of his alliance with the destructive minority that sought its own interests. Cox pressured Faisal to order the arrest of seven leaders of the agitators, but Faisal refused and said that he was sure that this measure would lead to a general revolution and that he could not die while this responsibility rested on his conscience. The king and Cox kept arguing the subject till the surgeon came and insisted on taking the king to the surgery stand. That was a tense scene in the presence of a crowd of slaves and servants outside the hall who were all armed and trained and in the presence of six Iraqi doctors inside the hall watching the surgery knife lest it should be misused. The king insisted on his stance to the last breath against the order which he regarded as a tragedy."[2]

The reader may notice that there is a similarity between these two accounts, and we can conclude in light of both of them that Cox wanted to take advantage of the time of the operation to get the king to agree to hit the leaders of the opposition and to finish their movement, but the king made him miss that opportunity.

It is noteworthy that Cox did not mention in his official reports what he did with Faisal, nor did Ms Bell refer to it in her letters, as if they

---

[1]Ameen al-Rayhani, *Faisal al-Awwal* (Faisal I), pp. 118-119.

[2]Graves (op. cit.), p. 317.

both realized how lowly the action was, so they kept it to themselves. Al-Rayhani comments about this, saying that Cox acted upon the well-known Arab axiom that says, "A good man hides his insult." He [Cox], therefore, did not mention this incident in his reports.[1]

Anyhow, Abraham quickly carried out the surgery as soon as Cox left the room. He conducted it according to the precision and craftsmanship for which he was known. Graves says, "The ulcer condition at the time of the operation was on the verge of danger; it was pierced, and any delay in conducting the operation could have led to death."[2]

It is worth mentioning in this regard that people during that time did not know what was going on. Various rumours spread among them about the king's sickness. Some of them said that the king was not sick, but the British forced him to pretend to be sick. Others said that the doctors recommended the operation as instigated by the British. [3] Muhammed al-Khalisi wrote the following about the king: "He feigned sickness and stayed in bed, pretending that he was on the verge of death, and I sensed evil behind that, and I think that Faisal is sick in his creed, conscience and manliness, not in his body."[4]

Hitting The Opposition

When Cox found out that the king did not agree to hit the opposition, he decided to undertake this responsibility on his shoulders. On August 26, Cox published a long statement addressing "all people of Iraq" which he filled with threats and intimidation. He followed this by shutting down both opposition parties and suspending both *Al-Mufid* and *Al-Rafidain* newspapers. When Ja`far Abul-Timman and Hamdi al-Pachachi went to the criminal investigations office to protest these unfair measures, the

---

[1]Ameen al-Rayhani (op. cit.), p. 118.

[2]Graves (op. cit.), p. 317.

[3]Abdul-Razzaq al-Hassani (op. cit.), Vol. 1, p. 96.

[4]Excerpted from the manuscript of Sheikh Muhammed al-Khalisi titled "Hero of Islam". [Actually, the manuscript to which the author refers to here is now in print, and I have a copy of it given to me by one of the instructors of the Khalisi University in al-Kadhimiyya which I visited once. – Tr.]

policemen were waiting for them, so they both were immediately arrested, and so were Mahdi al-Baseer, Ameen al-Charchafchi, Abdul-Rasool Kubba and Sami Khundah. They were all expelled to Hungam Island. After that, Habib al-Khayzaran was banished, too, and only three opposition men escaped arrest: Ahmed al-Sheikh Dawood, Abdul-Ghafour al-Badri and Ibrahim Hilmi al-Omar. The first and second of the men disappeared, so the police could not get a hold of them, whereas the third fled to Iran.

Cox issued his order to oust Hilla's administrative officer, Ali Jawdat al-Ayyubi, and fire the mayors who supported him, such as Khayri al-Hindawi and Shakir al-Mulla Hammadi. He also sent planes to strafe some tribes such as the Fatlah tribe in al-Muhannawiyya, the Aqraa tribe in Ifak, the Khafaja tribe in Shatra and the Azza tribe in al-Mansouriyya.[1]

On August 28, Cox sent an Indian man from among his employees named Muhammed Hussain Khan Kabuli to Sheikh Mahdi al-Khalisi and Sayyid Hassan al-Sadr in al-Kadhimiyya to warn them that they had to get their sons, Sheikh Muhammed and Sayyid Muhammed respectively, to leave Iraq within 24 hours and that if they did not do it, the high commissioner would be forced to undertake measures against them which do not suit the respect [normally reserved] for clergymen. So, both men had to respond to this warning. Both Muhammads—al-Khaliki and al-Sadr—left Baghdad the next day and headed to Iran, and many residents of al-Kadhimiyya and Baghdad came out to bid them farewell at the train station.

Ms Bell described in one of her letters that Cox hitting the opposition was a daring act and that it "saved the situation". Then she said, "The extremists' movement collapsed; as for the moderates, they raised their heads high. The party of Sayyid Muhammed al-Gailani [al-Naqeeb] kept growing noticeably, and this means that the king's sickness was a good chance that came on time." Ms Bell points out that after that Naji al-Suweedi went to her after having prepared an "excellent plan" to gather signatures throughout the country to strengthen British-Iraqi relations.[2]

---

[1] Abdul-Razzaq al-Hassani (op. cit.), Vol. 1, pp. 96-99.

[2] Burgoyne (op. cit.), Vol. 2, p. 293.

Stance Of Yasin Al-Hashimi

At a time when the king was still bedridden following his surgical operation, Yasin al-Hashimi went to Ms Bell in her office to talk to her about the general situation. Al-Hashimi kept speaking ill of the king's "fickle" behaviour, blaming the British for being unable to control him.

Ms Bell wrote in a letter dated August 31 about al-Hashimi's visit, saying that he expressed his concern about the country's fate. He had read the treaty and was of the opinion that Iraq could not expect more tolerant terms. Al-Hashimi wondered, "Why did the king not accept it?" Then he addressed Ms Bell, saying, "It is your [Britons'] fault; why did you not control him, and why did you permit him to be under the influence of people who want to lead us and his own self to destruction?" Ms Bell kept explaining to al-Hashimi how she, Cornwallis, and Clayton were flattering the king in a futile attempt to convince him. Then Ms Bell wondered, "How can we work with the king when in the vital issues, he agrees with Cox and Cornwallis, but he so quickly changes his mind as soon as both men get out?" Al-Hashimi answered her, saying, "Yes, I know that someone goes to him, a man from the marketplace, and in one word makes him change his mind." Then al-Hashimi said, "It is [an issue with] the king, but the country comes before him." Ms Bell then praised Yasin al-Hashimi's strength of character and intelligence, saying, "I think that Yasin is the man of destiny, for he has more intelligence and energy than any other Arab I know, perhaps not stronger in conduct than Ali al-Sulayman, but he has a broader knowledge of matters than him. The king knows his strength, and he fears it, but due to his great conceit, he thinks he can subdue and use Yasin. I think that Yasin will gain favour with the king by pretending to surrender to him, but when he for sure takes control of the situation, he will hold the king by the neck and force him to adopt the policy which he wants. It is then that the king will twist like a snake, and Iraq's fate will be determined on this basis where history repeats itself in Iraq, so Yasin becomes the actual ruler, whereas the king becomes a mere symbolic head. I am sorry I have to believe that this is the fate that suits the king, for he is conceited, weak and cowardly, and nothing good will ever come out of him."[1]

It is obvious from this statement that Ms Bell discovered in Yasin al-Hashimi the man the British were looking for, the one who could stand in the face of Faisal and force him to surrender to the policy which they wanted in Iraq. In those days, the British were losing patience with Faisal, as if they had to choose one of two options: they should either oust him, or paralyze him by putting a strong man before him who would challenge and subdue him. Perhaps they found in the second option that which would bring them ease without stirring an uproar against them, and here is Yasin al-Hashimi having come to them ready to perform the desired role.

One of the amazing coincidences is that only a few days after al-Hashimi's visit to Ms Bell, a letter reached her which al-Hashimi had sent when he was in Nasiriyya to a friend of his in Baghdad. In it, al-Hashimi cursed the British and described them as the "oppressors", invoking Allah Almighty to grant success to kicking them out of the country. This friend handed this letter to the general director of security, who in turn handed it over to Ms Bell. It was then that Ms Bell realized that her discovery was not sound, and that al-Hashimi was not the man who could be trusted.[2]

The King Changes Stance

On September 10, 1922, following the king's recovery, Cox visited him to congratulate him on recovering. He kept talking to him frankly, saying that the British government would no longer tolerate his communication with any nationalist movement, nor will it tolerate any delay that may take place about certifying the treaty. He also asked him to be a constitutional king—that is, similar to the king of Britain—so he would stop unnecessarily interfering in the affairs of the administration and of the officials. It is said that Cox gave the king the option to either apologize for what he had done in the past or to surrender and that the king

---

[1]Burgoyne (op. cit.), Vol. 2, p. 295.

[2]*Ibid.*, Vol. 2, p. 298.

preferred to apologize.[1] It is also said that the king apologized for his past actions by saying that he did them because there was no constitution and the administration was not synchronised and that as soon as the constitution and treaty were passed, he would gladly do what he was asked.[2]

Cox gave the king a drafted statement that agreed with the suppressive measures which Cox had carried out during the king's sickness and thanked him for them, and the king did what Cox wanted him to do. Below is the text of the statement:

Dear Sir Percy,

Now I have healed, praise be to Allah Almighty, and my doctors have permitted me to resume my state business. I see it my duty before I undertake this responsibility to offer Your Magnificence my heartfelt thanks and to express to you my great admiration for the strict policy and necessary measures which Your Magnificence had undertaken in your capacity as a representative of the government of His Majesty, in order to safeguard the public interest and to maintain order and security during my sickness which took place all of a sudden during the period which usually ends between an administration's resignation and the forming of another. In conclusion, I reiterate my sincere thanks to Your Magnificence for your valuable assistance.

Your Sincere Friend, Faisal
Baghdad, 11 September 1922[3]

According to Graves, the relationship between the king and Cox became friendly after that.[4]

---

[1]Ghassan Atiyyah, *Iraq*, Beirut, 1973, p. 378.

[2]Philip Ireland (op. cit.), p. 283.

[3]Abdul-Razzaq al-Hassani (op. cit.), Vol. 1, p. 97.

[4]Graves (op. cit.), p. 323.

When it was time to look into the formation of a new administration, Cox was of the view that the *naqeeb* should form it for the third time and that most of its members should be from among those who had served in the previous *naqeeb* administration. The king agreed to all that Cox had asked of him.

On September 30, the new administration was formed under the presidency of the *naqeeb*. In it, Abdul-Muhsin al-Sa`doun was the interior minister, Sasson Hisqail was the finance minister, Tawfiq al-Khalidi was the minister of justice, Ja`far al-`Askari was the minister of defence, Sabeeh Nash'at was the minister of transport and labour, and Muhammed Ali Fadhil was the minister of endowments. On October 17, a royal decree was issued which appointed Abdul-Hassan Shalash al-Najafi as minister of education, but he asked to be excused from having to undertake this cabinet post due to his many commercial businesses; therefore, the post of minister of education became vacant.[1]

On October 13, the treaty was published in Baghdad with the king's signature at the bottom. The king broadcast a statement to the people in which he praised the treaty, describing it as having been built on mutual interests between Iraq and Great Britain, and that the people would undoubtedly appreciate its value and would increase their upholding of the friendship of "our main ally" since its friendship is necessary to safeguard this kingdom's independence and to ensure its economic and urban development.[2]

About those tense days through which the king went, Ameen al-Rayhani narrates, "People before his sickness used to go to him with enthusiasm and say, `Hoist the flag, we are your men, we sacrifice our lives for your sake.'" Faisal mentioned, for example, one of those commandos who was a senior opposition leader and the most enthusiastic among them, but he disappeared before Cox could carry out his order to banish the leaders, and then he returned thereafter to congratulate the king for his recovery. The king, therefore, asked him, "What have you done with the British? Have you changed your mind about getting them out of the country?" Without being confused, the man answered him

---

[1]Abdul-Razzaq al-Hassani (op. cit.), Vol. 1, p. 101.

[2]*Al-Iraq* newspaper of October 14, 1922.

immediately, saying, "They said to us that you yourself were banished from the land, so we took to silence."[1]

Perhaps it is suitable to mention one interesting dialogue which took place during those days between the king and Ms Bell about Yasin al-Hashimi. Al-Hashimi was a candidate for the post of minister of interior in the new cabinet, and the king was willing, but Ms Bell was not. Ms Bell went to the king to convince him that al-Hashimi was not suitable for that cabinet post; therefore, she showed him the letter in which al-Hashimi was damning the British, and then she said to the king, "We do not care if anyone says to us: 'You are oppressors and villains.' Perhaps we would answer him by saying, 'By God, only God knows.' But when he speaks similarly to what al-Hashimi has done, that is: 'You are the only means to save my homeland,' then he writes at the same time in a way that describes us as being oppressive, invoking God for success in kicking us out of the land, this is something which cannot be forgiven." The king tried to justify al-Hashimi's behaviour, so he said to Ms Bell, "What al-Hashimi did is normal in Eastern life, for the slavery from which the people have suffered during six centuries has made one obligated to be hypocritical and to play on two ropes in order to protect himself through trickery. Even I do that! We have not been accustomed to living in freedom, so we may be free in our conduct. One who wants to rule the people of the East must look at them through their own glasses." Ms Bell says that she was convinced of the truth of what the king said in defence of al-Hashimi but remained insisting on not letting al-Hashimi assume any cabinet post then. She was of the view that it might be possible for him to be a cabinet minister, later on, believing that in the end, he would reach the top.[2]

I think that in his defence of al-Hashimi's conduct, the king was defending his own. Apparently, Ms Bell realized it; therefore, she said that al-Hashimi would, in the end, reach the top, as if she was saying to the king, "He will reach the top just as you reached it."

---

[1]Ameen al-Rayhani (op. cit.), Vol. 1, p. 101.

[2]Burgoyne (op. cit.), Vol. 2, p. 298.

Chapter Five

The Banishment Of Sheikh Mahdi Al-Khalisi

On October 20, 1922, Abdul-Muhsin al-Sa`doun, in his capacity as the interior minister, issued orders to the administrators to start holding the founding assembly's elections, and on the 24th, al-Sa`doun announced a general declaration which was concluded by the following text:

> "Here, I would like to reiterate and plead to the honourable members of our people not to heed the distortions and falsifications which some of those who do not care about the real interests of the people may dare to disseminate, that they should unite their views and place their trust in those whom they expect to try to achieve their wishes. The final statement belongs to the founding assembly which is being elected; may Allah enable everyone to earn what is good for the country."[1]

The New Opposition

The British and the king used to think that the opposition was no more

---

[1] Abdul-Razzaq al-Hassani, *Tarikh al-Wizarat al-Iraqiyya* (history of Iraqi administrations), Saida, 1965, Vol. 1, p. 112.

and that the elections would be held according to their own plan. Then it became clear to them in a few days how wrong their view was. The opposition was resurrected anew in a stronger thrust, and this time it was led by the *mujtahids* in al-Kadhimiyya and Najaf, in the vanguard of whom was Sheikh Mahdi al-Khalisi.

The first indications of the opposition appeared in the form of a referendum directed to the *mujtahids* on the 15th of Rabi` al-Awwal of 1341 A.H., which coincided with [Sunday] November 5 [according to the Gregorian calendar, or to October 23 according to the Julian calendar] of the year 1922 the text of which was:

> "Our distinguished scholars and Islam's Proofs [Hujjatullahs], may Allah Almighty enable us to enjoy your shade all the time. It has come to our attention that due to your religious function and spiritual leadership, you have banned all the Iraqi nation from having anything to do with this election, prohibiting [them to] assist it in any way, and making [it such that] helping it [would be deemed] defiance of Allah and of His Messenger; therefore, we plead to you to explain the authenticity [of such a notion] so we may follow your commands which Allah Almighty has commanded that we should obey; may Allah prolong your shade."

This referendum was appended with the answers of the three senior *mujtahids* as follows:

> "*In the Name of Allah, the most Gracious, the most Merciful.* Yes, we have issued a prohibition of the election at the present time due to what is obvious for everyone who resides in the desert or is an urban settler; therefore, anyone who joins it or assists it is akin to one who fights Allah, His Messenger and obedient servants, Allah's blessings be upon them all. [Signed:] the humblest person: Abul-Hassan al-Mousawi al-Isfahani."

> "*In the Name of Allah, the most Gracious, the most Merciful.* Yes, we have ruled that the entire Iraqi nation is prohibited

from joining it and that anyone who enlists in this matter or assists it with the least assistance opposes Allah, His Messenger and the Pure Imams, Allah's blessings be upon them all; may Allah protect everyone from so doing. [Signed:] the humblest person: Muhammed-Hussain al-Gharawi al-Naeeni."

"In the Name of Allah, the most Gracious, the most Merciful. Yes, we have prohibited the entire Iraqi nation from participating in this election: Anyone who joins or assists it opposes Allah and His Messenger, and the most Exalted One has said the following in His Holy Book: *'**Do they not know that the fire of Hell is for those who oppose Allah and His Messenger? There they shall dwell. That is the supreme disgrace'*** [Qur'an, 9:63]. May Allah protect everyone from it. [Signed:] the one who rests his hope [on Allah's mercy] Muhammed-Mahdi al-Kadhimi al-Khurasani al-Khalisi, may he be forgiven."[1]

The matter did not stop there; rather, *fatwas* kept being issued from time to time, and there was a group of enthusiastic youths who dedicated their efforts to monitor all of that: they would write the formula of the referendum and present it to the *mujtahids* in order to get from them the desired *fatwas*. In his memoirs, Muhammed-Mahdi Kubba says the following:

"Together with a group of al-Kadhimiyya youths, in addition to some al-Khalisi School students, I was diligent in writing the wordings seeking edicts and in meeting scholars of theology and getting them to issue edicts, delegating some youths to write them on paper and to make carbon copies of

---

[1] Excerpted from the royal palace's documents, Folder 3, Document 70.

them, then to distribute them among the people and send them to Baghdad and other parts of the country."[1]

On their part, the *mujtahids* kept becoming more and more strict in prohibiting the holding of elections. For example, in a *fatwa* which he lately issued, Abul-Hassan al-Isfahani said, "To all our Muslim brothers: this election kills the Islamic nation; therefore, anyone who casts a vote after having known about the prohibition of the election, his wife becomes unlawful for him; he must not be visited; it is not proper to respond to his salutation, and he must not enter the public bathhouse used by the Muslims. This is our viewpoint, and Allah is the One Who knows what is right." Sheikh Mahdi al-Khalisi issued a *fatwa* in which he clearly referred to Cox banishing, displacing and strafing with planes and to the *naqeeb*'s party supporting him; this is its text:

"Since the elections are based on the premise that they oppose the wishes of the Iraqi nation through the military authority and the moderate free party which was founded via coercion and force while [simultaneously] shutting down the parties that agree with the nation's wishes, subjugating its people, disuniting it, and strafing with planes those who lag behind the free party, so much so that those who were killed by their bombs were children, the elderly, the innocent, women, and others from among those who, on account of the grief for their death one would die, he would not be blameworthy according to my view; rather, he would have been worthy of such a deed. Having anything to do with the elections and with everything that is based on this premise that harms the future of Iraq, actually, it harms all its affairs, being prohibitive according to the Shari`a and to the consensus of the Muslims, we deem that he gets out of the responsibility of the Muslims. It is from Allah that we seek

---

[1]Muhammed-Mahdi Kubba, *Muthakkarati fi Sameem al-Ahdath* (my memoirs in the heart of events), Beirut, Lebanon, 1965, p. 27.

success; He suffices us, and Great is the One on Whom we rely."[1]

What is noteworthy is that most, almost all, al-Kadhimiyya scholars supported al-Khalisi in prohibiting the elections, forgetting their personal disputes and local [internal] competition, becoming all in a single row and opposing the government. We found their signatures on the issued edicts; they are Sayyid Hassan al-Sadr, Sheikh Abdul-Hussain Al Yasin, Sayyid Muhammed Mahdi al-Sadr, Sheikh Mahdi al-Marayati, Sheikh Mahdi Jarmuqah, Sayyid Mahdi al-Khurasani, Mirza Ibrahim al-Salmasi, Sheikh Isma`eel al-Assadi, Sheikh Radhi al-Khalisi, Sheikh Muhammed al-Assadi and Sayyid Asadullah al-Haidari. This proves the strength of the opposition, which later surfaced.

Sheikh Mahdi al-Khalisi began to openly speak ill of the king, denouncing his stance vis-à-vis the treaty and describing him as reneging on his promise which he had made when he first came to Iraq. In his memoirs, Muhammed-Mahdi Kubba indicated that al-Khalisi announced [once] among a crowd in his school, "We swore the oath of allegiance to Faisal to be a king over Iraq with conditions, and he has violated those conditions; therefore, we are not obligated for any allegiance to him, nor is the Iraqi nation." This statement by al-Khalisi created a buzz in various circles, and the king heard about it, so he became very resentful of him, hiding his grudge towards him.[2]

Al-Sa`doun Succeeds Al-Naqeeb

Al-Naqeeb became fed-up with this intense opposition that the *mujtahids* were leading, using their edicts as weapons [to demonstrate it]. Some opposition leaflets kept attacking the person of the *naqeeb*, describing him as a renegade from Islam. The famous popular poet, Abboud al-Karkhi, composed a poem denouncing the *naqeeb*, which was widely circulated, particularly these two lines of verse:
O Naqeeb, O Naqeeb,

---

[1]Excerpted from the royal palace's documents, Serial 115, Document 1.

[2]Muhammed-Mahdi Kubba (op. cit.), p. 26.

Amazing how you have no friend:
When you abandoned your grandfather, Muhammed,
You took Cox as your beloved one instead.

Ameen al-Rayhani narrates that he visited the *naqeeb* during that period and found him angry and confused. The *naqeeb* said to him the following: "In the country, there are many nationalists, and they all are politicians, but there are no eyes in their heads that show them that in which they really are. Where are they with regards to the country, and where is the country in their regard? They were in the past under the Turks' feet, and now they sell the country to the Turks for one fils in order to seek revenge against those whom they think are their foes. We undertook the matter on our shoulders, and we seek success from

Abdul-Muhsin al-Sa`doun
(Courtesy: Wikipedia Commons)

none other than Allah, relying only on Him, the most Praised One, the most Exalted. Have you, Afandi, met with the nationalists and heard their rhetoric? Tomorrow, we shall meet with their senior leaders in Karbala and Najaf. We describe this *ijtihad* as ignorance, and we describe it as stubbornness. The British people have the knowledge, and they have wealth, and they also have wisdom; as for the nationalists, what thing do they have? Do they love the country more than us, which is our land before it is theirs, and most of them are still foreigners?"[1]

The *naqeeb* was always keen on remaining in charge. Ms Bell wrote about him once, saying, "There is one matter: the *naqeeb* will not relinquish the presidency of the cabinet unless he bears a burden while

---

[1]Ameen al-Rayhani, *Mulook al-Arab*, Beirut, Lebanon, 1951, Vol. 2, pp. 397-398.

both his feet are forward."[1] But the British people started feeling that he was no longer good for them: the political situation needed a strong and strict man of a type other than that of the *naqeeb*. It can be said that the *naqeeb* was suitable for presiding over the cabinet at the beginning of the formation of the government when the British wanted for it a man who enjoyed sanctity or social veneration. As for now, after the *mujtahids* have raised their strict sermons, the situation needs a strict man, not a man with veneration.

The king was not comfortable with the *naqeeb* and wanted to replace him with one of his aides, namely Ja`far al-`Askari, but the British regarded al-`Askari as being weak and unable to deal with the situation, and they may have regarded him as a tool in the king's hand. The British during that period started looking at Abdul-Muhsin al-Sa`doun [right photo] as the most suitable man for the job, and they kept paving the path for him to succeed the *naqeeb* as head of the administration as soon as possible.

The British, as we have already seen, were looking for a man who could stand in the face of the king, and they found that man in the person of Yasin al-Hashimi, but they soon discovered that they were wrong about him. Apparently, the British finally found in al-Sa`doun the suitable man they were looking for.

Actually, al-Sa`doun is different from al-Hashimi: he is frank, he neither flatters nor does he tend to tolerate or pretend. This he has inherited from his Bedouin legacy on which he grew up during his childhood. Moreover, he has a strong character; he is dignified, firm and persistent: if he sets his mind on something, he goes on with it regardless of whether people like it or not.

It is noteworthy that al-Sa`doun believed that the citizenship concept was yet to crystallize in Iraq, that the people of Iraq were not a single nation but varying nations[2], and that Iraq was surrounded by enemies from every side, such as Ibn Saud, the Turks, the Iranians and the French; therefore, Iraq's interests, according to al-Sa`doun, was strongly linked to cooperation with the British. It is not wise that Iraq should face

---

[1]Burgoyne, *Gertrude Bell*, London, U.K., 1961, Vol. 2, p. 289.

[2]Excerpted from a manuscript by Khayri al-Omari.

all these enemies alone, knowing that it does not have the strength that assists it to withstand them. If the British withdrew from Iraq, its surrounding enemies would eat it up in a short period of time. Al-Sa`doun used to express these opinions without being hypocritical about them, unlike some politicians who are used to announcing to the public what is different from that which they hide in their hearts. Add to this, he did not feel too weak to face the king, and he often stood on par with him, opposing or defying him. On November 1, 1922, Ms Bell wrote saying, "Al-Sa`doun is one of the people whom I love more than others, for he is a daring man who is not afraid and does not entertain the least hesitation about standing in the face of the king when he differs from him about an opinion, something which he used to do quite often."[1]

On November 6, al-Sa`doun submitted his resignation from the interior ministry, justifying it by his fellow ministers opposing his plan to use harshness in holding the elections and in punishing those who boycotted them. Only 10 days after his resignation had passed, the *naqeeb* submitted the resignation of his entire cabinet. The king immediately accepted the *naqeeb*'s resignation. Two days later, the king commissioned al-Sa`doun to form a new cabinet.

Ameen al-Rayhani comments about the *naqeeb*'s resignation, pointing out that the British kept quiet and did not care about it. He indicated that the people kept wondering: "Where is the loyalty of the British people?" In his broad tone, al-Baghdadi said, "They use him, bother him, then leave him."[2] In other words, once the British could do without the *naqeeb*, they abandoned him!

The New Cabinet

The Sa`doun cabinet was comprised of al-Sa`doun as prime minister and deputy minister of justice, Naji al-Suweedi as interior minister, Sasson Hisqail as finance minister, Yasin al-Hashimi as minister of labour and transport, Abdul-Lateef al-Mandeel as minister of endowments, Abdul-

---

[1]Burgoyne (op. cit.), Vol. 2, p. 303.

[2]Ameen al-Rayhani, *Faisal al-Awwal*, Beirut, Lebanon, 1958, p. 143.

Hussain al-Chalabi as minister of education and Nouri al-Sa`eed as deputy minister of defence.

What is noteworthy is that al-Sa`doun wanted, in the beginning, to assign the post of minister of labour and transport to Abdul-Muhsin Shalash, to whom he sent a telegram in this regard on November 17, but Shalash asked to be excused from having to accept it. It is believed that he was apprehensive of the wrath of the *mujtahids* and of that of public opinion. It was then that al-Sa`doun assigned that ministry post to Yasin al-Hashimi.

Abdul-Hussain al-Chalabi's appointment as a cabinet minister was met with strong denunciation in al-Kadhimiyya, and people kept taunting him and speaking ill of him in an ugly way. They regarded him as one of the assistants and supporters of al-Khalisi, then they found him suddenly changing and becoming one of the men of the government. One day, a group of the people of al-Kadhimiyya lurked for him at the gate of the Holy Shrine, and they were led by Sheikh Hassan, son of Sheikh Mahdi al-Khalisi. When al-Chalabi wanted to enter the Shrine in order to pass through to his house as he used to do every day, those men encountered him with the claim that he was an apostate who was not permitted to enter mosques. Two of his men took to defend him, and trouble almost broke out had he not faced the matter with calm and clemency and went home through the alleys that are adjacent to the Shrine. Finally, he preferred to reside outside al-Kadhimiyya in the Ayl Mansion.

Al-Sa`doun was determined to hold the elections despite edicts issued prohibiting them. When the government officials started the preliminary procedures for them, they were met with a strong boycott in some parts of the country, particularly in the holy places.

The boycott was not confined to only the Shi`a areas but went beyond them to some other areas as well. In Mosul, for example, posters called for the boycott, and taunts faced those who were administering the elections. Some Christians took part in this boycott: a poster appeared on the door of the municipality house saying that the Christian clergymen issued edicts about boycotting the elections and assisting the Muslims in this regard in order to hold on to national unity, safeguard common interests and the age-old harmony. On December 28, Mosul's administrative officer wrote the interior ministry saying that the inspection board in Mosul no longer desired to continue its work and started fearing the consequences of the edicts, that the boycott movement did not stem from inside the governorate but was coming from the capital, and that the slow pace of the elections in the governorates and the reports coming from them were major causes for confusing the minds in Mosul.[1]

It is interesting to mention that the *naqeeb*'s political party, the Free Party, adopted an opposition stance to the government during the elections. The *Asima* newspaper, this party's spokesman, criticized the electoral process. Apparently, the *naqeeb*'s party adopted this stance in order to highlight the inability of the Sa`doun cabinet to carry out the same action which al-Sa`doun used in the past to accuse the *naqeeb*'s cabinet of being unable to carry out.[2]

Al-Sa`doun decided to take charge of the interior ministry so he could personally oversee the progress of elections. Ms Bell wrote a letter dated January 16, 1923, saying, "The Prime Minister, Naji al-Suweedi and Abdul-Lateef al-Mandeel came to me for lunch. Upon his arrival, the Prime Minister announced that he feared he had a shiver, so I told him that the cherry brandy was an excellent medicine. Luckily, I had some of it from the leftovers of a past banquet, so they all took a good part of it, even those who did not have a shiver. After that, we had a very friendly meal. They confided in me that they were considering making a change in the cabinet posts so Naji Beg would shift to the justice ministry and the interior ministry would be given to the Prime Minister. They requested me to prepare the mind of the high commissioner for this change, so I immediately agreed because Muhsin Beg would be much better than Naji for the interior ministry since he is less sensitive about the political impacts. Sir Percy Cox agreed, and the nominations have now been made..."[3]

---

[1]Muhammed Muzaffar al-A`dhami, "Al-Majlis al-Ta'seesi al-Iraqi" (Iraqi founding assembly), an unpublished university thesis, Vol. 1, pp. 357-358.

[2]*Ibid.*, Vol. 1, pp. 356-357.

[3]Burgoyne (op. cit.), Vol. 2, p. 307.

A Policy Change

When al-Sa`doun took charge of the interior ministry, he was expected to undertake tough measures to complete the elections and to punish those who boycotted them. But what actually took place was quite the opposite. Late in January, it was noticed that the electoral process in all parts of Iraq had come to a halt, and the government did nothing about it; rather, it kept quiet about it, as if it was pleased with it.

Moreover, some men of the opposition who were jailed in Hungam [Island] were released. On February 19, four of them reached Baghdad. They were: Ameen al-Charchafchi, Habib al-Khayzaran, Abdul-Rasool Kubba and Sami Khundah. Three others arrived after that; they were: Hamdi al-Pachachi, Ja`far Abul-Timman and Mahdi al-Baseer.

Also, the government decided to deal with the restlessness in the Muntafiq governorate because of the policy of Maj. Yates. Abdul-Aziz al-Qassab, who was an administrative officer in Karbala, was transferred to the same governorate. In mid-March, Cornwallis went to the Muntafiq to discuss the matters in person, and he agreed to the solutions which al-Qassab had submitted for the problems of the governorate. When Cornwallis returned to Baghdad, an order was issued to oust Maj. Yates appointed another man in his place. Al-Qassab describes the new adviser as good-hearted.[1]

All of this indicates that the Sa`doun cabinet changed its policy and started following the way of leniency and tolerance toward the opposition. Here, this question confronts us: what is the reason that made the administration change its policy with the knowledge that al-Sa`doun had resigned from the previous administration in order to protest its leniency policy?

We can attribute this change to two reasons: the first is the aggravation of the Turkish threat at Iraq's northern borders at the time, and it was a very serious threat as we will discuss. It can be said that the Sa`doun cabinet found it necessary to appease the opposition in order to unite the ranks to face that threat.

---

[1]Abdul-Aziz al-Qassab, *Min Thikrayati* (from my memories), Beirut, Lebanon, 1962, pp. 231-235.

As for the second reason, it is the change in the then British policy towards Iraq. On November 23, 1922, the cabinet of Lloyd George resigned, and the new British cabinet refused to ratify the treaty signed with Iraq. Then a strong campaign surfaced in Britain against the government for having spent huge sums of money on Iraq. Some members of the parliament demanded a withdrawal from Iraq at the first opportunity, prompting the new British administration to summon Cox for consultation. Cox flew to London on January 19, 1923, and he was succeeded in his post by Sir Henry Dobbs as a representative.[1] Apparently, the Sa`doun administration did not find in those circumstances what would justify its insistence on continuing the elections, and it may have preferred to wait till public opinion in Britain regarding the treaty settled down.

Turkish Threat Exacerbated

Mustafa Kamal Pasha [Ataturk] had scored a sweeping victory over the Greeks in September 1922. This victory created a great echo in some Iraqi circles, especially among those who were nostalgic about the Turkish era, hoping it would return. The Turks were very proud of this victory, so they started mobilizing their troops on Iraq's northern borders in order to retake Mosul and perhaps all of Iraq.

In October of 1922, secret reports reached Cox saying that recruitment was taking place on a broad scope in Ibn Omar Island, Sirt and Mardin.[2] In December, a telegram reached Cox from the British Consul in Aleppo saying that Turkish forces under the command of Ozdemir Ali Shafiq Beg staged a night attack on the British camp at the northern borders and on the flight station in Zakho and that the Turkish authorities in Midyat put their hand on 750,000 kilograms of grains and placed a tender for the purchase of 2,000 water bags in order to use them to make rafts. They also mobilized all the population to pave roads and build fortifications.[3]

---

[1]Cox and Dobbs, *The Making of Iraq*, Mosul, pp. 64, 67.

[2]Excerpted from London's National Records Center Document No. FO 371-7781.

[3]*Ibid.*, Document No. FO 371-9002.

On January 21, 1923, reports reached Baghdad about four Turkish regiments and attachments having arrived at Ibn Omar Island, prompting the British command in Baghdad to dispatch some of its forces to Mosul. As for the Iraqi army, it was assigned the task of protecting the transport lines. On January 20, Prince Zaid went to Mosul to oversee defence matters on the northern borders and was later joined by Capt. Clayton. The Turks kept sending their agents and proponents to Iraq secretly to contact some chiefs of Iraqi tribes, especially Kurdish tribes, some opposition leaders, and *mujtahids.* Many of their letters fell in the hands of the British.[1]

Ms Bell wrote to her family on January 30, saying, "Are we about to be invaded? If we are subject to an invasion, will we be left alone to defend ourselves according to our resources? If the Turks do not send a brigade or two, we are fine, but if they do, the matter will be different. Despite all the bragging of 'Ismat Pasha, they do not start the attack because they think that the local tribes will be the ones to start it, but these tribes are hesitant about responding to the pressure. The most that can be said is that if the Turks are scheming, we must likewise scheme. But if they are serious, we hold a losing hand." Then Ms Bell says, "Today, the king invited me for tea. He was upset. He wanted to know if we are after all ready to defend the country or if we wanted to leave the matter to him. He told me that whenever necessary, he might accept holding a referendum provided it did not include the Turkish areas, most of whose residents are Arabs, such as Nasibin and Mardin, that the armed forces of both sides must withdraw, and that a neutral country must oversee the referendum. But he will also ask us to strengthen his side by abolishing the mandate. If we do not accept this suggestion, or if the British forces in Mosul are in danger, or if the Arabs are left alone to defend their homeland, he will personally go to the borders to spend his life in it steadfast to the end." Ms Bell comments about Faisal's last statement saying, "By my soul, I seek nothing better than going with him."[2]

The Turkish propaganda in Iraq at the time derived its strength from religion with the claim that the Turks are Muslims and the British

---

[1]Burgoyne (Op. Cit.), Vol. 2, pp. 308-309.

[2] *Ibid.*

people are apostates; therefore, Iraq is obligated by the Shari`a (Islam's legislative system) to be ruled by the Turks rather than by the British. This propaganda in Iraq was widely received, and it was adopted by the *mujtahids* in particular because they, due to the nature of their profession, do not recognize national or political borders which divide the Muslims: Muslims in their view are one nation in which there is no difference between a Turk, an Arab or a Persian, and a Muslim is preferred over an apostate in any case.

Ms Bell wrote on April 12, "The *mujtahids* issued a *fatwa* prohibiting the defending of Iraq from the Turks, and this edict was posted on the gate of the Kadhimiyya Shrine; a copy of it reached me early this morning. The question is: what will the Iraqi government do in this regard? According to the opinion of Mr. Cornwallis, the *mujtahids* who signed the edict must be banished to Iran as Iranian subjects, but this decision is serious: if the king lets matters take their course, the few coming days may be quite serious because the month of Ramadhan is approaching with its religious fervour."[1]

Sheikh Mahdi al-Khalisi was very much inclined towards the Turks as we have already pointed out. It is said that during that period, he was secretly corresponding with them. A noteworthy story spread in al-Kadhimiyya in this regard: a man of Turkish origin named Rif`at Afandi was working for the British intelligence service. He used to go to al-Khalisi after a long absence carrying for him letters that he claimed were sent by Mustafa Kamal Pasha [Ataturk]. Al-Khalisi believed in this scheme, so he would write answers to the letters, which he would then give to Rif`at Afandi in order to get them to reach Mustafa Kamal Pasha, but Rif`at Afandi was getting them to the [British] high commissioner.

We do not know how true this story is, and we did not find in the British documents or in Ms Bell's letters what supports it, and it may be one of the opponents' exaggerations. But it is not unlikely in light of Sheikh Mahdi al-Khalisi's extreme bias towards the Turks.

There is another story narrated to me by one of the residents of al-Kadhimiyya whom I trust: Sheikh Mahdi al-Khalisi received during that period a letter from the Turks, which he put underneath the bed on which he sat according to people's customs at the time. Among those who used

---

[1] *Ibid.*, Vol. 2, p. 313.

to frequently go to his meeting place was a man named "Sh" who worked for the British intelligence and who wanted to get that letter, so he went to Sayyid Muhammed Ridha al-Haidari, whom he offered the sum of 500 rupees in exchange for helping him get the letter from underneath al-Khalisi's bed. But Sayyid Muhammed Ridha rebuked and kicked the man out, so the man returned after some time to say that he was able to get the letter and, with it other letters in exchange for the sum of only 100 rupees.

Back To Prohibition

On March 31, 1923, Cox returned to Baghdad carrying an Appendix for the treaty as a "protocol" containing the consent of the British government to reduce the treaty's period from 20 to 4 years. The king and ministers augured well with this "protocol". On April 30, the king announced to the public a declaration which he opened with this statement: "Through the care of Allah, the most Great, the most Exalted One, and the spirituality of His Chosen Prophet, our government has been able to undertake another big stride along the path of realizing the nation's aspirations by contracting the new Appendix to the Iraqi-British treaty."[1] As soon as this declaration was published in the newspapers, telegrams started showering Baghdad from various parts of Iraq congratulating the king and the administration for this "blessed step".

Meanwhile, it so coincided that the British forces were able to expel the Turkish forces from Rawanduz and some northern areas, thus lessening the Turkish threat, and the Turkish propaganda shrunk to a great extent. It was then that the king and the prime minister felt that the circumstances were suitable to return to the subject of elections and to start its process anew.

The king summoned a number of the mid-Euphrates sheikhs. Among them were: Abdul-Wahid al-Hajj Sikar, Muhsin Abu Tibeekh, Alwan al-Yasiri, Qati` al-Awwadi and Sha`lan Abul-Joon. He convinced them that the "protocol" was a gain for Iraq and that starting the elections was necessary, so the chiefs agreed with his viewpoint with the exception of Abu Tibeekh, who declared that he was unable to oppose the scholars

---

[1] Abdul-Razzaq al-Hassani (op. cit.), Vol. 1, p. 124.

of theology who had decreed that the elections were prohibited, but he will [nevertheless] exert his effort to reach a compromise between the will of the scholars and the policy of the government.[1]

The king dispatched Alwan al-Yasiri and Qati` al-Awwadi to Sheikh Mahdi al-Khalisi in an attempt to convince him to withdraw his edict prohibiting the elections, but they did not succeed in their attempt, and it is said that al-Khalisi charged them of being apostates. In this regard, a story is told that took place with al-Yasiri: having failed to convince al-Khalisi, he went to visit the Shrine of Imam al-Kadhim. When he reached the Shrine's gate, he saw al-Khalisi coming out of it surrounded by his retinue, so al-Khalisi said to him, "How can it be permissible for you to come to visit the Imam while you are an apostate?" Al-Yasiri responded to him with a hurtful word. It is then that a member of the retinue shouted in a loud voice that the public could hear: "Get out, Kafir [apostate, unbeliever]!" Al-Yasiri had to flee from the shrine without his shoes for fear of the public's ire.

Sheikh Mahdi al-Khalisi began making preparations for repeating the announcement of prohibition edicts that had been made public. On May 16, the interior ministry's criminal investigations office was notified that a letter from Najaf reached al-Kadhimiyya regarding the [said] prohibition and that Sheikh Mahdi al-Khalisi consulted with al-Kadhimiyya's scholars around him, who all agreed with him. On the eve of May 17, posters appeared pasted on the gates of the Kadhimiyya Shrine reminding people of the mujtahids' prohibition of the elections and which read, "The government is now trying to fool the people with an appendix to the treaty, and it is exerting its utmost to hold the elections, ignoring the edicts of the *mujtahids*; so, be alert, folks, do not be fooled by decorative speech, be aware and on the look out, O men of reason."[2]

On May 30, a believer submitted a request for a *fatwa* which he directed to the *mujtahids,* the text of which was: "O Islam's Proofs, the Signs of Allah among the people, may Allah strengthen the creed through you and protect the Shari`a. Is it permissible to be involved in some way

---

[1] Muhammed Mahdi al-Baseer, *Tarikh al-Qadhiyya al-Iraqiyya* (history of the Iraqi issue), Baghdad, Iraq, 1923, Vol. 2, p. 501.

[2] Muhammed Muzaffar al-A`dhami (Op. Cit.), Vol. 2, p. 405.

in the elections of the Iraqi founding assembly, or is it not permissible for any Iraqi individual? Please issue your *fatwa* for us, may Allah sustain your shade on the worlds." The *mujtahids* wrote down their edicts under this solicitation for *fatwa*, stating that their previous ruling prohibiting the election remained firm and had not changed. They were: Abul-Hassan al-Isfahani, Hussain al-Naeeni, Hassan al-Sadr, Muhammed-Mahdi al-Sadr, Ali al-Shirazi, Mahdi al-Marayati, Ibrahim al-Salmasi, Muhammed al-Assadi, Muhammed-Mahdi al-Khurasani, Sadiq al-Khalisi, Ibrahim al-A`raji, Radhi al-Khalisi, Assadullah al-Haidari and Isma`eel al-Assadi. The last of them, Sheikh Mahdi al-Khalisi, wrote down saying, "Yes, the judgment by Islam's Proofs and Signs of the Knowing Sovereign continues to be in effect, and anyone who opposes it opposes Allah, and he is on the verge of being a polytheist."[1]

Fatwas of this type kept being issued and pasted on mosques' walls and gates, and copies of them were sent to the governorates. Some enthusiastic youths would volunteer to post them on walls, choosing the early hours of the morning, pretending they were going to perform the *fajr* prayer ritual at mosques, and when they found the streets empty, they would quickly stick the *fatwas* then disappear.

The patience of the British ran out, and so did that of both the king and Abdul-Muhsin al-Sa`doun, but they differed about how to deal with it. Al-Sa`doun was of the view that toughness should be used with the *mujtahids* without fear or hesitation, whereas the British hesitated, feeling apprehensive of such a policy and believing that it could lead to a tribal revolution and security disturbance. As for the king, he still hoped he could establish an understanding with the *mujtahids* and somehow convince them.

It is noteworthy that most *mujtahids* were carrying Iranian citizenship. Some of them were actually of Iranian origin, and some of them took Iranian citizenship during the Ottoman period in order to avoid being conscripted. Al-Sa`doun found in this gap a venue to get them. He was of the opinion that the *mujtahids* were Iranians, foreigners in Iraq without the right to interfere in the politics of this country. But if they wanted to work in politics, they had to accept Iraqi citizenship; otherwise, the government had the right to expel them from the land.

---

[1]*Ibid.*, Appendix No. 16.

Al-Sa`doun was determined to carry out his opinion. On June 9, an amendment was issued to the Baghdad Penal Code. Through this amendment, the government had the right to banish foreigners because of the misdemeanours which they committed. On June 17, the council of ministers held a special session in which it decided to start the elections and to use toughness with those who opposed them by banishing the foreigners from among them outside the country and referring the Iraqis to courts.

During that period, the *Asima* newspaper wrote and advocated for fighting the intruders who had no connection with Iraq and demanding the government to keep anyone who is not an Iraqi or an Arab person from interfering in the nation's affairs.[1]

Preliminaries

Muhsin Abu Tibeekh, as we have already pointed out, had violated what his fellow mid-Euphrates sheikhs had agreed on with regard to starting the elections. It is said that the king was resentful of his stance and asked him to leave Iraq for days and to return when the situation calmed down. Abu Tibeekh decided to leave for Syria on June 14.

Sheikh Mahdi al-Khalisi wanted to turn the occasion of bidding Abu Tibeekh farewell into a political demonstration in defiance of the king and the government. On the morning of the day set for Abu Tibeekh to leave, a large meeting took place in the courtyard of the Kadhimiyya Shrine, so much so that the courtyard was overcrowded with people despite its spaciousness. It was attended by al-Khalisi, many tribal chiefs and men of the opposition. Salman al-Qatifi[2] stood up and delivered an effectively enthusiastic speech, and the attendants kept shouting for the downfall of the government and lauding the life of the *mujahidin*. When the party concluded, the masses surrounded Abu Tibeekh as they headed to the train station in the Karkh flank. Some of them rode Tramway carriages while others rode cars as the rest walked. When they reached

---

[1] *Al-Asima* newspaper of June 14, 1923.

[2] He is the man who later was known as "Salman al-Safwani". He was then one of al-Khalisi's students and was close to him.

Alawi al-Hilla area in al-Karkh, the Karkh residents asked Salman al-Qatifi to repeat the speech which he had delivered at the Kadhimiyya Shrine, so he responded to them and ascended a platform made of benches provided by nearby cafés. Abu Tibeekh ascended and stood beside him. Al-Qatifi hardly began delivering his speech when police commissioner Abdul-Razzaq al-Fadhli advanced toward him and said in a loud voice, "In the name of the government and of the law, I prohibit you from delivering the speech, and if you do not desist from delivering it, I shall use force." A fierce argument erupted between al-Qatifi and al-Fadhli, so Abu Tibeekh interfered and requested al-Qatifi not to deliver his speech in order to avoid bloodshed. The masses were then agitated and pushed themselves against the police. Bullets were shot here and there without hurting anyone. The police were able to snatch Abu Tibeekh into a car, and he was thus taken to the train station. Men from among the Kadhimiyya residents were able to snatch away al-Qatifi and take him to al-Kadhimiyya, where he disappeared.[1]

This incident was to the government like the straw that split the back of the camel: it was regarded by the government as defiance of it and boldness which must not be tolerated, so it set its mind on banishing Sheikh Mahdi al-Kahlisi, issuing its secret orders to police commissioner Abdul-Razzaq al-Fadhli to get ready to arrest him at the nearest opportunity.

Al-Fadhili had at the time 20 infantry and 20 cavalry policemen. The government asked him if he had enough or if he needed more force. He answered, saying that he had enough and that he did not want more so he would not attract people's attention to him lest they should get ready to resist. Al-Fadhli talked to me about those days, saying that he started preparing himself to arrest al-Khalisi, waiting for the right time. Among what he did in this regard was sending some members of undercover police in plainclothes to mingle with the public inside and outside the Shrine. He let some of them pretend to be beggars sitting at the Shrine's gates and pretending to beg. When a supporter of al-Khalisi came to stick a poster of *fatwas* or announcements on one of the Shrine's gates, they

---

[1]Excerpted from the handwritten manuscript of memoirs of Salman al-Safwani; these are important memoirs which we hope will be published.

would seize him or point him out to the nearby policemen who would catch him.

On the afternoon of June 21, a young man from the Khalisi family came. His name is Ali Naqi, a grand nephew of al-Khalisi. He wanted to post an announcement on one of the Shrine's gates, and he was noticed by a couple of undercover policemen who tried to arrest him, but some residents rushed to help him flee. Then a third policeman came to help his fellows, and the three were finally able to catch and take him to the Sarai police station. During the interrogation with him at the station, he admitted that it was his duty to post the *fatwas* that the *mujtahids* had issued, giving the names of some of them. He also admitted that he was not working alone but was assisted by Salman al-Qatifi and two sons of al-Khalisi, namely Hassan and Ali.

As Ali Naqi was stating his admissions at the police station, Hassan al-Khalisi went to the Shrine to post an announcement on its Bab al-Qibla gate. When a policeman attempted to arrest him, Ali shouted at the people saying, "Kill this man. He is a Jewish unbeliever!" It was then that people assaulted the policeman, seized him, took him inside the Shrine's courtyard and beat him. Hassan took out a knife from his pocket and said to him, "I am going to kill you." But the policeman was able to slip away from the people's hands with a great deal of difficulty, returning to the police station barefoot, his face yellowish. A group of policemen rushed to arrest those who attacked the policeman but did not find any of them and thereafter kept looking for Hassan al-Khalisi and his brother, Ali, as well as for Salman al-Qatifi. When the latter were found, they were escorted with Ali Naqi to Baghdad, where the four men were jailed in the Sarai.[1]

Al-Khalisi Arrested

Arresting al-Khalisi's sons was akin to checking the pulse. When the government saw that arresting them did not result in the uproar that it feared, it decided to arrest al-Khalisi himself, setting the eve of June 26 as the date to do it.

---

[1]Muhammed Muzaffar al-A`dhami (op. cit.), Vol. 1, pp. 418-419.

Some evidence indicates that the king at the time was puzzled and hesitant. Deep down, he held al-Khalisi in contempt and preferred to banish him out of Iraq, but he feared the consequences. As for Abdul-Muhsin al-Sa'doun, he was determined to banish al-Khalisi and was confident that no danger would result from it. It is worth mentioning in this regard that Sir Henry Dobbs had assumed the post of acting high commissioner since early last May. Like his predecessor, Cox, he was apprehensive of banishing al-Khalisi, but al-Sa'doun pledged to him that he could do it without stirring any security disturbance, and Dobbs felt comfortable with his words, leaving the matter to him to do it according to his own responsibility.

The king wanted to be distant from Baghdad when al-Khalisi was to be banished, so he decided to conduct a tour to Basra. He arranged with al-Sa'doun to send the latter a telegram from Basra if he finally consented to banish al-Khalisi and that the code between them would be "the hen" as a reference to al-Khalisi.

At 1:00 pm June 18, the king left Baghdad aboard a riverine ship belonging to Abdul-Qadir al-Khudhayri. His retinue was comprised of Rustam Haidar, Naji al-Suweedi, Safwat al-Awwa, Abdullah al-Madhayfi and Nasir ad-Deen al-Naqeeb. His companions were: Tahsin Qadri and Tawfiq al-Damaluji. It is thought that, from the time of his departure from Baghdad and till his arrival at Basra, the king's mind was preoccupied with the Khalisi matter, not knowing if it was right to banish al-Khalisi; therefore, he instructed Naji al-Suweedi to send a telegram to al-Sa'doun to advise him to "leave the hen alone."[1] But al-Sa'doun refused to listen to the king's advice, and he sent him a telegram informing him of the necessity of banishing al-Khalisi and that the government could no longer be patient with him. This is the text of al-Sa'doun's telegram:

"We submitted in our previous telegram that some people tried to stick up [posters of] *fatwas* in al-Kadhimiyya banning the elections, and the one who posted them is al-Khalisi's grandson, Sheikh Ali, so the police immediately arrested him. A short while later, Sheikh Hassan, son of Sheikh Mahdi, tried

---

[1]Khayri al-Omari, *Shakhsiyyat Iraqiyya* (Iraqi personalities), Baghdad, Iraq, 1955, Vol. 1, p. 52.

to stick another *fatwa,* so the uniformed policeman who was standing nearby tried to prevent him, but he refused and even urged the public to attack the policeman. He attacked him with them holding a knife in his hand with which he stabbed the policeman, whereupon he, too, was arrested. When Sheikh Ali was interrogated, he admitted that all those actions were carried out on orders of al-Khalisi and both his sons, Sheikh Ali and Sheikh Hassan, in Baghdad and al-Kadhimiyya. Anyway, the government cannot put up with his actions. I see it necessary to quickly expel him, his sons, al-Qatifi and Sheikh Ali, al-Khalisi's grandson. The high commissioner agrees to their expulsion, provided it will not be to Iran. If you consent, they will be sent to Basra and from there to Jidda by sea. No report has yet reached me from Muhsin Shalash."

The king answered in a telegram saying,

"If the action towards Sheikh Mahdi [al-Khalisi] is necessary, I wish it should be done with all respect and in a way that does not undermine his personal dignity and that his family must not be harmed or scared." The king followed it with another telegram in which he said, "You have the absolute authority with regards to what you see as fit to do in al-Kadhimiyya and Baghdad in order to maintain security and the government's honour, and a strict plan must be undertaken. After al-Kadhimiyya, inform the *mujtahids* of Najaf through the administrative officer of what has taken place with al-Khalisi and his followers and assure them to continue to maintain tranquillity and to carry out their religious duties while notifying them of the government's sorrow for having been forced to undertake these measures despite the peaceful means which it has followed up to the present. Announce this in the newspapers in an appropriate way."

On June 25, the government issued an official statement in which it condemned the *mujtahids* in an ugly way, describing them as intruders and having nothing to do with the Arab cause and not concerned about the true interests of the people, and that they created statements which they claimed were derived from the religious canons, but they meant by them nothing other than undermining the elections, misleading public opinion, and blocking the people from ascending to power. The statement also said, "The clemency and patience demonstrated by the government encouraged those foreign maniacs to go to extremes in misleading the masses to the extent that they recently encroached on the sanctity of the holy shrines with movements which fully violate the religious ethics, movements which men of piety and creed avoid, by posting on the shrines of the Imams, peace be upon them, and on walls of sacred places posters which corrupt and agitate the public under the guise and in the name of the creed, thus violating the sanctity of the holy places and exposing them to such misleading aims which were not based except on ill intentions and on harming the people's interests." The statement concluded thus: "On this occasion, it must be known that the government cannot tolerate such actions and will punish anyone who plays havoc with the people's legitimate rights."[1]

The *Asima* (capital) newspaper commented on this statement saying,

> "Boycotting the elections is the greatest manifestation of the foreign nature of the intrusive notion which is not sincere to Arab nationalism and to Iraq's independence." The newspaper demanded the government to strike with an iron fist at the sinful hands that mixed poison with fat in order to be able to crush Arab nationalism throughout Iraq.[2]

At a late hour on the eve of June 26, al-Khalisi was arrested, and everything was done quietly!

---

[1]Abdul-Razzaq al-Hassani (op. cit.), Vol. 1, pp. 130-133.

[2]*Al-Asima* newspaper of June 25, 1921.

How The Arrest Was Made

Al-Khalisi used to go every night to his school after sunset and evening prayers, and his school was adjacent to his house. He would deliver some lessons to the school's students, then he would go home. Abdul-Razzaq al-Fadhli put his plan to arrest al-Khalisi at a late hour of the night so the streets would be empty of pedestrians.

On the night when it was decided to arrest al-Khalisi, al-Fadhli commissioned one of the undercover policemen to monitor the school and to inform him when al-Khalisi would leave it for home. At about eleven o'clock, when al-Fadhli was sure that al-Khalisi was at home, he hurried to him in two cars accompanied by one police officer and five policemen as well as the mayor of the Shuyookh quarter.

We have two different narratives about how al-Khalisi was arrested. One of them is narrated by Abdul-Razzaq al-Fadhli, and the other is narrated by Salman al-Safwani. Here we state both narratives, quoting their handwritten memoirs:

> Al-Fadhli says: "As regarding how he—meaning al-Khalisi—was taken [into custody], I went to his house after 10:00 pm when he had returned home from his school. I knocked at his door, so he talked to me from the house's second story and asked me, 'What do you want?' I said, 'Please open the door so I may notify you of the order which I have now received from the government.' The man came down, so I said to him, 'The assembly of ministers is now in full session at the palace and is asking you to attend; so, please come with me because they have sent you a special car.' He said, 'I am a man of religion, and I am not supposed to get out of my home after dark.' I answered him, saying, 'Sir, you are a politician since you have interfered in matters in which you have no right to get involved; therefore, you have to come with me immediately.' He said, 'Let me enter the bathroom, then perform my ablution and go with you,' whereupon I consented. He wanted to lock the [house] door, but I prevented him. He actually entered the bathroom as I stood at the door and waited for him for almost half an hour, but he

did not get out. I had to send an Afghani Commissioner, Sayyid Hassan, to the bathroom to see what happened to al-Khalisi. When he entered, he found out that the man's nerves had convulsed, and he could not walk. Since the time when al-Khalisi was supposed to arrive at the train station was about to pass, I seated him in the car and went to the station."

As for the second narrative it is narrated by al-Safwani, who quotes al-Khalisi himself. He said the following:

"I was asleep on my house's rooftop and was awakened by a continuously violent knocking at the door, so I rose from my bed and stretched my head on the side of the door where I saw the house surrounded by armed forces, and so were the roads leading to it. I inquired from over the roof about who the knocking man was, and he asked me to get down and open the door quickly. I then realized that the large force was brought to arrest me without any doubt. I thought of playing the role of either the eagle or the sparrow: when the sparrow falls into the hand of the hunter, it tries to resist in order to free itself and fly, and it uses its beak, claws and wings, which are all its weapons of resistance. But the result is that it loses its feathers, its legs break and it is exposed to death. As for the eagle, it takes to calm when it falls in the hand of the hunter, surrendering to fate and destiny in anticipation for an opportunity to win its freedom. I could cry out for help and get my folks in al-Kadhimiyya to come to my rescue, and they would quickly leap to save and defend me. But what would the result be other than bloodshed, and the matter would end by arresting me in abjection and humiliation? I quickly and calmly chose to be an eagle, and I told my family not to raise their voices. I quickly put on my clothes and opened the door where I was likewise quickly snatched into a car to the train [station]."

When al-Khalisi arrived, the train station was pitch black, and it was surrounded by a large force of soldiers and policemen. A special train was prepared in it comprised of one engine and three carriages, one of which was set aside for transporting al-Khalisi, and it was a first-class carriage. As for the other two carriages, they were third-class carriages for transporting the force in charge of guarding the train along its path.

The four men who were jailed at the Sarai in Baghdad were brought and lodged in the carriage where al-Khalisi was. The darkness was quite intense, so the men did not know that al-Khalisi was in the same carriage with them. Salman al-Safwani says the following in his memoirs: "I was the only smoker among my fellows, so I lit a match to see, and what I saw was horrific: I saw imam al-Khalisi with his head uncovered and sitting in the corner of the carriage putting his head in his hands, lowering his head, and there were signs of grief and exhaustion on him. I advanced towards him, greeted him and kissed his hands, and thus did my fellows. I sat next to him in total silence, not believing whether I was awake or in a dream."[1]

The train carried them towards Basra. On the morning of the next day, the newspapers in Baghdad published an official declaration as follows:

> "Convincing evidences have been plentiful that Sheikh Mahdi al-Khalisi and both his sons as well as Sheikh Salman al-Qatifi and Sheikh Ali Naqi are the ones who did what was reported in the previous declaration; therefore, they have been expelled from Iraqi lands. The government would like to announce once more that it is determined to hand over the legal authority to the true representatives of the people, and it cannot tolerate any foreign whims playing havoc, under the guise of religious authority, with the vital matters relevant to the nation's rights."[2]

The *Mujtahids'* Movement

When the report spread in al-Kadhimiyya in the morning, people refused to open their shops in protest, and they started crowding in the Shrine.

---

[1] *Al-Hawadith* newspaper of April 11, 1930.

[2] *Al-Iraq* newspaper of June 27, 1923.

Abdul-Razzaq al-Fadhli demonstrated noticeable activity to disperse the crowds, spreading an air of terrorism in the town. He sent out callers to call in the markets, threatening anyone who would continue to close his shop with strict penalties. He also sent members of the police force to write down the names of the owners of the closed shops and to look for them. His efforts in this regard resulted in people gradually opening their shops. When it was hardly midday, the town returned to its normal status and nothing remained in it save some rumours which people were whispering here and there as they turned right and left for fear someone would see them.

The same took place in Baghdad: unrest spread in some markets, especially in the brass market and in some neighbouring markets, but the tough measures which the government undertook made people rush to open their shops as their brothers in al-Kadhimiyya had done.

A group of clergymen in al-Kadhimiyya tried to carry out a movement declaring their solidarity with al-Khalisi, protesting his banishment. They met at the house of Sheikh Mahdi al-Marayati in the Tell quarter and sent other clergymen messages asking them to join their movement, but those folks asked to be excused and did not support them. It is said that a senior *mujtahid* was not satisfied with not supporting them and rather articulated harsh words abusing Sheikh al-Khalisi for his interference in politics. He said that he had repeatedly advised him, but he did not listen. Thus, the movement died in infancy, and its advocates dispersed.

But the matter in al-Najaf went on contrary to what had taken place in al-Kadhimiyya: as soon as the report reached al-Najaf in the morning of June 27, the markets became restless, people assembled, and the *mujtahids* declared their solidarity with al-Khalisi and that banishing him was an insult to the religion and to its adherents, and they decided to migrate from Iraq in protest.

On the afternoon of that day, those *mujtahids* left Najaf. In their vanguard were Sayyid Abul-Hassan al-Isfahani and Mirza Hussain al-Naeeni. They went to the Sahla Mosque [in Kūfa] for *i`tikaf*, seclusion, for one night, as customary. They were visited there by a crowd of the people of Kufa. On the morning of the next day, the *mujtahids* went to Kufa, and from there, they rode steamboats to Twairij. From Twairij, they rode in cars to Karbala.

The government had prepared itself for the matter in advance. On June 26, Mawlud Mukhlus reached Karbala after a royal decree had been issued appointing him as the administrative officer of that governorate. This administrator began undertaking tough measures as soon as he reached Karbala. He sent a telegram to Najaf's mayor saying, "You must not permit anyone to travel to Iran with the Iranian scholars. Also, you must not allow anyone to get out of Najaf except with the government's permission. Ban the transportation means from transporting passengers who have no permit from the police administration till another order is issued. Convey this to the police directorate." The mayor responded to him, saying, "No resident of al-Najaf travelled to Iran with the Iranian scholars. Rather, they travelled to Karbala, and they all are in Karbala today; nobody remains here who was to join them. As for absolutely preventing all passengers and travellers from going to Karbala and elsewhere, this produces embarrassment and hearsay, while the condition—praise to Allah—in the county is complete calm and tranquility; so, please be clear about who should be prevented and who should not, and we await your order."[1]

When the *mujtahids* reached Karbala, a special tent was prepared for their stay, and people were prevented from contacting them. They were joined by a number of Karbala's *mujtahids*. The administrative officer tried to reason with them, but they insisted on leaving Iraq. The government, therefore, sent a telegram to the administrative officer ordering him to facilitate the travel of those among them who were bearing Iranian citizenship. As for the rest, they must be kept in Iraq and placed under police surveillance.

On July 1, Salih Hamam, Karbala's police director, undertook the travel procedures of the *mujtahids* who were bearing Iranian citizenship, and they were nine in number: Abul-Hassan al-Isfahani, Hussain al-Naeeni, Jawad al-Jawahiri, Ali al-Shahristani, Abdul-Hussain al-Shirazi, Ahmed al-Khurasani, Mahdi al-Khurasani, Hassan al-Tabatabai and Abdul-Hussain al-Tabatabai. There were 25 men among their followers. They were all lodged in cars under strict police protection. When they

---

[1]Abdul-Rahim Muhammed-Ali, "Al-Najaf wal Majlis al-Ta'seesi (Najaf and the founding assembly)" in the *Rabita* magazine of Najaf of September 1975.

reached the Khirr [1] near Baghdad, they were taken to the Dora roundabout, where they crossed the Tigris. This was meant to get them away from the eyes of the public so nobody would come to know of their arrival. On the morning of July 2, a special train took them to Khanaqin, from which they were taken behind the borders.

On July 3, the *Iraq* newspaper published a report under the heading "Some Scholars Travel to Iran", the text of which was:

> "It has been rumoured in the capital that some *mujtahid* scholars in al-Najaf al-Ashraf were determined to depart from Iraqi lands, and we investigated the matter with the press directorate which officially informed us that some of the respectful Iranian scholars, following the publication of the government's declaration about foreigners interfering in the country's political affairs, had demonstrated their desire to return home to Iran. His Excellency, the administrative director of Karbala, met them in the name of the Iraqi government and explained to them that the government did not harbour anything bad against them and that they were fully encompassed with respect and regards so long as they maintained their service of the religion by guiding people to matters of the creed. The scholars demonstrated their extreme desire to return home; therefore, the government conducted all the required facilities for providing convenient travel for them."

On the same day, that is, July 3, Jalal ad-Deen Khan Kayhan, the general Iranian Consul in Baghdad, wrote the high commissioner protesting the deportation of the *mujtahids*. In his letter, he wrote saying that the *mujtahids* were roughly treated as though they were criminals and that this was regarded as an unjustifiable insult to representatives of

---

[1] There used to be a small river in Baghdad called "Nahr al-Khirr نهر الخر" up to the 1950s over which a bridge was installed. The river was dumped and the bridge removed when the Mansour fashionable quarter of Baghdad was established. The location of that bridge is what is now known as the Harthiyya in the Karkh flank. The author here is referring to the location of that bridge. – Tr.

the Islamic faith in general and of the Shi`a sect in particular. The high commissioner answered him by saying that Sheikh Mahdi al-Khalisi was expelled by the Iraqi government in accordance with the residency law because he interfered in the electoral process in an illegal way, issuing *fatwas* excommunicating those who would participate in them. As for the other *mujtahids*, the government did not deport them: the administrative officer of Karbala tried to convince them to stay [as they would be] encompassed with the government's respect if they restricted their efforts to religious matters only, but they insisted on returning to their homeland, Iran, and the Iraqi government provided them with all means of comfort during the trip and preparing for them a special train, despite the fact that they had tried to stir demonstrations against the government as they were on their way from Najaf to Karbala. The high commissioner concluded his letter with an apology for being late in sending his answer since that delay was necessary for the high commissioner to look into the complaints which the general Iranian Consul had stated.[1]

An Incident In Hilla

When the *mujtahids* were deported on July 1, Hilla was set in motion to protest. The religious scholar in Hilla at the time was Sheikh Muhammed Sammakah. He was a representative of one of Najaf's senior *mujtahids*. This man kept instigating people to demonstrate in support of the *mujtahids* and to protest their deportation. This was not taken well by the governorate's administrator, Naji Shawkat, so he instructed the police director to expel the man to Baghdad.

Sheikh Muhammed Sammakah was expelled on the eve of July 2. Naji Shawkat tells us in his memoirs about how he was arrested, saying,

> "I asked the police director to visit the man at his house
> following his return from his evening prayers at the mosque
> and to escort him to the train station. The man was
> accustomed, after performing the prayer ritual at the mosque
> near his house, to remain awake for some time with those

---

[1]Excerpted from the National Records Center in London, Document No. FO 371 – 9047.

who brought him for prayer, after which he would go home. Apparently, the police director was new to the procedures and precautions in such circumstances, so he did something reckless which almost got us into trouble: he accompanied three policemen and surrounded the said mosque, coercing the *mjutahid's* representative to go to the train station. Thus, he snatched him away from his group and supporters, taking him to the station. Soon those supporters came out to the street, staging boisterous demonstrations, and it was almost 10 in the evening. As I was waiting for the results of the deportation, my servant said that the residents started surrounding my house and that their number kept increasing. I used to live in the house alone, and I had nobody with me in it other than the said servant, so I put out the lights in my room which oversees the street. I kept watching what went on in the street, and my pistol was in my hand. Suddenly the servant said that those who gathered asked him to open the door so they would be able to enter and meet me. The situation was extremely critical and was aggravated by the fact that I did not receive from the police director anything about what went on and which was concluded, and I saw that it would be better not to meet people so they might not ask for something which I would not accept, such as refusing to deport the deputy of the *mujtahid.* I, therefore, asked my servant to climb to the house's rooftop and to slip to the assistant police director who was in a nearby house to summon him to meet me immediately after undertaking the measures which he saw fit to keep the crowds around the house away. The said assistant deserved my good impression of him, for he was able to disperse the crowds that assembled in the streets. At 11:00 pm, the situation started improving, and the crowd began dispersing."[1]

---

[1]Naji Shawkat, *Sira wa Thikrayat* (a biography and memories), Beirut, Lebanon, 1975, p. 69.

Naji Shawkat says that the British adviser in the governorate, namely Maj. Longrick, who became famous later because of the books he wrote about Iraq, visited him in his house at 11 that night and kept asking him about the reasons that prompted him to deport the sheikh without taking his opinion into consideration in his capacity as governorate adviser. He hinted to me that he could not bear the responsibility for the deterioration of the general situation. He advised him to abolish the deportation order and to release the sheikh immediately. The administrator told him that he was ready to bear every responsibility for what would take place as a result of his action and that he would notify the administration in Baghdad that he undertook the deportation decision without consulting the adviser. Then the administrator asked the adviser not to accept any meeting with anyone in this regard on the basis that he—the administrator—had undertaken it at his own responsibility.

The next day, the town of Hilla was calm. When the administrator reached his office for his usual job, he was visited by Salman al-Barrak, who asked him to permit a delegation of residents to visit him. The delegation was comprised of 20 individuals. When they entered the administrator's office, they kept pleading that he help them repatriate the deported sheikh, so the administrator said to them, "If you pledge to me to end the boycott of the elections and to ensure their usual process, I promise you to return him one week later." They expressed their readiness to cooperate with the government in this regard, so the administrator sent a telegram to the interior ministry asking to lift the surveillance from the sheikh and to permit him to return due to the disappearance of the causes that led to his deportation. Longrick visited the administrator after that and said to him, "You have noticeably succeeded in your plan, and I was afraid of the consequences of this deportation."[1]

The King In The Mid-Euphrates Region

We had said that the king wanted to be distant from Baghdad when al-Khalisi was arrested, so he went to Basra. The king did not leave Basra except after making sure that al-Khalisi was arrested and that everything

---

[1] *Ibid.*, pp. 69-71.

went well. On the eve of June 27, the king and his retinue left Basra. One of destiny's ironies is that al-Khalisi's train reached the Basra [train] station as the king's train was leaving it. Salman al-Safwani says, "The train stopped at the Basra station where we met His Majesty's private train exiting Basra. Those inside it were eying us through the carriages' windows which were brightly lit with electrical lights."[1]

On June 28, a great celebration was held for the king in Diwaniyya which was attended by many chiefs of mid-Euphrates tribes. Baghdad's newspapers were verbose in detailing that celebration, describing the attendants as heroes of the 1920 Revolution. Below is the text of what the *Al-Iraq* newspaper had published in this regard, as reported by its correspondent in Diwaniyya:

Sheikhs of Shamiyya, its heads and tribal chiefs met, and they included the tribes of: al-Zawalim, Albu Hassan, al-Safran, al-A`ajeet, Banu Zraij, al-Agra`, Albu-Hahthah, `Ifach, Albu-Dayr, al-Daghara, al-Khuza`il, al-Shibl, al-Fatla, Banu Hassan, Al-Sa`eed and others in a large pavilion in the afternoon. They met with His Majesty the king, to whom they swore their most solemn oath that they would sacrifice themselves for the sake of following the policy of His Majesty and in obeying his commands, that they were ready to fight any idea or plot jeopardizing the country's main Arab national interests and crush anyone who promoted such jeopardizing, and that they would not tolerate a single day's delay in holding the elections. Among what leader Sheikh Sha`lan Abul-Joon said was: "We are Your Majesty's strong arm in achieving the nation's absolute independence through the means which you prefer; we are at your command this day and tomorrow as we were yesterday." His Majesty responded to him by saying that the government that day belonged to the nation, "As for myself, I am only its senior servant who tries to realize its aspirations of freedom. I am very pleased with your sense of nationalism in the necessity of holding the reins of its affairs. If we squeeze the dust of this land which has freed itself, the ancestors' blood will drip from it. This land can never surrender to a foreign call or expose its entity to peril. The nation needs a constitution made by its representatives according to its own will, customs and traditions." It was then that enthusiasm intensified, and everyone said, "Āmeen" for all words of His Majesty. They

---

[1] *Al-Hawadith* newspaper of April 11, 1930.

added saying, "Our tribes, in their entirety, are your sharp-edged sword in supporting your wise policy, and this we pledge before Allah and before the world."[1]

What was published by the Baghdadi newspapers was, of course, meant to tell the public that the mid-Euphrates tribes, especially those that had participated in the 1920 Revolution, stood beside the king and supported his deportation of al-Khalisi and the expulsion of the *mujtahids*. It is noteworthy that the newspapers were not satisfied with what they published but kept publishing lengthy articles after that indirectly speaking ill of the *mujtahids*, describing them as foreigners, that they had a narrow mentality and wanted to undermine the state's entity which was established on the skulls of thousands of martyrs.

The most violent articles published on abusing the *mujtahids* were written by Salman al-Sheikh Dawood, which he signed with his initials "SD". Below is a sample of one of his articles, and it is titled "Moral Cowardice" in which he said:

> "Although these oscillators had lived under the Arab shade of Iraq, inhaling the air of this land, they never stopped fighting it and scheming against it under a decorative cover, the brightness of which steals the vision of the simpletons of this land, the cover of religion, religious unity, etc. which cannot be achieved due to the spread of the principle of nationalism. I am sure they meant nothing but weakening the blessed Arab movement. Thus, they betray the land, the spacious shade of which they enjoy in order to serve a foreign nation which has been one of the greatest factors in crushing the Arabs' state and in annihilating their [Arabs'] prosperous civilization. Despite the attitude of hostility towards this land, these individuals, when confronted, demonstrated all cowardice and submission [to foreigners]."[2]

---

[1] *Al-Iraq* newspaper of June 30, 1923.

[2] *Ibid.*, July 5, 1923.

In another article under the heading "The Simpleton Mentality," Salman al-Sheikh Dawood attacked the *mujtahids* whom he described as working in politics without having any knowledge of modern sciences, which are necessary for everyone who works in politics: they do not know the peoples' history and psychology; rather, they do not even know the borders of their own homeland, nor do they know of their folks' history but a page full of entertaining stories and myths."[1]

The *Mujtahids* In Iran

When the *mujtahids* were expelled out of Iraq through Khanaqin, they went to Kermanshah, which they reached on July 7. In that town, a huge reception was made for them in which the people and government officials participated. The *mujtahids* stayed in Kermanshah for one month. The British Consul in that town sent a telegram on July 17 to Sir Percy Lorraine, the British Minister Plenipotentiary in Tehran, describing what went on in the town during their stay. He said, "The *mujtahids*' wrath was directed at the Iraqi government. They told a crowd of people that they would never return to Iraq except with conditions which include the deposition of King Faisal and that they had letters from senior tribal chiefs in Iraq who supported their demand." In his telegram, the British Consul pointed out an interesting phenomenon: the Communist Party in Kermanshah suddenly became quite religious, and its members declared their attachment to one of the *mujtahids*, namely Sayyid Ali al-Shahristani. They kept attending the mosque every day for his sake, and the head of the party became like his spokesman. The Consul said that this phenomenon could lead to serious consequences, and it gave room to the Bolsheviks to infiltrate. The Russian Consul, accompanied by his interpreter, Mirza Ibrahim Khan, visited the three *mujtahids*: Sayyid Abul-Hassan al-Isfahani, Mirza Hussain al-Naeeni and Sayyid Ali al-Shahristani. But al-Isfahani and al-Naeeni did not speak to him. As for al-Shahristani, his meeting with him was cordial. Then the British Consul mentioned in his telegram that Mirza Ibrahim Khan succeeded a few days earlier in instigating the residents against Britain, so the markets were

---

[1] *Ibid.*, July 10, 1923.

shut down and a demonstration went out, but the military authority prevented it on instructions from Sayyid Ali al-Shahristani.[1]

The *mujtahids* left Kermanshah for the town of Qum. In the towns and villages through which they passed, huge unmatched receptions were made for them, so much so that some people were throwing themselves before the *mujtahids'* cars in order to demonstrate their readiness to sacrifice their lives for their sake. On August 17, the *mujtahids* reached Qum where they settled. It is a sacred town that has an opulent Shrine for one of the daughters of Imam al-Kadhim, and it houses a large seminary for the study of religious sciences.

The anti-Britain movement kept escalating in various parts of Iran, especially in the capital, Tehran. The Communist Party undertook an important role in this process. When the month of Muharram started on the 14th of August, the mourning speakers and preachers kept instigating the public against the British people, calling on them to stage demonstrations and to boycott British-made goods.

Sheikh Muhammed al-Khalisi was deported to Iran the year before, as we pointed out in the previous chapter. He settled in Tehran. When the *mujtahids* were expelled, Sheikh Muhammed took advantage of the opportunity. He is an articulate speaker, and he kept launching violent campaigns against Britain and its supporters. Sir Percy Lorraine stated the following in a telegram to London: "Sheikh Muhammed al-Khalisi is regarded as the main instigator against the British in Tehran, and he is in close contact with the Russian Consulate." He also stated that the Soviet officials in Iran utilized the incident of expelling the *mujtahids* as a weapon in their hands to instigate the public against Britain.[2]

Sir Percy Lorraine had to go to Baghdad in a military plane sent for him from Baghdad in order to talk to the Iraqi officials to convince them to return the *mujtahids* to Iraq. But he returned without any result. On August 30, Lord Curzon, the British foreign minister, sent a lengthy

---

[1]Excerpted from the Public Records Directorate in London, Document No. FO 37-9047.

[2]Excerpted from the Public Records Directorate in London, Document No. FO 371-9047.

telegram in which he explained the tense situation in Iran as a result of deporting the *mujtahids*. Below is a portion of that telegram:

"Dear Lord: the incident of the *mujtahids* leaving Iraq and the results of their reaching this land has been the topic of a series of telegrams which I see it necessary to submit to you. The circumstances of their exit and the way they were treated demonstrated a difference of opinion between this commission and the high commissioner in Baghdad. From the viewpoint of British policy in Iran, there can be nothing worse than this incident. After a long period of unpleasant relations with the Iranian government, hostility towards Britain started weakening, while the reputation and influence of the Soviet Commission reached the bottom, and the path was open to restore cordial relations between Britain and Iran on the basis that Britain is the only state that can and would like to help Iran along the path of administrative progress and economic development due to the traditional sentiments it has in this regard. But the banishment of Sheikh Mahdi al-Khalisi and the exit that followed it of the senior *mujtahids* accompanied by 26 of their followers in the protest resulted in a great uproar in Iran based on the claim that those men were holy individuals who were forcibly kicked out of Iraq by the British, and the British have thus dealt the worst insult to the Shi`a creed, removing the mask from what they used to claim to be loving Islam and [now] introducing themselves as its bitter enemies. It is not necessary to add to this the fact that the Bolsheviks have taken advantage of it fully: now they have a weapon in their hand for the propaganda which they did not expect, so they have used it with all their power to stir hostility towards Britain and ire against it. On my arrival to Baghdad and exchanging of opinions with Sir Henry Dobbs and other British officials in Iraq, I found the subject to be more precise than I used to imagine: the Iraqi officials undertook the banishment measures on their own and at their own responsibility, and they are very happy with the results and were not pleased with my coming to Baghdad, for they are concerned the British pressure on them would lead to a return to the way in which they used to be and to sacrificing what they believe to be their own interest. In reality, their situation forces them to resign when they are under pressure, and they emphasize that there is no other government that can replace them. If this takes place, the British authority will find it necessary to return to direct administration, something which the British government of His Majesty does not accept. On the other hand, the Iraqi government does not have the intention or the desire for the *mujtahids'* return to Iraq during any set time period. Thereupon, I felt that I should insist on my viewpoint which is: the circumstances in Iran, according to my understanding of them, do not lead except to a total failure in reaching a middle way for the solution."

Sir Percy Lorraine pointed out in his telegram that during his stay in Baghdad, he met King Faisal in the presence of Sir Henry Dobbs, Abdul-Muhsin al-Sa`doun and Cornwallis. He found al-Sa`doun very rigid about the return of the *mujtahids*, whereas the king was inclined to look into whatever would calm down the serious situation in Iran. They finally agreed to look into the matter of the return of the *mujtahids* after the end of the elections of the founding assembly and the ratification of the treaty and its appendix. Lorraine stated that after his return to Tehran, he met the Shah, and he also met the ministers and discussed the subject with which their minds were preoccupied. He said to them, "The interest of the Iranian and Iraqi governments in this regard is one and the same, which is: the religious authority must be concentrated in the hands of the senior *mujtahids* in Iran such that making them above the civil government's authority is something odd which no modern government can tolerate for long; therefore, it is natural for the Iraqi government to resist such hegemony with all the energy it has." Lorraine says that this statement had its impact on the Shah and his ministers.[1]

---

[1]Excerpted from the Public Records Directorate in London, Document No. FO 371-9048.

Al-Khalisi In Basra

The train that transported Sheikh Mahdi al-Khalisi and his four fellows from Baghdad reached Basra's station on the eve of June 27, as we pointed out before. These men were moved from the station directly to a mansion on Shatt al-Arab in the direction of the Sarai called "Agha Ja`far Mansion". The government claimed at the time that it housed them in that mansion in order to provide for them the means of comfort and opulence since that mansion was regarded in those days as the most opulent in Basra. But Salman al-Safwani denies the authenticity of the government's claim. He has said, "True, it housed us in that luxurious mansion, but it put us in a basement room the outer appearance of which is mercy and the inner is a painful torment."[1]

Al-Safwani describes what they went through in that room, saying:

> "There was nothing in that room, not even a straw mat, for us to sit on. We, therefore, slept while seated that night, supporting ourselves upon the room's windows, and the heat was intense. The mosquitoes were large and many swarms of them kept attacking us mercilessly, so we could not close our eyes. Moreover, we were not fed since the night imam al-Khalisi was arrested, and a hungry person cannot sleep. If one of us went to the toilet, he was escorted by an armed Indian soldier. Those soldiers were extremely fierce. In the morning, a few loaves of ordinary bread were brought to us and a piece of white cheese that had become like a rock and a few slices of cucumbers, so we could not eat any of that food. At noon and in the evening, we were brought the same, so we did not eat of it and decided to stage a hunger strike. Our strike lasted three days, during which we were completely exhausted. On our strike's third day, a British police inspector came to us and cast a look at the room in which we were lodged. He smelled a foul stink coming from the room's corner next to

---

[1]*Al-Hawadith* newspaper of April 11, 1930.

the door. He drew closer to it and saw some bread, cheese, and cucumbers piled up on each other without anyone touching it till it rotted. He saw how the room was empty, even of straw mats and that we had nothing to sleep on. Signs of resentment appeared on his face, and he left the room without saying one word. A few hours later, the inspector returned to us. He had gone to Basra in a steamboat. The soldiers brought us furniture that filled a full house: carpets, beds, bottles, chairs, tables, utensils, ration items and different types of food with amazing generosity. We were told that the government had assigned a chef to cook food for us according to our taste. Since I was the only smoker among my fellows, it was decided to supply me with 4,000 cigarettes per month of paper-wrapped Iraqi cigarettes. Those cigarettes benefitted us because we had no paper to write on. I used to keep the wrapper of every cigarette to record my brief daily diary on it when the surveillance eyes were not looking."[1]

Al-Khalisi and his fellows remained in that "luxurious" mansion till June 30. On the eve of that day, they were asked to get ready to move elsewhere. A steamboat was prepared to move them. The boat was full of sacks of rice, sugar and tea as well as cans of cooking oil in addition to a herd of cattle, and they were all set aside to feed them. The boat took them to a ship called Vasna, which was docked at a distant location in Shatt al-Arab. They boarded the ship, where a first-class wing was set aside for them. Each of them was given 500 rupees as pocket money.[2]

Before the ship had sailed, another steamboat came close to it carrying Ahmed al-Rawi who was at the time al-Muntafiq's police director, accompanied by two of the king's slaves, namely Salim and Barjas. Al-Rawi climbed with the two slaves to the ship and introduced himself to al-Khalisi, saying that he belonged to a house of knowledge and

---

[1]Excerpted from the handwritten memoirs of Salman al-Safwani.

[2]Salman Al Ibrahim al-Safwani, *Mahkoomiyyati* (my sentence), Saida, Lebanon, 1952, p. 24.

religion, that he was the son of `*allama* Sayyid Ibrahim al-Rawi, that he was deputed by the king to escort them, and that he [the king] had sent with him two of his own slaves as evidence for honouring and caring for them.

It is noteworthy that Ahmed al-Rawi was sent by the king to bring Prince Ghazi [son of King Faisal I], his mother and sisters from Hijaz, but the king commissioned them to undertake another mission when he came to know that he would ride in the same ship carrying al-Khalisi. Al-Rawi told me that the king had instructed him to treat al-Khalisi well, ordering him to provide for him all means of comfort. Actually, al-Rawi did not fall short in serving and looking after al-Khalisi, exerting in so doing his utmost effort.

Al-Khalisi A Pilgrim

When the Vasna ship reached Bombay, al-Khalisi and his fellows were taken to another larger ship, one of those that carried passengers between India and London. A first-class wing was set aside for them, and each of them was given, for the second time, the sum of 41 pounds as pocket money.[1]

As the ship was on its way to Aden, Sheikh Khaz`al, the emir of Muhammara, sent a letter to King Faisal asking him to let him host al-Khalisi. The king asked to be excused. This is the text of the letter that the king sent Khaz`al:

To the Greatness of the Holiest Sardar, Sheikh Khaz`al Khan, Governor of Muhammara,

Dear Brother,
I received in the most felicitous hour your honourable letter in which you hint at your desire to keep Sheikh Mahdi as your guest, so I thanked your Greatness, and noble feeling towards me and towards the sheikh referred to. But unfortunately, the Sheikh had travelled from Bombay to

---

[1]*Ibid.*, p. 24.

perform the pilgrimage prior to the arrival of your respectful letter. I, by Allah, am very sorry for what has happened, but it is the will of Allah and the responsibility bound upon me for the country and its benefit that necessitated that the Sheikh should leave the country at this time because of his strong opposition to the elections for the founding assembly. Despite that, I appreciate the terseness of your invitation and will do everything to realize your desire in this regard. In conclusion, please rest assured of the continuation of my affection and respect for your honourable person.

Your Brother Faisal, July 28, 1923[1]

The ship reached Aden on July 16. The men descended from it to the port, and Ahmed al-Rawi kept looking for an Islamic hotel for their stay but could not find one because the port's hotels were all foreign [Western-styled]. But luck helped them at the right time when a great Aden merchant saw them. He used to be in the past a resident of al-Kadhimiyya, and his name was Hassan Ali. He introduced himself to them and took them to his place, where he provided them with the means of comfort.

Through the governor of Aden, a telegram reached al-Khalisi from the Iranian government inviting him and his sons to its country, but al-Khalisi rejected the invitation and said that the pilgrimage season was approaching, so he had to perform the pilgrimage obligation first, then he would consider the invitation thereafter.

It was very difficult at that time to reach Mecca before the start of the pilgrimage season. There was only a single ship going to Hijaz, and it was the last of the pilgrims' ships. Moreover, it was overcrowded with passengers and did not have a vacancy. But the governor of Aden was able to prepare a place in the wing of the ship's captain for al-Khalisi and his companions, and thus they were able to reach Jeddah [sea port] at the right time.

When the ship was close to Jidda, the mayor of Jeddah came out to welcome it in a steamboat together with the customs' director and the

---

[1]*Ibid.*, p. 24.

minister of health. They all welcomed al-Khalisi on behalf of King Hussain and declared to him that he and his companions would be guests of the king during their stay in Hijaz.

Al-Khalisi stayed in Jidda for only a few hours. He was in a hurry to reach Mecca else it should be too late for the pilgrimage. Donkeys from al-Ahsa were prepared for him and for his companions to transport them to Mecca which they reached after a tiresome trip that lasted nine hours. As soon as al-Khalisi was out of Jeddah, the British Consul in Jeddah received a telegram from Sir Percy Lorraine in Tehran that said:

"Please let Sheikh Mahdi al-Khalisi send a telegram to the Iranian prime minister expressing his appreciation for the Iranian government's interest in him and declaring in it that the British government offered to send him to Iran but he preferred to seize the opportunity to perform the pilgrimage. It is very important to let al-Khalisi send such a telegram so the agitation that is intensifying here among the circles of clergyman may abate."

The Consul responded to this telegram, saying that he was sorry for being unable to do what he was asked as he should because al-Khalisi remained in Jidda for only a few hours, having reached it in the late morning, then left it in the afternoon; therefore, it is impossible for the Consul to visit al-Khalisi. He, therefore, commissioned Sayyid Ahmed al-Rawi to do it. Al-Rawi has stated that al-Khalisi was quite suspicious and evasive and would not do anything before consulting with the Iranian Consul. Al-Rawi was finally able to obtain from al-Khalisi a sheet of paper that he signed, but it seemed it was not of much benefit for the British government. The Consul concluded his telegram by praising Ahmed al-Rawi, saying that he deserved recognition for the effort he exerted in getting that sheet of paper and that he, therefore, commended the high commissioner in Baghdad to recognize the competence of this man, requesting him, if he found it appropriate, to also attract the attention of the Iraqi government to the same as well.[1]

---

[1]Excerpted from the National Records Center in London, Document No. FO 371 – 9047.

On al-Khalisi's arrival to Mecca, he did not visit King Hussain as official traditions require. Al-Khalisi was of the opinion that scholars are not permitted to visit kings; rather, kings are the ones who should visit scholars. Al-Rawi says that he was able in Mina to convince al-Khalisi to attend the royal pavilion which was prepared for the army's parade. It was there that al-Khalisi met and hugged the king. The king demonstrated a great deal of respect for al-Khalisi, and he always addressed him as "Mawlana [our master] al [the] Sheikh".

Salman al-Safwani narrates an interesting anecdote that took place when al-Khalisi and his fellows were sitting beside King Hussain in the royal pavilion: they saw Prince Ghazi peeping through a curtain, and he was then a lad of eleven years old, so the king called on him using the name "Awn" saying, "Come, Awn, salute your uncles who summoned your father to Iraq." The king kept talking to them about the reason why he called Prince Ghazi "Awn". He said, "When his mother was pregnant, our uncle, al-Hussain, peace be upon him, appeared to me in a vision and said that she would give birth to a male child; therefore, I should call him Awn. When the boy was born, the family wanted to name him Ghazi because his father was at the time an invader in the Asir [province], insisting on this name. I, therefore, said to them, 'You can call him whatever you want, but I shall call him only Awn in response to the request of our Uncle al-Hussain.'"

Al-Khalisi In Qum

Having completed the rituals of the pilgrimage and visited the grave of the Prophet, al-Khalisi decided to respond to the Iranian government's invitation, so he boarded a ship that took him and his fellows to Bushahr. Salman al-Safwani parted with them when he went to Basra and from there to Baghdad in a lengthy story about which there is no room here to narrate.

When al-Khalisi reached Bushahr, a huge reception took place in it for him: all the residents of the town came out to welcome him. Many delegations had come from nearby areas for the same purpose. During the reception, an amazing incident took place which is difficult to explain: an Englishman who was working for the Abadan Oil Company infiltrated the ranks of the welcoming masses and held tightly to al-Khalisi's car, then he fired one shot from his pistol, which missed al-Khalisi. The masses fell on the man desiring to kill him, but the soldiers rushed to save him. When Sir Arnold Wilson came to know about it, and he was at the time the director of the said oil company, he sent a message to al-Khalisi expressing his regret and apology for what had taken place, saying that the man was during the incident drunk and unaware of what he was doing, and that he fired him from his job and sent him back to London. When the news reached Tehran, a great uproar took place among the people, and sedition almost broke out, but the government calmed the people, assuring them that al-Khalisi was not harmed and that wine had overpowered that man who did not intend to do what he had done on purpose, whereupon people calmed down.[1]

After staying in Bushahr for a short while, al-Khalisi left it for Shiraz and from there to Isfahan then to Qum. Great receptions took place for him in all the cities and villages through which he passed. His arrival at Qum took place in late October of 1923, when he met the *mujtahids* who had arrived there before him.

Al-Khalisi hardly settled in Qum when a dispute began between him and the *mujtahids* who desired to return to Iraq. The latter had sent King Faisal two messengers to negotiate the matter with him; those were: Mirza Mahdi al-Khurasani and Sheikh Jawad al-Jawahiri. When al-Khalisi came to know about the dispatching of those messengers, he felt very depressed. It is said that several arguments took place between him and the *mujtahids*. Sheikh Muhammed al-Khalisi pointed it out in his memoirs; he said the following:

> "When my father reached Qum and saw the weakness and fear that overtook the scholars due to their communication with Faisal and determination to return to Iraq, he very strongly blamed them, explaining to them that the Shari`a and the Divine Command did not support such an action, and that they should stay in Iran and try to reform it and to reform Iraq and all Islamic lands through it because if it was reformed, it would be the centre of reform movements in all Islamic lands due to its geographical location and full

---

[1]Excerpted from the handwritten memoirs of Sheikh Muhammed al-Khalisi.

independence, and that surrendering to the British people and to Faisal was prohibitive, especially after their banishment of all those scholars and disregard for their holiness. He explained to them that their submission to injustice and surrender to humiliation by returning to Iraq would bring about evil to the Islamic world and that all other classes of Muslims would surrender just as those scholars had surrendered, and in this lay the annihilation of the Muslims in general and of Iraq and Iran in particular, that this was one of the most strongly prohibited things by the Shari`a and a man who rejects injustice, or a man of reason who knows the value and status of life, would not do it. My father kept advising the scholars and guiding them but to no avail, till he lost hope and said, 'I wish you never came to Iran nor took part with me, and that you left me alone to face the British. Now, if you are determined to do what violates the interest of Islam and to do something which I see to be a serious prohibition, I have to part with you and stay in Iran till Allah judges for me, surely He is the best of those who judge.' He parted with them angrily and went to Khurasan. The scholars remained in Qum, making preparations to return to Iraq, surrendering to the order of the British, accepting humiliation and disgrace, and waiting for permission from Faisal and the British to return to Iraq. Their judgment lies with their Lord; He best knows their condition."[1]

Sheikh Muhammed al-Khalisi renders the *mujtahids'* desire to return to Iraq to three reasons:

FIRST: The *mujtahids*, especially Sayyid Abul-Hassan al-Isfahani, who never spoke well of Iran, thought ill of the Iranians.

SECOND: The *mujtahids* thought that the presidency [of the Shi`a theological seminary] was not done except in Najaf. They came to know that Sayyid Muhammed al-Fairoozabadi started working towards seeking the presidency in it for himself. He started writing letters to Iran belittling

---

[1] *Ibid.*

the expelled *mujtahids* and saying that the scholarly seminary in Najaf [hawza] was busy with research and study and that the scholars in it were in the best of condition.

THIRD: Sheikh Abdul-Kareem al-Yazdi, who was the most senior among the *mujtahids* of Qum, did not desire the *mujtahids* to stay there because they would compete with him for the presidency, so he opposed them from behind a curtain.[1]

It must be mentioned in this regard that Sir Percy Lorraine pointed out to such details in his letter to Lord Curzon dated August 30, 1923, in which he said, "The *mujtahids* have in Iraq houses, real estate and a lot of charity funds for distribution; therefore, it is in their interest to return to their 'pasturage' as soon as possible. Add to this, senior *mujtahids* in Iran, though obliged to welcome and respect the deported [Iraqi] *mujtahids*, regard them as parasites and as competing with them for status and privilege."[2]

Al-Khalisi In Khurasan

Al-Khalisi decided to split from the *mujtahids* and to go to Khurasan. In mid-October of 1923, he left Qum. On his arrival at the town of Shah Abdul-Azim, which is located to the south of Tehran, crowds went to him from Tehran to greet him and to kiss his hands. Reza Khan, who had fairly recently assumed the position of Prime Minister, came to him, too, and held private talks with him for more than two hours.

Al-Khalisi reached Khurasan in early 1924. After completing the ceremonies of the *ziyara* of the Shrine of [Imam] al-Ridha, he intended to settle in the town. He sought *istikhara* [a plea to the Divine One for help in making a decision] to Allah through the Qur'an, and this verse of the

---

[1]Excerpted from the manuscript of the book titled "Batal al-Islam" (Islam's Hero) by Sheikh Muhammed al-Khalisi [which is now in print]. – Tr.

[2]Excerpted from the National Records Center in London, Document No. FO 371 – 9048.

Almighty came up: "*A good town, and a forgiving Lord.*" Thus, he resolved to reside in it.[1]

The first thing al-Khalisi did in Khurasan was the forming of a society which he called "Society for the Salvation of Both Harams and of Mesopotamia". On January 26, he issued a declaration in Arabic inviting the Muslims in all Islamic lands to be members of this society, urging them to purge the holy places in Hijaz and Iraq of the pollution of the unbelievers. This declaration was translated into Persian, Turkish, Pashtu and Urdu and was published in a booklet circulated among the public, and it was smuggled to India.

Al-Khalisi was interested in strengthening the Iranian government and in the growth of its armed forces in order to make them a base for the Muslims in fighting the unbelievers. When he was in Shiraz on his way to Qum, he issued a *fatwa* authorizing the Iranian government to levy *zakat* and *khums* funds from the Muslims and to spend the funds on the armed forces in charge of protecting the borders.[2] When he settled in Khurasan, he issued a second *fatwa* on spending the revenues of the endowments of [Imam] al-Ridha to meet the deficit in the budget from which the Iranian government was suffering during those days.[3]

We need not say that the issuing of both of those *fatwas* created many enemies for al-Khalisi, especially among the clergymen. There was a large number of clergymen and others who were benefitting from the *khums* and *zakat* funds as well as from the revenues of al-Ridha's endowments, and they did not relish the government faring with those funds without assigning them a share of them. Add to this, many clergymen, especially in Khurasan, found in al-Khalisi a competitor who threatened their religious position in the public's circles, excelling over them and attracting their hearts to him.

Al-Khalisi's contenders kept looking for the opportunity to scheme and to get him. The opportunity came to them on February 23, 1924 when al-Khalisi issued a *fatwa* to make the Nowruz Feast a religious

---

[1]Excerpted from al-Khalisi's previously mentioned book.

[2]*Report on the Administration of Iraq – 1923-1924*, London, 1925, p. 13.

[3]Abdul-Razzaq Ameen, *Thikra al-Khalisi* (in memoriam of al-Khalisi), Baghdad, Iraq, 1925, Vol. 1, p. 13.

mourning day. On that day, the "East Iran" newspaper, which was published in Khurasan, issued a special edition in the editorial of which it wrote in large letters this statement: "A National Feast – or an Islamic Mourning Day?" The newspaper directed this question to al-Khalisi: "Is it permissible to celebrate the next Nowruz Feast when Mecca, Medina, Najaf, Karbala, Kadhimiyya and Samarra are under the rule of the enemies of Islam and these places' holy soil is trampled upon by the foreigners' steeds?" Then the newspaper published al-Khalisi's answer in which he said, "Celebrating the Nowruz Feast this year must be as though it coincided with the month of Muharram on the day when Imam al-Hussain and his brother, Abul-Fadhl al-Abbas, were killed."

It is well known that Nowruz has always been regarded as a great national feast in Iran. Iranians narrate in its religious traditions and legacies. One of the strange coincidences is that Nowruz in that year coincided with the middle of Sha`ban, the day when the Shi`as celebrate the birth of Sahibul-Zaman [the 12th Imam al-Mahdi], and it also coincided with the day when the Bahaais commemorate the death anniversary of Abbas Afandi. Al-Khalisi's opponents kept spreading among the public a rumour saying that al-Khalisi was Bahaai and that he wanted to turn the feast into sombre grief mourning the death of Abbas Afandi. This charge was circulated among many people, especially those who held al-Khalisi in contempt because of his daring *fatwas*.

The people of Khurasan split into two opposing groups: one group was supportive of al-Khalisi, whereas the other was against him. What increased the hostility among both groups is that the Russian Consulate supported al-Khalisi, while the British Consulate supported his opponents.

When Nowruz day approached on March 21, some of those who make *taqleed* of him [who follow him] went to al-Khalisi to ask him for permission to celebrate the birth of Sahibul-Zaman, so he granted them permission, provided such a celebration should take place one day after the Nowruz day. A celebration was actually held on the next day in the evening at the Koher-Shah Mosque and was attended by the general governor, senior government officials and the town's dignitaries. At that time, a hostile demonstration came carrying statues of Abbas Afandi and Ali Muhammed al-Bab, and it came near the celebration's place. It started celebrating the Nowruz feast and taunting Bahaaism. Then it went towards al-Khalisi's house, shouting slogans against him and setting out fireworks. After that, it kept touring some town streets and assaulting some Bahaais, then it dispersed after setting the statues which it was carrying ablaze.

Al-Khalisi's followers did not remain silent about this insult. They came out the next day in a demonstration in support of al-Khalisi, and the demonstrators kept shouting slogans against Bahaaism and against the republic idea that some Iranians were advocating and which he regarded as a plot to eradicate Islam. The demonstration passed by the Shrine of Imam al-Ridha and some main streets, assaulting some Bahaais as the previous demonstration had done. An army force was summoned to disperse the demonstrators, and there was a fistfight between the soldiers and the demonstrators. The soldiers fired in the area, and then the demonstrators dispersed after a large number of demonstrators had been arrested and released the next day.[1]

Al-Khalisi felt fed up with Khurasan and its people and decided to leave the town for Tehran. He stated that the folks of Khurasan had insulted him more than the British people. When the news of his intended departure spread among the public, many Khurasanis went to him to declare their repentance for what they had done and to insist that he should stay. A confidential British report stated that the Russian Consul played a role in convincing al-Khalisi to stay in Khurasan.[2]

Al-Khalisi's Demise

Sheikh Mahdi al-Khalisi died of a heart attack on the eve of [Sunday] Ramadhan 11, 1343 A.H., which coincided with April 5, 1925 A.D. [according to the Gregorian Christian calendar, or on the 23rd of March according to the more popular Julian Christian calendar]. Khurasan had never before witnessed the like of the funeral awarded to al-Khalisi on that day: markets shut down, government offices closed their doors and both Russian and Afghani consulates declared mourning.

---

[1]Excerpted from the National Records Center in London, Document No. FO 371 – 10140.

[2]*Ibid.*

On the eve of April 7, a telegram reached al-Kadhimiyya from Khurasan announcing al-Khalisi's death, so the town was shaken by this report, and weeping and wailing were heard loud throughout it. The next day, the markets shut down to declare their mourning and chest beating processions were formed by various shop owners. The mourners walked towards al-Khalisi's School, wailing and beating their chests. A procession from al-A`dhamiyya came to share with the people of al-Kadhimiyya their grief. This was their chant:

O pillar of Islam, protector of the Shari`a,
You orphaned people are Sunnis and Shi`a.

I was then a 12-year-old lad, and I remember something interesting: When people were talking about al-Khalisi's banishment and death, they likened it to the martyrdom of [Imam] al-Hussain. They were saying that Yazid son of Mu`awiyah is now George V, that Ubaydullah ibn Ziyad is Faisal, and that Omar ibn Sa`d is Abdul-Muhsin al-Sa`doun. As for Shimr Thul-Jawshan [who killed Imam al-Hussain], he now is Abdul-Razzaq al-Fadhli. People forgot to state that they themselves were the people of Kufa.

Fatiha *majalis* (mourning gatherings) for al-Khalisi were held in most Iraqi cities and were continued for a long period of time. Also, mourning commemorations were held. The first commemoration was organized by Hizb al-Nahdha (renaissance party) on the eve of April 9 in which Abdul-Razzaq al-Ruwaishdi, Jameel Sidqi al-Zahawi, Nu`man al-A`dhami, [Mulla] Abboud al-Karkhi, Muhammed Abdul-Muhsin, Ibrahim Hilmi al-Omar, Hassoun al-Qazwini and Khamees Al Twaij participated. On the eve of the 20th of April, Nadi al-Islah (reform club) in Baghdad organized a second commemoration in which Ja`far al-Shibeebi, Mahdi al-Baseer, Abdul-Hussain al-Azari, Qasim al-Alawi and Ma`ruf al-Rusafi participated.

Al-Khalisi's School in al-Kadhimiyya became like the Ukaz Market due to the large number of poets who kept going there to deliver their poems [eulogies] from its pulpit. The government did not undertake any measure to prevent the poets from delivering their poems there. Rather, it left them to do whatever they pleased because it realized that they did not pose any danger.

It is noticeable that the poets did not depart in their poems from the traditional frame to which they were accustomed in composing eulogies since time immemorial. Almost all their poems were similar in their meanings, revolving around the greatness of the lost man and his feats, how a cornerstone of the creed has now crumbled, how the world is now dark due to his death, and how people after him are now confused, not knowing which direction they should go, and such themes which repeat themselves when any great man dies. The difference between one poet and another is in the way he coins the resounding expressions describing such themes and the exaggerations he uses for his portrayals.

Men of letters and the intelligentsia were busy those days comparing one poem after another, forgetting the goal for which al-Khalisi died. Whenever they met, most of their talk would revolve around the poets who delivered their poems that day, the verses which won the most admiration, and they may argue, dispute and raise their voices just as what used to take place in the early "golden" ages.

I remember in this regard that a poet from Najaf named Sayyid Sadiq al-Hindi delivered a poem eulogizing al-Khalisi, which remained for a long period of time the centre of people's talk and admiration. The following are some example verses of it so the reader may become acquainted with the ideological level in which people at the time were living:

Are you the wonder of the cosmos?
An angel you manifested yourself in human form?
Or did the Great One send you as a model
In whom people see how iman *truly is?*
Or does this age have anyone else besides you
Who has won the race in both abodes?
You kept your praiseworthy life story to people
To recite as they recite the Qur'an.
O Noah of this age, how have you left us
From the tumult of perils in a flood?
O Khalil of this land, the Nemrud of grief
Ignited the hearts over you with fires.

O Kaleem[1] of this land who
Towards patience directed the snake miracle.

The death of our people you did resurrect,
As if Jesus is now brought back with such an act.[2]

Actually, such has been the method of Arab poetry since its first ages: people were distracted by it from the problems and tragedies that surrounded them. This is why the rulers always encouraged it and paid generously for it, finding in it the best way to divert the public's attention, drugging it. It is true when one says, "Poetry is the opiate of the Arabs."

---

[1]The one referred to as "Kaleem Allah" is Prophet Moses who spoke to Allah and turned a rope into a snake. – Tr.

[2]Abdul-Razzaq Ameen (op. cit.), Vol. 1, pp. 54-55.

Chapter Six

The `Askari Administration

The success of Abdul-Muhsin al-Sa`doun in banishing al-Khalisi and deporting the *mujtahids* raised his status with the British people, making him, in their eyes, the man who could be relied on to implement their policy on the one hand and resist King Faisal's manoeuvres on the other. The king sensed the danger resulting from it, and he started feeling jealous of al-Sa`doun's status rising with the British.

What increased the king's worry is that the new high commissioner, Sir Henry Dobbs, very much admired al-Sa`doun and saw in him the man in whom the nobility and simplicity of the Bedouins were personified.[1] The king and his aides, therefore, kept spreading bad rumours against al-Sa`doun and trying to belittle him in national circles, creating difficulties for him.[2]

Throughout the summer of 1923, the king kept waiting for an opportunity to oust al-Sa`doun's cabinet. In late October, he stirred a ministerial crisis in order to oust it. On the 31st of the same month, Ms

---

[1]Khayri Ameen al-Omari, *Shakhsiyyat Iraqiyya* (Iraqi personalities), Baghdad, Iraq, 1955, Vol. 1, pp. 49-50.

[2]Khayri al-Omari, *Hikayat Siyasiyya* (political anecdotes), Cairo, Egypt, 1969, p. 199.

Bell wrote saying, "The king stirred this day as a ministerial crisis as is his habit from time to time. The administration, in general, is as best as can be obtained. As for the king's complaints, they are mostly unreasonable."[1]

The administration crisis stemmed from a letter sent by Rustam Haidar on behalf of the king to the ministerial council saying, "The Sa`doun cabinet pledged from its start to tackle the economic hardship gripping the country, but it has done nothing other than increasing the burden of taxes on the nation's shoulders; therefore, His Majesty the King asks the cabinet to provide him as soon as possible with an explanation of the actions it has thought of or undertaken to avert the danger of the status of the economy." Al-Sa`doun felt angry about this letter and saw it as though the king was blaming him for the cabinet falling short of carrying out its obligations; therefore, he sent an answer to the king saying, "If His Majesty the King regards the administration as falling short of carrying out its duties, it then has no choice except to submit its resignation. But if the King truly wants to find out what the administration has done to solve the economic crisis, we request His Majesty to stop the said letter and to send another in its place." When this answer reached the king, he retreated and sent a message to al-Sa`doun to apologize and to say that he did not mean to blame him for the administration falling short in its business, "as Your Excellency thought; rather, I wanted to attract your attention to the severity of the economic hardship and to the need to double the efforts to deal with it."[2]

Hardly two weeks passed since the end of the administration crisis when it returned again, and the king kept hunting for reasons to oust the cabinet. On November 14, Ms Bell said, "On Monday [November 12, 1923], I went to see a polo match for the Arab Army, and the king was there, so I rode in his car and tried to convince him not to oust the [Sa`doun] cabinet but to no avail."[3]

Al-Sa`doun was forced to submit his resignation on November 15. The king rushed to commission one of his men on whom he relied—

---

[1]Burgoyne, *Gertrude Bell,* London, 1961, Vol. 2, p. 319.

[2] Abdul-Razzaq al-Hassani, *Tarikh al-Wizarat al-Iraqiyya* (history of Iraqi administrations), Saida, Lebanon, Vol. 1, pp. 144-145.

[3]Burgoyne (op. cit.), Vol. 2, p. 320.

namely Ja`far al-`Askari—to form a new cabinet. Al-`Askari was at the time Mosul's administrative officer, and only a short period had passed since his appointment there. A telegram reached him from the king, ordering him to return to Baghdad immediately.

The `Askari administration was put together on November 26. In it, Ali Jawdat al-Ayyubi was the interior minister, Nouri al-Sa`eed was the defence minister, Abdul-Muhsin Shalash was the minister of finance, Ahmed al-Fakhri was the minister of justice, and Sabeeh Nash'at was the minister of transport and labour. On the same day, a royal decree was issued to assign the ministry of endowments to Salih Pash-A`yan. But the post of minister of education remained vacant since the intention was to assign it to a Shi`a man so the cabinet would have two Shi`a ministers instead of one, and the search started for that man.

Salih al-Husari narrates saying, "The opinions were clashing with each other about the man who would be the minister of education, so Ali Jawdat al-Ayyubi suggested the name of a man from Karbala whom he knew when he was the administrative officer there, namely Muhammed Hassan Abul-Mahashin, whom he described as "faqeer", easy-going, i.e. obedient and does not incline to dispute with his fellows. On January 3, the royal decree was issued to appoint Abul-Mahasin as the minister of education. It became clear later that this man was not "faqeer" as they imagined him but was more opposing and violating than other ministers.[1]

The British report submitted to the League of Nations said the following about the `Askari administration: "The forming of the new administration gave the Shi`a sect the opportunity for reconciliation for which it discreetly yearned. When it became clear that the cabinet contained two Shi`a ministers, one of them for finance, a delegation of Shi`a chiefs went to meet the king to whom they submitted a statement in which they expressed their conviction that the Shi`as were wrong in opposing the British policy and that they were determined to undertake a radical change in their stance towards it."[2]

---

[1]Sati` al-Husari, *Muthakkarati fil Iraq* (my memoirs in Iraq), Beirut, Lebanon, 1967, Vol. 1, pp. 371-384.

[2]*Report on the Administration of Iraq – 1923-1924*, London, 1925, p. 17.

We do not need to say that this delegation which the British report pointed out, did not truly represent the Shi`as but was rather comprised of those dignitaries and chiefs who were accustomed to meeting the rulers and to articulating sugar-coated speeches which such rulers desired to hear, and they were quite few in those days, and they still are!

Negotiating With The *Mujtahids*

Al-Sa`doun, as we have seen, was very rigid against the *mujtahids*, having no desire to be lenient in the matter of their return from Iran, and the British supported him in this regard, whereas the king was the opposite: he wanted to contact and negotiate with the *mujtahids* in order to repatriate them, and perhaps he wanted to do that to spite and challenge al-Sa`doun.

Sir Percy Lorraine sent London a telegram from Tehran dated August 30, 1923, in which he said the following:

> "I have heard from reliable Iranian sources that the issue of the *mujtahids* may soon be settled through direct talks between them and two messengers sent by the king to them in Qum. Some Iranians have indirectly tried to drag me to take part in the talk about the terms through which the *mujtahids* could return, but I refused to do anything in this regard and said to the individual who came to meet me that I had no authorization from the Iraqi government which is mainly responsible in this regard to participating in any such negotiation."[1]

In mid-November—that is, shortly before the fall of the Sa`doun administration—letters fell in the hands of the British which the *mujtahids* had sent to their representatives in Iraq in which they said that King Faisal promised them the following: 1) The Sa`doun administration will fall; 2)

---

[1]Excerpted from the National Records Center in London, Document No. FO 371 – 9048.

A Shi`a administration will be formed under the presidency of a Shi`a man; 3) All deported *mujtahids* will be returned to Iraq; 4) The treaty will be rejected.

In their letters, the *mujtahids* said that despite their lack of trust in the king's promises, they sent within the folds of their letters a *fatwa* which is signed and sealed by them announcing the lifting of prohibition from the election in case the king fulfils his promises. When Sir Henry Dobbs became familiar with these letters, he went to the king and said to him that his game with the *mujtahids* was not without risk and that they might use it as a weapon against him. Ms Bell says, "The king took the matter in light spirits and said to Dobbs that the *mujtahids* exaggerated in their demands and that they could be left to cook their soup slowly and he would cut off his negotiations with them.[1]

The king cut off his negotiations with the *mujtahids* according to his pledge to Dobbs, but he kept, as was his habit, mobilizing some nationalist entities to demand the return of the *mujtahids* in order to take it as a pretext for opening the subject again with Dobbs. On January 6, the *Istiqlal* newspaper said that a group of the capital's enlightened men and thinkers contacted it to express their appreciation of the present government for its determination to return Sheikh Mahdi al-Khalisi and his fellow mujtahids. They also expressed their elation with the government's good intentions, and they wanted it to support its statements with actions. On the 10th of the same month, the newspaper went back to indicate that several letters reached it from Hilla, Najaf and Karbala thanking the new administration for its determination to return Hujjatul-Islam al-Khalisi and the rest of the renowned scholars and that they wished these hopes would materialize.

At any rate, the king was able in early February of 1924 to reach an understanding with Dobbs about returning the *mujtahids* on the basis that the elections were about to come to an end and there was no reason to be rigid against their return. The following was stated in the British report submitted to the League of Nations about this subject:

---

[1]Burgoyne (op. cit), Vol. 2, p. 321.

"It was decided in February of 1924, after the consent of the high commissioner, that there was no objection to the *mujtahids'* return with the exception of Sheikh Mahdi [al-Khalisi], provided they pledge to the king that they would avoid interfering in politics. Their banishment, though voluntary, had led to aversion between the Iranian and Iraqi governments, and the influx of students and pilgrims from Iran had stopped. This has resulted in financial hardship in the holy shrines and in the railways sector, too. Moreover, there is a feeling that the *mujtahids'* evil power has been uprooted due to their foolish action in protesting and the regret that followed it. The Iraqi government deserves to be congratulated for its tough stance, which ended with its victory over the trouble-making *Iranian* clergymen."[1]

The king met with Dobbs on February 9 to reach an understanding about the plan which must be followed to repatriate the *mujtahids.* Dobbs was apprehensive about the return of the *mujtahids* to Iraq, or if they were near the borders, before the inauguration of the Founding Assembly, which was set for the middle of March. The agreement, therefore, took place between them for the king to send a message to the *mujtahids* to tell them that they must not leave before a letter from the king reached them permitting them to enter Iraq. But if they reached the borders prior to the arrival of the permission, the Iraqi government would deny them entry. The king estimated with Dobbs the length of the period which such a letter would need to reach them and for the answer to return in addition to the verification of the pledge that the *mujtahids* would provide. They found out that this would be no less than six weeks which would be sufficient for the Founding Assembly to have been inaugurated prior to their arrival.[2]

After the agreement between the king and the high commissioner on the above had been reached, something happened that led to blocking

---

[1]*Report on the Administration of Iraq – 1923-1924,* London, 1925, p. 13.

[2] Muhammed Muzaffar al-A`dhami, "Al-Majlis al-Ta'seesi al-Iraqi" (Iraqi Founding Assembly), an unpublished university thesis, Vol. 2, p. 561.

the negotiations with the *mujtahids*: the *mujtahids* wanted al-Khalisi to return with them, whereas the king and the high commissioner were concerned about al-Khalisi's return and insisted not to permit it anyhow. A report of the Iraqi intelligence dated March 5 indicated the following:

"The contact with the *mujtahids* in Iran about the terms that would enable them to return to Iraq has been delayed. Letters from them have arrived in which they protest. They say that it is a shame for them to return without Sheikh al-Khalisi. The king was addressed in this regard, but he kept his grounds. A telegram was sent to the *mujtahids* in this regard, and Sheikh Jawad al-Jawahiri wrote Mirza Hussain al-Naeeni requesting him and his fellows to seize this opportunity; otherwise, they would lose their status in Iraq, the status which other *mujtahids* started quickly seizing. On the other hand, al-Khalisi's family kept pressuring the *mujtahids* to convince them not to return without Sheikh al-Khalisi. The king says that Reza Khan sent him a telegram expressing the desire of the *mujtahids* to return according to the terms presented to them, and that Sheikh Jawad and Mirza Mahdi would leave Baghdad for Qum on March 1 accompanied by Sayyid Baqir Wahid al-`Ayn as a representative of the king. The latter will carry with him a draft of the pledge which the *mujtahids* must sign. He would then bring it with him or send it to Baghdad when the king sets a date for the mujtahids to return to Iraq."[1]

On March 1, Sheikh Jawad al-Jawahiri and Mirza Mahdi al-Khurasani travelled to Iran accompanied by Sayyid Baqir Wahid al-`Ayn.[2] These men exerted a great effort to convince the *mujtahids* to return to

---

[1] Excerpted from the National Records Center in London, Document No. FO 371 – 10147.

[2] This Sayyid Baqir is the one who came later to be known in documents by the title "Sar Kashik." Before then, he carried the said title "Wahid al-`Ayn", which means "the one-eyed", the surname of his father,.

Iraq without al-Khalisi, and they succeeded. It is believed that Reza Khan supported their effort, for a secret British document pointed out that Reza Khan used to advise the *mujtahids* to return without paying attention to al-Khalisi, and he used to tell them that al-Khalisi was a silly man without sensibility and that he was a tool in the hands of his son, Sheikh Muhammed.[1]

The Mujtahids' Return

The *mujtahids* wrote a pledge saying that they would no longer interfere in the Iraqi government's policy. I found among the documents of the royal palace four letters sent to the king and signed by Sayyid Abul-Hassan al-Isfahani, Mirza Hussain al-Naeeni, Sayyid Abdul-Hussain al-Tabatabai and Sayyid Hassan al-Tabatabai, and they all carry almost the same text. It is believed that they contained the pledge required of them. We contend ourselves here with reporting only al-Isfahani's letter, the text of which is:

> *"In the Name of Allah, the most Gracious, the most Merciful*
>
> Your Majesty the King of Iraq, Allah supports his domain and authority:
>
> After saluting you and inquiring about your conditions, the mercy of Allah and His blessings be upon you, we submit that I took your letter dated Rajab 26 sent with both Honorable Hujjatul-Islam Sheikh Jawad Sahibul-Jawahir and Honorable Mirza Mahdi Ayatollah Zadah, may their blessings prolong, in full respect. What you stated in it and deposited into its folds is now known to us, and they both informed us of the matters that went on between you and the reasons that necessitate a delay in our movement and the request of Your Majesty for support. Also, the one protected by Allah, Sayyid

---

[1]Excerpted from the National Records Center in London, Document No. FO 371 – 10147.

Baqir Sar Kashik, carried out his duty and conveyed his oral messages. We had undertaken on our shoulders not to interfere in political matters and to stay aloof from everything the Iraqis demand, and we are not responsible for it. Rather, the one who is responsible for the people's needs and for ruling it is Your Majesty, but supporting the Hashemite monarchy, as required by the Islamic creed, is our Islamic principle. As regards your command to unite the word and to firm the ties of friendship between Iran and Iraq, it is one of our religious duties. When we entered Iran, we kept exerting our effort in this regard, and the result of our blessed actions will appear. Peace be upon you, the mercy of Allah and His blessings.

"On Sha`ban 21, 1342 - The Humblest Abul-Hassan al-Mousawi al-Isfahani"[1]

(Seal)

On April 5, Sheikh Jawad al-Jawahiri and Mirza Mahdi al-Khurasani wrote the king a letter announcing the success of their mission. Here is its text:

In the Name of Allah Almighty

Your Majesty, the King of Iraq, may Allah Almighty support him and safeguard his domain and authority,

After saluting you and inquiring about your conditions, the mercy of Allah and His blessings be upon you, we submit that we are very eager for those Hussaini traits, may the Lord of the World protect and support them. We then submit that Brother Sayyid Baqir, after arriving at Qum, went to Tehran and met the Honorable Prime Minister, may he be protected. He did excellently in oratory and debate and established affection between the Arab and Iranian governments. The

---

[1]Excerpted from the royal palace's documents, Series 3, Document 59.

Prime Minister greatly demonstrated his appreciation of Your Majesty and showed respect for Sayyid Baqir on account of his affiliation with Your Majesty and due to his suitability and good manners regarding what you ordered him, and he must submit the details to Your Majesty. Then, Master, he conveyed the greetings of both Ayatollahs, the Sayyid and the Mirza, may their shade prolong, for your high status and for detailing their answers after we offered to serve them both, that His Majesty says that the greatest gift I desire is Iran's recognition of the Arab government being official, they both, may Allah prolong their shade, said: 'Prior to your arrival, we talked about this request, and the report was that after the Assembly convenes, the decision will be made in this regard.' Most [of our] representatives have likewise been advised. Since we are proud of the Arab government, especially since its king is supported by the Hashemite [family] Tree, we see that Iraq is our homeland, its government is our government, and its king is our king, we hope for an increase in the [prestige of the] Iraqi government, thus our heads will rise, and Your Majesty knows best. The director of the Iranian general security is the one who now is serving the great scholars, and he sent requesting to meet you. He bears the affection of the head of the Iranian government for Your Majesty and will be with the scholars in al-Najaf al-Ashraf. If Allah Almighty so wills, we shall succeed in the honour of serving you and in submitting the details; peace be upon you, the mercy of Allah and His blessings.

On Sha`ban 29, 1343 – Jawad son of the late Sahibul-Jawahir, may his soul be sanctified – (date seal)"[1]
(Seal)

In the morning of April 21, the *mujtahids* reached Khanaqin accompanied by Sardar Rif`at, director of the Iranian general security. The

---

[1]Excerpted from the royal palace's document, Series 3, Document 55.

town had made preparations to welcome them, decorating its streets with Arab flags and palm fronds. They were welcomed by Sheikh Muhammed Hassan Abul-Mahasin, minister of education, Tahsin al-`Askari, representative of the interior minister, and Husam ad-Deen Jum`ah, representative of the police for escorting Sardar Rif`at. The *mujtahids* spent that night in Khanaqin and then rode the train the next morning on their way to Baghdad. When they reached the Baaquba [train] station, they got down to pray, and they were welcomed there by finance minister Abdul-Muhsin Shalash, Sheikh Jawad al-Shibeebi and others.

A large crowd of the people from Baghdad and al-Kadhimiyya as well as delegations from the governorates, assembled at the train station in Bab al-Mu`adham. Tents were set up there in preparation for welcoming the *mujtahids* on their arrival by train. When the train approached the masses, the latter's voices rose to glorify and magnify the Almighty, and they kept looking at the train expecting it to stop, but they were surprised when the train did not stop but kept going. The train stopped at the river bank near the house of the prime minister. There, the ministers were ready to welcome it, and so was the king's envoy, Safwat al-Awwa, and others.[1] From there, the train crossed the Tigris River via the ferry and then took them to Karbala.

The Return Of Both Muhammeds

Sayyid Muhammed al-Sadr and Sheikh Muhammed al-Khalisi were banished to Iran in August of 1922, as we stated in the fourth chapter. It is known that both of these men did not like each other; therefore, they were not harmonious when they reached Tehran, and there is no room here to mention the matters that went on between them there.

Sheikh Muhammed al-Khalisi was in Tehran, persistently fighting the British, and it is said that he contacted the Bolsheviks in order to cooperate with them in this regard. As for Sayyid Muhammed al-Sadr, some evidence point out that he kept contacting King Faisal in order to facilitate his own return to Iraq.

---

[1] *Al-`Ālam al-Arabi* (the Arab world) newspaper of April 24, 1924.

Since late 1923, *Al-Istiqlal* newspaper kept pointing out that Sayyid Muhammed al-Sadr's health had deteriorated in Tehran because the weather did not suit him. On December 30, 1923, the newspaper stated that a delegation from among the capital's youths met the king and acquainted him with al-Sadr's health condition and that the king expressed his sorrow and declared his desire for al-Sadr's return to Iraq, but he said that al-Sadr neglected to provide the pledge which is usually taken from deportees and that this is the reason why his return is so late; otherwise, he would have returned some time back. On March 9, 1924, the newspaper published a report under the heading "A Serious Leader is Coming Back: Sayyid Muhammed Sadr ad-Deen", in which it said, "The hearts have been filled with joy, elation has painted itself on the faces of all patriots in general and the people of al-Kadhimiyya in particular, a report has been announced about the return of this great leader to his homeland, Iraq." On the 26th of the same month, the same newspaper published saying, "The health of Sayyid Muhammed al-Sadr greatly deteriorated last winter, and the doctors in Tehran objected to his staying there; therefore, he decided to return to Iraq for good. The Iraqi government does not oppose it, so good news to the nationalists and to his great father, the `allama imam."

On May 29, *Al-Aalam al-Arabi* newspaper stated that Sayyid Muhammed al-Sadr would reach Baghdad the next morning and that a committee was formed to welcome him. The newspaper published the reception's agenda, which was put together by the said committee. It was decided that Muhammed Hassan Habbah[1] should go to Khanaqin to welcome him on behalf of the said committee, and that Abdul-Hameed Kannah should go to Baaquba, and the private school students should line up to greet him on his arrival at the Bab al-Mu`adham [train] station and Abdul-Majeed Zaidan should deliver a welcoming speech before him on behalf of the committee.

Al-Sadr reached Baghdad at the determined time, and a huge reception was made for him at the station. When he reached his house in al-Kadhimiyya, the house was overcrowded with congratulating people.

---

[1]This is what the Arabic text reads and which I think is a typographical error: the name should be Muhammed Hassan Kubba, a poet to whom reference is made above in this book. – Tr.

Some poets delivered poems praising and welcoming him, including one by Sheikh Radhi Al Yasin, the first lines of which were:

O leader of Iraq! The separation has been too long,
Iraq has so much missed you, its patience ebbed.

It was noticed that after his return to Iraq, al-Sadr started undertaking a route in politics different from the one he used to tread before: it is the route of "affirmation" instead of that of "negation", according to his biographer, Abbas Ali. This writer said the following: "His Eminence returned after the period which he had spent in Tehran to occupy his place in leading the national front with his inspired talents and brilliant mind. In this stage, he was closer to the policy of affirmation than that of negation because he saw it thereafter to be more successful in getting what he wanted for this homeland: honour, sovereignty and independence."[1]

Anyhow, this shift in al-Sadr's conduct was met with indignation and strong criticism by many people in al-Kadhimiyya and elsewhere. They were used to making opposition [to the British] synonymous with nationalism: an opponent is, to them, a nationalist. If he abandons opposition, he, in their view, becomes a traitor.

Such is the story of Sayyid Muhammed al-Sadr. As for Sheikh Muhammed al-Khalisi, his is another story. He returned to al-Kadhimiyya suddenly on the eve of April 16, 1932. Apparently, he entered Iraq when the government was unaware. As soon as the news of his arrival at al-Kadhimiyya spread in the morning of the next day, people kept going in hordes to al-Khalisi's school to greet him. They were passing by him in ranks as he stood to welcome them at the door of the school's internal courtyard. Each of them would kiss his hand and walk away in order to make room for the next.

But Sheikh Muhammed did not stay in al-Kadhimiyya except for three days. At noontime, April 16, when he was returning home after performing the noontime prayer rite at the Safawi-built Mosque, he was intercepted by a police commissioner who told him that the interior

---

[1] Abbas Ali, *Za`eem al-Thawra al-Iraqiyya* (leader of the Iraqi revolution), Baghdad, Iraq, 1950, p. 158.

minister and the police director, as well as Baghdad's administrative officer wanted to meet him now in Baghdad to discuss with him an important matter. The Sheikh asked the commissioner for a brief respite so he could eat his lunch at home, and the commissioner permitted him to do that, but when he found out that he was late at home, he entered his house and asked him to hurry to get out with him. Then he took him to the Sarai centre in Baghdad. Some people of al-Kadhimiyya went behind him, and they were joined in Baghdad by another crowd of Baghdadis. After the interrogation with him, he was seated in a car accompanied by a commissioner and two armed policemen. The car drove in the direction of Baaquba, then Khanaqin. Some residents tried to crowd themselves in order to prevent the car from moving, but the police resisted them. An officer shouted, rebuking them, and then he started beating them with a baton, forcing them to disperse.[1]

When Sheikh Muhammed reached the Iranian borders, his passport was returned to him with an official letter from the interior ministry that said: "Since the foreigner named Sheikh Muhammed son of Sheikh Mahdi al-Khalisi whose features are fixed below falls under the text of Clause C of the 11th Article of the Iraqi Residency Law for the Year 1923, and since the said person is not welcome to stay in the Iraqi country, I, the interior minister, acting on the authority granted to me by the said Article of the Iraqi Residency Law for the Year 1923, order the said person to be deported beyond the Iraqi borders and that he must remain outside unless an order is issued by us to the contrary. Issued by the office of the interior ministry on April 20, 1932. Signed: Naji Shawkat."

Sheikh Muhammed al-Khalisi remained in Iran till the year 1949. He received there from the government of Reza Shah persecution, intransigence and deportation. Then the policy in Iraq finally dictated that he should be permitted to return, so he returned to Iraq and was welcomed from the borders officially and publicly. People went in crowds to see him when he came back; they loved and admired him, but they started dispersing from him little by little. We shall talk about the story of how they crowded around him and then how they dispersed from him in a forthcoming volume of this book [series].

---

[1]Excerpted from the handwritten memoirs of Sheikh Muhammed al-Khalisi.

Process Of Elections

The Sa`doun administration had, since July 12, 1923, started the Founding Assembly elections, and the electoral process continued during the `Askari administration. It is noted that the *fatwas* that the *mujtahids* had issued banning the elections created some impact on a number of cities such as Najaf, Karbala, Hilla, Kadhimiyya and Hayy. The greatest impact had taken place in Najaf, where a secret meeting took place attended by many Najafis and headed by Abdul-Kareem al-Jaza'iri, Jawad al-Jawahiri, Muhammed Ali Bahr al-`Uloom, Muhsin Shalash, Abbas al-Kilidar and Hadi al-Naqeeb who decided to boycott the elections, signing a dossier in this regard. Only al-Kilidar refused to sign it.[1] On July 28, Najaf's mayor and Karbala's administrative officer submitted a letter stating the factors that led to the hindering of the electoral process in al-Najaf; these were:

FIRST: Some candidates from the inspection board had fled abroad, leaving their fellows in an embarrassing situation that they could not override for fear public opinion would be stirred against them with criticism.

SECOND: They waited for the results that would happen in the places where the Ja`fari [Shi`a] sect is followed with regards to the elections, so they would not be the ones to initiate this matter and thus would later be blamed for it.

THIRD: Some candidates from the inspection board openly violated the elections and influenced the minds of simple people who feared ill consequences. Among those who openly violated, I mention Sayyid Kamal ad-Deen, headmaster of the Ghari School. This man was truly an extremist in opposing the government's aspirations and an opponent of its goals. Had he not thus wished, the elections would have made an important stride along their path; therefore, please bring the individual referred to and keep him in the governorate's centre until the elections are completed, provided he is banned from socializing with anyone for fear

---

[1]Muhammed Muzaffar al-A`dhami (op. cit.), Vol. 2, pp. 481-482.

he disseminates his harmful ideas among and influences simple-minded people.[1]

The government wanted to send a military force to Najaf, but Mawlud Mukhlus sent it a telegram on August 5 advising it not to send the force because this would attract attention. On August 9, Mawlud Mukhlus went in person to Najaf and was able to remove the difficulties that blocked the electoral process.[2]

What is noteworthy is that as the struggle in Najaf was going on as we have stated, there was a struggle of another kind between the king and the high commissioner about the electoral process in some areas, especially Baghdad, Mosul and some districts of Dulaim [now the Anbar province]. It reached the knowledge of the high commissioner that the king was covertly encouraging some candidates in those areas who are known for their hostility to the British people. On August 31, the high commissioner sent a letter to Cornwallis saying,

"I hear from various sources that the common view is that His Majesty the king desires most of the extremists to be in the Assembly. Such a majority will refuse to ratify the treaty. So, if this result actually surfaces, it of course, will lead to calamities. I see it my duty to officially warn the government of His Majesty King Faisal about what I think will probably take place unless the matters do not change the next week."

This was a warning to the king at the time. When the king became familiar with it, he answered it in the following as he addressed Cornwallis:

"You, Dear, undoubtedly fully know the great efforts which I have exerted for the success of the elections, and you are fully familiar with what I have done in various places and clubs which I recently visited for the same objective. God knows

---

[1]Abdul-Raheem Muhammed Ali, *Al-Najaf wal Majlis al-Ta'seesi* (Najaf and the Founding Assembly), *Al-Rabita* magazine in Najaf in its issue dated September 1975.

[2]Muhammed Muzaffar al-A`dhami (op. cit.), Vol. 2, pp. 481-483.

that I had no goal behind the efforts which I exerted in encouraging the elections other than the treaty would as a result, win the support of the vast majority of the country's residents. Huge difficulties faced me along this path, but I did not care about them because I believed, and I still do, that the ratification of the treaty is the pillar of this kingdom. My actions aim at achieving a sacred duty for which every difficulty becomes easy. For the sake of this duty did we deport the scholars [of theology], and for its sake have I put up hardships and stood in several courts the results of which, I believe, has not been bad; rather, they have led to the people of Mosul welcoming the elections after some of them were boycotting them while some others were reluctant in their regard, then some Shi`as of the cities joined in. You must remember what I said to you some time back, that is, that we have to make sure about each member of the Assembly before he is elected so we may be fully safe when the treaty is ratified. Any of us who nominates someone must feel secure about him and responsible for his view in the Assembly." Then the king concluded his letter by saying that he was very much in pain that His Excellency the high commissioner thought less of "my [king's] loyalty to my homeland and to my friend, Britain, or that I try to renege on a promise which I regard as the pillar of life for my kingdom which is threatened from all its ends."

When the high commissioner became acquainted with this answer, he wrote expressing his regret about the king having misunderstood him, saying that he did not doubt the king's intentions towards the treaty, but there was a large segment of the people that believes that the king supports the candidates who oppose the treaty, and this impression will quickly disappear when they become familiar with the government's real desire in a permanent way.[1]

---

[1]*Ibid.*, Vol. 2, pp. 530-534.

The Founding Assembly Convenes

Once the elections had taken place, it was decided that the convening of the founding assembly should be on the 27th of March of 1924. First, views differed about the assembly's physical quarters. Some people say that the quarters should be in the vocational school that Madhat Pasha built in 1870 on the bank of the Tigris near the Officer's Club between the fort and the Qashla. But the assembly of ministers did not accept this opinion. The interior minister suggested that the Cinema Royal building in the Bab al-Agha quarter should be set aside for the assembly. His suggestion was not accepted. Finally, the view settled on the "Strangers' Hospital" building, which was built by Madhat Pasha on the bank of the Tigris River in the Karkh flank. Renovations and required additions were made to it in preparation for the inauguration.

The inauguration day of the said Assembly was declared an official holiday, and the interior ministry ordered all administrative officers of governorates to celebrate it. Also, the ministerial assembly asked the capital's municipality to decorate Baghdad city day and night, the sentences of prisoners were lessened, and some of them were released.

Prior to the inauguration day, the king threw a lunch banquet at his mansion, to which he invited the assembly members. The members swore an oath of loyalty to the king and the country. There was a problem that upset them, which was electing the assembly's head. The British wanted Abdul-Muhsin al-Sa`doun to be the head, whereas the king wanted the head to be Yasin al-Hashimi. Ms Bell wrote on the eve of March 26—the night that preceded the opening of the Assembly—saying the following:

> "I am writing this in the middle of the night because I am unable to sleep. On Monday, there was a lunch invitation at the king's mansion, and I sat beside the king and found him sparkling. He concluded a magnificent work with the assembly's members, for they swore loyalty to him and to the country that day, and tomorrow the assembly will open at 10:00 am. We had a day full of annoyances and commotion about the issue of the presidency of the assembly. If they do not elect Muhsin Pasha [Abdul-Muhsin al-Sa`doun], it will

not be good. But Ja`far changes his mind once every quarter of an hour and influences the king. I told everyone that they must elect Muhsin; as for the rest, it is left to the gods. It is like the wooden bottle game: you keep yourself busy with one side of the arrangement and turn to see that the other side has collapsed."[1]

On the morning of the day set for the inauguration, a number of soldiers were lined up in the street leading to the assembly to salute the king on his arrival. Also, school students lined up. The masses crowded on both sides, as is their tradition when they wanted to be onlookers. At 9:00 am, members of the assembly started coming one after the other. When it was about 10:00 am, the commander of the British forces arrived in the company of the high commissioner. Exactly at ten o'clock, the royal convoy arrived, and the king was riding in his red convertible car wearing his Arabian outfit and bearing a gold sword, and in his belt, there was a dagger also made of gold. The masses let boisterous applause, the army band played a salutation to him, and cannons were fired.

When the king entered the assembly's hall, the members stood out of respect for him. Then the king delivered the throne's speech in which he expressed his pleasure at the opening of the first consultative assembly in Iraq, saying that there were three essential matters which the assembly had to decide; these were: 1) the ratification of the treaty, 2) the coining of the constitution, and 3) the coining of a law for parliamentary assembly elections. The king called in his speech on assembly members to ratify the treaty because it hinged on the solving of the country's essential issues with assistance from the British government and the League of Nations. Then he pointed out that the constitution, which he described saying:

> "Islam's rulings are based on *shura* (consultation), and the greatest sin the Islamic sects committed was swerving from this verse of the Almighty: 'They settle their matters by consulting among themselves.' Therefore, every Muslim individual who knows what his religion commands must

---

[1] Burgoyne (op. cit.), Vol. 2, p. 336.

support this divine rule, and every laziness about it is disobedience of Allah's command. In order to follow this serious matter, in order to emulate the nations that are deeply rooted in civilisation and acting on the wishes of the Iraqi nation, we call on you, honourable representatives, to issue this law and to put a system for the electing of the parliamentary assembly."[1]

Once the king finished delivering his speech, he left the hall, so Ja`far al-`Askari presided over the session temporarily for the electing of a head for the assembly. When the ballots were sorted, it became clear that al-Sa`doun had won 50 votes, whereas al-Hashimi won 23, and Ibrahim al-Haidari won eight votes. Al-Sa`doun, therefore, ascended the presidency podium and thanked the assembly members for their vote of confidence. He also thanked Britain for fulfilling its pledge to facilitate the meeting of the assembly.

Ms Bell attended the inauguration party. After that, she wrote describing what happened, saying, "The king delivered a great speech, but he was very nervous while delivering it." Then she described the moment in which al-Sa`doun was elected as being exciting, pointing out an interesting phenomenon that took place during the polling; she said, "Some tribal sheikhs who were sitting in front of us carried their ballot cards directed at us before they cast them in the polling box in order to show us that they wrote al-Sa`doun's name on them."[2]

Opposition Once Again

It was decided that the assembly should look into the issue of ratifying the treaty before looking into the coining of the constitution. It was noticed that this matter was not in harmony with the constitutional rules in democratic countries: it is not appropriate to look into ratifying a treaty with a foreign country prior to determining the country's status vis-à-vis the form of government in it and determining its various powers. At any

---

[1] Abdul-Razzaq al-Hassani (op. cit.), Vol. 1, pp. 168-169.

[2] Burgoyne (op. cit.), Vol. 2, p. 336.

rate, it was agreed on between the king and the British that the matter of the treaty, due to its importance for Iraq's special situation, should receive precedence.

It is noteworthy that the British were optimistic with regard to the treaty, thinking that the assembly would ratify it quickly and that there was no opposition after the deportation of the *mujtahids* during the term of the previous administration.[1] Add to this, the British were comfortable with most assembly members, especially tribal sheikhs, whose number in the assembly was 40. They had met before the assembly's inauguration and pledged among themselves to support the treaty and that none of them would do anything contrary to the unanimous consent of everyone.[2]

The British realized a short while later that they were mistaken in their optimism. It became clear to them that the opposition was able to rise anew and more forcefully, that many members with whom they were comfortable would-be leaders of the opposition or at least encouraging it.

The early signs of the opposition were articulated by Naji al-Suweedi following the submission of the treaty to the assembly on April 2. Al-Suweedi then submitted a proposal in which he said, "The treaty must be announced to the people, the only means to say its word in its regard. The representatives have no right to look into the treaty except after they become familiar with the people's opinion because they are obligated to work according to the opinion of the people, according to their hopes and wishes." When this proposal of al-Suweedi was submitted to the assembly for voting, it was endorsed by the assembly.[3]

It can be said that this proposal sentenced the treaty from the start to rejection, for if the treaty was presented to the people, according to al-Suweedi's suggestion, it would naturally stir in the circles of the educated a movement opposing the treaty, and these will mobilize the masses. It is then that the opposition infection will transfer to the inside of the assembly, and some representatives will criticize the treaty in order to win the masses' admiration, and other representatives will go along with

---

[1] Elie Kedourie, *The Chatham House Version*, London, 1970, p. 265.

[2] Philip Ireland, *Iraq* (trans. Ja'far al-Khayyat), Beirut, Lebanon, 1949, p. 310.

[3] Abdul-Razzaq al-Hassani (op. cit.), Vol. 1, p. 171.

them. Thus the representatives will be split according to the masses into two opposing teams: patriots and traitors, and the matter may end in the treaty being rejected by most of the voters.

What we have stated did actually take place. On April 6—four days after Naji al-Suweedi had submitted his proposal—the *Istiqlal* newspaper published an editorial under the heading "To the Attorneys from among the Sons of the Two Rivers" signed by "S", who is believed to be attorney Dawood al-Sa`di. In it, he pointed out the attorneys' calm during those historical days when the nation's assembly determined the destiny of the homeland. It also pointed out to the attorneys in all world countries as having won the ultimate prize in their struggle for their homelands. Then he addressed the attorneys thus: "The homeland is drawing its last breath, and you have to carry out your sacred duty and share the assembly's members in pleasure and in pain, for the people are patiently monitoring your efforts."

On May 9, Dawood al-Sa`di and Rasheed Rushdi submitted a request to Baghdad's administrative officer to hold a meeting at the Hilal Hotel in the Maidan Quarter to honour the representatives and to listen to the speeches of some attorneys about the country's general policy. The administrative officer agreed to the request in the beginning then withdrew it following an instruction issued to him by the interior ministry. On the next day, representative Abdul-Razzaq al-Ruwaishdi raised this point in the assembly and asked the government to permit the holding of the meeting in order to become familiar with the opinion of the attorneys who are law specialists and are fully familiar with the articles of the treaty. Nouri al-Sa`eed stood to demand the closure of the subject because looking into the treaty is the specialization of only assembly members, and nobody else has the right to take part in it. Representative Salih Shkarah stood to rebut Nouri al-Sa`eed, saying that the treaty concerns the entire nation and that it is the duty of the assembly to reach an understanding with the people on the pages of newspapers and not in meetings. After a sharp argument among the representatives about this subject, it was decided to refer it to the president of the assembly to look into it. In the next session, Yasin al-Hashimi announced that the government did not prevent the meeting but asked it to be postponed. Then al-Sa`doun, in his capacity as head of the assembly, announced that the issue was concluded and that there was no objection to inviting the attorneys and to meeting with the representatives.

The attorneys decided to hold the meeting on April 17 in the Cinema Royal instead of the Hilal Hotel and that it would be at two hours after sunset because the time was the month of Ramadhan. In the morning of the next day, the *Iraq* newspaper carried out a discussion by Nouri al-Sa`eed in which he admitted the faults of the treaty, but he said that the ratification of the treaty, despite all of that, would lead to solidifying Iraq's political entity. As for rejecting it, this would hurl the country into a pit that we all fully know that it contains the disappointment of our national aspirations and the loss of all the great efforts that our nation has till now exerted. Nouri al-Sa`eed meant by this the rejection of the treaty would lead to the loss of the Mosul area, which Turkey was demanding as well as other perils that threatened the country from all its sides.

The meeting was held at the set time and was attended by assembly members and a large number of attorneys, dignitaries and the intelligentsia, so much so that the cinema's hall was overcrowded. The party was opened by a martial song by students of the Tafayyudh Private School, then Dawood al-Sa`di stood and delivered a speech in which he welcomed those invited, explained the political situation then said, "Representatives, rest assured that the Iraqi nation stands before you as though it charges you of a major crime whereas you in reality are innocent. It expects you to issue a decision either of its death or of its innocence." His speech, as reported by *Al-Aalam Al-Arabi* newspaper, was met with enthusiastic applause, a great commotion and loud shouts. He was followed by attorney Shafiq Nouri al-Sa`eedi who recited in a loud, enthusiastic voice a statement by the attorneys, which included a scathing criticism of the treaty and a complaint about the injustice of its articles. Then Yasin al-Hashimi rose to speak on behalf of the assembly members. Addressing the attorneys, he said, "By Allah, do hold many such meetings in every hard time." Then he said, "We swore to the truth and to loyalty to our kingdom and king no matter how harsh the restrictions and the threats may be." His speech won thundering applause and shouting.[1]

Ms Bell described in one of her letters the meeting held at the Cinema Royal, saying, "A group of villain attorneys who have no practice

---

[1]*Al-Aalam al-Arabi* newspaper of April 20, 1924.

held a party to which they invited the representatives. Two of those asses delivered violent speeches against the British in general, and the treaty in particular, portraying the treaty differently from what it is, such as the British individual cannot be stopped in Iraq if he breaks the law. The attendants kept beating their chests at that. Yasin al-Hashimi spoke and thanked the attorneys for their invitation. Then he added, saying, 'We must not forget that Britain is the only friend of Iraq.' But this statement does not do al-Hashimi any good because he was, in the beginning, the one behind the holding of this party, and he now wants to calm it down so he would have a foothold on both sides."[1]

The Opposition's Method

The new opposition differs from its predecessor in the method. During the time of the previous opposition, the *mujtahids* were satisfied with issuing their *fatwas* prohibiting a political matter, and those *fatwas* had a great impact on people because one who violated them would gain social renunciation and contempt in addition to the lasting penalty that awaits him in the Hereafter. As for now, the new opposition uses another method derived from the nature of life, not from one in which there is a share of the Hereafter: it has resorted to terrorism once and to tribal *nakhwa* (distress call) another.

Tawfiq al-Fukaiki, then a law student, says in his memoirs that he and fellow students used to go to the homes of some prominent representatives using with them the *nakhwa* methods known to the tribes, such as tying a knot in the *kaffiya* or refusing to drink coffee, etc. They did that with Salim al-Khayun, Zamil al-Manna` and Salman al-Zahir. Al-Fukaiki narrates about Salim al-Khayun that King Faisal asked him later, "What prompted you to reject the treaty after I had the impression that you accepted it?" Salim al-Khayun answered him, "Sir, a short law student from among the students of the College of Law named Tawfiq al-Fukaiki embarrassed me. He and his fellows refused to drink my coffee. They were not satisfied with that, so he knotted my *kaffiya* according to the tribal

---

[1]Burgoyne (op. cit.), Vol. 2, p. 340.

way, so I had to promise him to reject the treaty, and it seems that this student is familiar with Arabs' traditions."[1]

The opposition started using women and children to influence the representatives. Abdul-Hadi al-Zahir said to me that Abdul-Ghafour al-Badri used to bring Bedouin women with strong personalities whom he collected from some places such as Albu Shibl and Dooriyyin to send them to the homes of sheikh representatives. When one of them entered the sheikh's house, she would scream in his face according to the tribal way, saying, "I rely on your honour, father of so-and-so, do not sell us to the soujar (soldier?!), a thousand regrets!" This method often influenced the sheikhs because it left an impact on their Bedouin hearts.

Ms Bell wrote on June 4, saying that Ajeel al-Yawir [of the Shammar tribe] went to visit her that morning and said, "Khatoon[2], I have come to inform you that there is no force on the face of the earth that can make the assembly ratify the treaty. You do not know what goes on in the city. A man from among the people of the market stands day and night in front of my house. He is not old; rather, he is a boy wearing shabby clothes. Every time I enter the house or get out of it, this boy meets me to hold (shake) my hand, or he kisses my cloak or its edge, then he cries saying, `Sheikh, father, do reject the treaty, do not sell us to the British!' He does not know the content of the treaty, and he was hired to stand at my house door to say what he says." Then Ajeel al-Yawir concluded his statement by saying, "If there is one boy who stands before my house, there are three or four others who stand before the house of each member of the assembly."[3]

Assassination Attempted

Ms Bell wrote in a letter saying that Cornwallis called her in the morning

---

[1] Abdullah al-Jibouri, *Tawfiq al-Fukaiki*, Baghdad, Iraq, 1971, pp. 38-39.

[2] Iraqis refer to Ms. Gertrude Bell using two names: "Khatoon", Turkish for Lady, and "Umm [mother of] Naji due to Ms. Bell's friendship with an old Baghdadi man to whom she refers as al-Hajj Naji al-Karradi, al-Karrada area of Baghdad being his residence, and whose orchard she enjoyed very much". – Tr.

[3] Burgoyne (op. cit.), Vol. 2, p. 343.

of April 18 and told her that the number of the tribal sheikhs who supported the treaty was now only six and that they were present at his place, desiring to issue a statement supportive of the treaty without paying attention to what the other evil sheikhs are doing. Then Cornwallis frets and says that we must start the matters anew, and we must form a party of tribal sheikhs the nucleus of which is made of these six men.[1]

We did not know who those six men who supported the treaty were, only two of them, namely Addai al-Jaryan and Salman al-Barrak. Both of these men, in fact, were bold in their support for the treaty, fearing none, caring the least about public opinion.

Apparently, the opposition was determined to terrorize these two sheikhs in order to make them a lesson to others. At 2:30 pm on April 20, as both sheikhs were walking together returning to their shared home—which is located in the Bab al-Agha quarter near Cinema Royal—two unknown persons fired shots at them. Addai was shot in his arm and Salman in his leg, but their wounds were not serious. They were immediately taken to a hospital. The assembly's session the next day was postponed in order to express resentment about the incident. Ms Bell commented on this incident, saying, "One of the features of our policy in Iraq is that when they [Iraqis] differ among themselves, they shoot each other, they do not shoot us; otherwise, I would have been the wounded person, not Addai."[2]

The police quickly arrested 21 opposition men. Among them were: Dawood al-Sa`di, Shafiq Nouri al-Sa`eedi, Rasheed Rushdi, Ali Mahmoud al-Sheikh Ali, Awni al-Naqashli, Anwar al-Naqashli, Sami al-Naqashli, Muhammed Abdul-Hussain, Abdul-Razzaq al-Hassani, Rasheed al-Sufi, Abdul-Hadi al-Zahir, Tawfiq al-Fukaiki, Sadiq Habbah, Nasrat al-Farisi, Fakhri al-Tabaqchali, Abdul-Rahman Khidhir, Talib Mushtaq, Muhyi ad-Deen Abul-Khattab, Hashim al-Sa`di, Abdul Majid Zaidan, Qasim al-Alawi and others. The interior ministry ordered the closure of both *Al-Istiqlal* and *Al-Sha`ab* newspapers.

Those arrested were presented to Addai al-Jaryan and Salman al-Barrak so they could both identify the two individuals who fired shots at

---

[1]*Ibid.*, Vol. 2, p. 340.

[2]*Ibid.*, Vol. 2, p. 341.

them. Salman pointed at Ali Mahmoud al-Sheikh Ali, saying that he was one of them. Then he pointed at Awni al-Naqshali, saying that he was the other, but he was not sure. After that, it became clear that Salman erred in identifying the men. It was said at the time that the real culprits were Shakir al-Qaraghuli and Abdullah Sirriyyah, who two months earlier had assassinated Tawfiq al-Khalidi as is well known.

On April 23, the investigation judge released 12 of those arrested. On the 25th, one other man from among them was released, namely Abdul-Rahman Khidhir. As for the rest, they were not released except on May 2. Abdul-Hadi al-Zahir told me that Shakir al-Qaraghuli and Abdullah Sirriyyah were sent to those captured prior to releasing them to say this: 'Do not be afraid, for we are ready, if necessary, to admit that we were the ones who fired at Addai al-Jaryan and Salman al-Barrak'."

Anyhow, this incident led to the spread of panic among the representatives. Each of them feared that his turn would come after Salman al-Barrak and Addai al-Jaryan; therefore, the number of the representatives who attended the assembly started decreasing as time went by till the number of those who attended the May 10 session reached only 53, whereas the number of all members was 100. Also, some representatives started submitting their resignation from the assembly's membership. One of them stated that he wanted to resign because of the continuous threats in letters which bear no signatures and because of the market posters.[1]

On May 21, Ms Bell wrote about her friend, al-Hajj Naji, who was one of the representatives known for supporting the treaty, saying, "I went to visit my dear old man and found him suppressing his agitation. He was sure his turn would be next. He said that everyone thought likewise. His distant home and regular movements make assaulting him easy. I tried to entertain him, but on my return, I felt quite worried about him, so I contacted Cornwallis so he could surround him with police protection, and if he could not do that, I would go to al-Hajj Naji and live with him for a period of time and not let him go to Baghdad except with

---

[1]Philip Ireland (op. cit.), p. 311.

me. We agreed on the view that most likely they could not fire at him as long as I was with him."[1]

Al-Hashimi's Behavior

During that period, we can describe al-Hashimi's behaviour as being duplicit: outwardly, he was an opponent of the treaty. Whenever he met with the attorneys who led the opposition, he would encourage them and bless what they were doing. But when he is alone with the king or with the British people or with some of his friends with whom he felt comfortable, he would praise the treaty and may even describe it as the best that could be obtained.[2]

There are two opinions explaining this duplicitous behaviour of al-Hashimi: one of them says that al-Hashimi did that after reaching an understanding with the king in order to benefit from the opposition by lightening the burden of some articles in the treaty and in amending it for the interest of the country.[3] The other opinion says that al-Hashimi wanted his opposition to ascend to power.

It seems that Ja`far al-`Askari supports the second opinion in explaining al-Hashimi's behaviour, for he feels that the opposition went out of its limit and became unbearable and that it aimed at distancing him from power so al-Hashimi would replace him. What strengthened his feeling is that al-Hashimi has quite often declared before the king and high commissioner that the `Askari administration was not controlling the assembly, as if he meant by that to say that he alone was able to convince the assembly to ratify the treaty.

In early May, Ja`far al-`Askari took the initiative to submit his resignation to the king. Having consulted with the high commissioner, the king summoned al-Hashimi and commissioned him to form a new cabinet. Al-Hashimi asked for 24 hours to study the situation. During that period, he contacted the high commissioner to ask him to amend some articles of

---

[1]Burgoyne (op. cit.), Vol. 2, p. 342.

[2]Khayri Ameen al-Omari, *Shakhsiyyat Iraqiyya* (Iraqi personalities), Baghdad, Iraq, 1955, Vol. 1, p. 109.

[3]Ali Jawdat, *Thikrayat* (memories), Beirut, Lebanon, 1967, p. 172.

the treaty so it would be easier for the assembly to ratify it, but the high commissioner rejected his request. Al-Hashimi finally had to ask to be excused from having to form a new cabinet, but he promised the king that a committee looking into the treaty, over which he presided, would submit a report to the assembly in favour of the treaty, so al-`Askari was convinced about continuing to preside over the cabinet till the ratification of the treaty.[1]

What is noteworthy is that al-Hashimi was during that period wooing Ms Bell in order to win her trust anew after having lost that trust, as we mentioned before. On May 21, Ms Bell wrote the following describing al-Hashimi,

"He has dark spots, yet I still like him. He has an attraction, and he gives one a sense of strength. I went to visit him at his house two weeks ago on the occasion of Eid, so he welcomed me in a way which I did not find in any other house and insisted on escorting me to see his wife and three little daughters. His family life is beautiful, and I think it is rare that we find in Baghdad a man who enjoys such family life."[2]

What is known about al-Hashimi was that his family life was not as Ms Bell imagined. His bickering with his wife was incessant, and he always used to complain about her. It is thought that he projected his family life to Ms Bell in such a beautiful way in order to psychologically influence her and make her inclined towards him, and it seems that he scored a pretty good measure of success in so doing.

On May 20, al-Hashimi submitted the report of the committee in charge of looking into the treaty to the assembly. Describing the treaty, he said, "We found in it what harms our sovereignty, undermines our rights and weakens our independence." He asked the assembly to reject it if the required amendments were not made to it. This was a surprise that

---

[1]Philip Ireland (op. cit.), p. 312.

[2]Burgoyne (op. cit.), Vol. 2, p. 342.

the king, the high commissioner and the administration did not expect.[1] But Ms Bell submitted her report to the high commissioner about what went on in the assembly, saying, "They will witness an amazing scene when the treaty will be ratified at the hands of Yasin al-Hashimi."[2]

Crisis Intensifies

The opposition's view was unanimous inside the assembly and outside it, so much so that the treaty had to be amended before its ratification. On May 26, the high commissioner submitted to the king what looked like a warning in which he said that the date of the next session of the League of Nations Council would be June 11, and if the treaty was not ratified by then, the British government would consider submitting another arrangement to the League's Council instead of the treaty.[3]

On May 27, minister of education Muhammed Hassan Abul-Mahasin submitted his resignation from the cabinet because of differences with his fellow ministers about the necessity of amending the treaty prior to submitting it to the assembly. Sati' al-Husari narrates an interesting anecdote in this regard: the prime minister said this to minister Abul-Mahsin prior to the latter's resignation: "You oppose us quite often. Usually, the minister who does not agree with his fellows withdraws and resigns. I think that you should resign." Abul-Mahasin responded to him by saying, "I do not resign, *you* should resign."[4]

May 29 was a boisterous day in Baghdad. It was decided that the assembly should look that day into the treaty for good by either ratifying or rejecting it. The opposition made preparations for that day, mobilizing public opinion to stand beside it and preparing the masses.

When it was daytime on that date, many markets were on strike, and people assembled in the Karkh flank around the assembly's building

---

[1]Sami Abdul-Hafiz al-Qaisi, "Yasin al-Hashimi", an unpublished university thesis, pp. 132, 135.

[2]Burgoyne (op. cit.), Vol. 2, p. 342.

[3]Abdul-Razzaq al-Hassani (op. cit.), Vol. 1, p. 183.

[4]Sati' al-Husari (op. cit.), Vol. 1, p. 384.

shouting, "Long Live Salim al-Khayun!" "Long Live Men of the Homeland!" "Long Live Independence!" "Do not Seal the Treaty, do not sign it!" The policemen tried to silence and calm them down, but their screams and shouts became even louder.[1] One of the interesting anecdotes narrated in this regard is that Sabeeh Nash'at, the minister of transport and labor, was coming in his car to the assembly when the masses surrounded his car, crowded on him and prevented his car from moving as they kept shouting "Down with the Treaty!" He, therefore, kept shouting, "Down with the Treaty!" in order to get rid of them, so they asked him for his word of honour that he would not ratify the treaty. He, thereupon, shouted in support of their statement, "God curse the mother and the father of anyone who ratifies the treaty!" He could not get rid of them except with a great deal of effort.

When the uproar outside the assembly intensified, some members came out to request the masses calm down. The head of the assembly, too, came out to make the same plea, but this did not have the slightest impact on them. When the police wanted to disperse them, they started pelting them with rocks, and some of them tried to enter the assembly's hall, whereupon Nouri al-Sa`eed summoned a force of cavalier soldiers to assist the police in dispersing the crowds. Those cavaliers first fired in the air, then they were forced to fire at the masses, causing some light injuries. Some soldiers entered the assembly carrying machine guns, and a clash almost broke out between them and the armed men who had come in the company of Salim al-Khayun and other tribal chiefs.

The assembly's discussions that day were not without enthusiasm. Salim al-Khayun distinguished himself in them with his speech which stirred the *nakhwa* according to the tribal way. Rayih al-Atiyyah and others rose to distinction, and then the session was adjourned to the 31st of May.

When the session was to be held on May 31, it became clear that many representatives were absent. The bell announcing the start of the session was sounded a full hour late. When the bell finally rang, it became obvious that the legal quorum was incomplete: the number of those

---

[1]Muhammed Muzaffar al-A`dhami (op. cit.), Vol. 2, p. 643.

present was only 49. This forced the assembly's president to postpone the session to June 2.

As the representatives were getting ready to exit the assembly's hall, they saw the high commissioner coming accompanied by Cornwallis, and this was a surprise to them. They all went to the rest area, and Dobbs started talking to them in an attempt to convince them to accept the treaty. He pointed out the talks of Sir Percy Cox in Istanbul about the Mosul issue, saying that the Turks were lenient about it, but when they came to know what happened in the assembly, they changed their minds and started demanding the Mosul governorate. Then Dobbs said that amending the treaty, which the representatives demanded, was possible but after its ratification. Then he took a sheet of paper and wrote this statement on it: "The British government is ready to look into amending both financial and military agreements in a way that agrees with what is known about the British people's generosity, especially since the 18th Article of the treaty itself permits this amendment provided it is done after its endorsement." Once Dobbs had finished writing the sheet, he delivered it to the president of the assembly, and then he left with his fellow, Cornwallis.[1]

Speech Competition

Dobbs thought that when he talked to the representatives, he convinced them and that they would quickly rush to ratify the treaty without hesitation. It later became obvious that their insistence increased on the necessity of amending the treaty, and they kept escalating their enthusiastic speeches in the assembly day after day.

One who becomes familiar with the written minutes of the assembly's sessions held after May 31 will find himself as though he is in a speech competition: each representative was trying to surpass his fellows in nationalistic enthusiasm and boldness of speech. Most representatives in those days had fallen under the impact of the general enthusiasm, which was charged with hatred of the treaty, regarding its ratification as a betrayal of the homeland. Any representative who was

---

[1]Abdul-Razzaq al-Hassani (op. cit.), Vol. 1, p. 180.

enthusiastic about denouncing the treaty would be surrounded by the masses with a halo of respect, and he would become, in their view, a conscientious nationalist, and every tongue would praise him. The listeners' balconies in the assembly were usually overcrowded with people who were watching the representatives in order to express their admiration of those who opposed the treaty from among them and curse those who supported it. A representative who spoke would pay attention only to the echo of his speech among the listeners and the talks of praise or denunciation which the latter would report to the masses outside the assembly.

When the founding assembly held its June 2 session, Rauf al-Chadarchi, Omar al-Alwan, Abdul-Razzaq Munir, Salih Shkarah, Muhammed Hassan Haidar and Ahmed al-Sheikh Dawood delivered their speeches. They violently attacked the treaty, and some of them assaulted Britain with it. Muhammed Hassan Haidar, for example, said, "Giving the rein of the country to a foreigner is treason. Treason means the loss of religion, honour and free living." Ahmed al-Sheikh Dawood described the treaty as "A lethal blow to our independence, killing our people, destroying our political entity." Then he concluded his speech by saying, "What has been dictated to us in this treaty cannot be described as an international covenant. Rather, it is a voucher of slavery and colonialism (applause); therefore, I request my brothers to stand and vote for sending the treaty back to the government. Stand, I plead to you in the Name of Allah." He meant by that to end the session and that the representatives should leave the hall. The president of the assembly objected to this, saying that the session must not conclude except after the voting is done. Salim al-Khayun responded to him by saying that the majority consensus had been reached about returning the treaty to the government. An argument took place as a result which ended after the session was postponed to the next day.

On the next day, enthusiasm was greater than it had been the day before. Among the first to speak was Abdul-Razzaq al-Ruwaishdi, Sha'lan Abul-Joon and Salim al-Khayun. Salim's speech was sentimental and full of verses of poetry. Describing himself and his fellow tribal sheikhs, he said that they represented the majority in the country, that they were the tying and untying folks, that they were the ones who sacrificed themselves and bought the country with their blood and with the blood of their fathers, "Therefore, far away it is from us to accept the treaty which came to enslave us (applause). I, therefore, state that the treaty is sent back to the government." Then he said that retreating from the demand of amending the treaty was infamy. He was thus pointing out to Naji al-Suweedi, who split from the opposition at that time after he used to be the one who had started it.

Nouri al-Sa`eed was the only representative who publicly expressed his opinion supporting the treaty without fearing the masses' wrath. Apparently, another crowd of people was interested in him. It was different from the crowd, which was interested in the rest of the representatives. He stood to defend the treaty saying, "I admit that it leads to restricting the country's independence, but this does not mean that there is no independence. The modern weapons are owned by superpowers, and the endeavour towards independence without weapons is not possible." Hassan al-Shabbout stood to rebut him, saying, "The financial agreement restricts Iraq's independence; so, how can Iraq arm itself when it does not have the funds?!"

It was then that some representatives from the north submitted a report which was recited on their behalf by Muhammed Sherif Beg, Erbil's representative. It said that they loathed expressing their opinion about the treaty since they did not postpone discussing it until after the Mosul issue was settled. Muhammed Sherif Beg said that he came to know that the Turks insisted on their demand to annex Mosul to them up to the Himrin Mountains [in Diyala]. He, therefore, requested the king and high commissioner to express an interest in keeping Mosul within Iraq; otherwise, the area would be endangered. Ahmed al-Sheikh Dawood stood up to emphasize that there was no relationship between the treaty and the Mosul issue except if Britain wanted to pressure the assembly and to influence it through this issue. Zamil al-Manna` stood up and enthusiastically said that there should be no fear regarding Iraq if Britain refused to assist it, for it could fight Ibn Saud, and the Iranians feared the Arabs. As for the Turks, they are restricted by international terms, and if they insist on being hostile towards the Arabs, the Arabs can repel them; therefore, he insisted on amending the treaty.

Then Omar al-Alwan spoke, and so did Asif Qasi Agha, Abdul-Wahid al-Hajj Sikar, Muhammed Hassan Haidar and Habib al-Khayzaran, striking this same chord. Among what Muhammed Hassan Haidar said was this: "I swear by Allah that if this treaty is ratified, there will be no friendship." Habib al-Khayzaran kept threatening a revolution erupting in case Britain insisted on not amending the treaty. Then he said that Britain would not relinquish Mosul because it contains sources of precious oil and that the benefits that Britain anticipates getting from Iraq are linked to defending it.

The discussions went on thus in the next sessions, which were held on June 5, 7 and 9. It was noticed that Abdul-Muhsin al-Sa`doun, while presiding over the assembly, was discreetly encouraging the opposing representatives, permitting them to demonstrate their enthusiasm as they liked. It is thought that he did so out of spite of the king and of his fellow, Ja`far al-`Askari.

Ms Bell wrote commenting about what was going on in the assembly, saying, "I agreed with the opinion of Cornwallis that we made a mistake. We realized that it would be in vain to ask people who are not politically educated to undertake a vital decision through their representatives in a matter which concerns their future. The factors of ignorance, personal greed and blind enmity would have a direct impact on the decision, and the issue would then be at a degree of ambiguity to the extent that its advocate cannot see his path."[1]

Loyal Newspapers' Campaign

There were in Baghdad at the time three newspapers that were loyal to the British. The first was the "Al-Awqat Al-Baghdadiyya" [Baghdad Times] which was issued by the British people. The second was the *Al-Iraq* newspaper which was owned by Razzouq Ghannam, who was a member of the founding assembly and was known for his support of the authority. The third, it was the *Mufid* newspaper which was owned by Ibrahim Hilmi al-Omar. This man was counted among the opposing journalists, but he finally changed his stance.

These newspapers were calling for ratifying the treaty before amending it. On May 26, *Al-Mufid* newspaper published an article under the heading "The Homeland is in Danger: Where are the Saviors?" It

---

[1]Burgoyne (Op. Cit.), Vol. 2, p. 343.

demanded in it the use of reason before sentiment, the balancing between the danger of refusing the treaty and the harm of its endorsement. It explained that the danger that would result from rejecting the treaty would be huge: the British would vacate Iraq and deprive it of their support on the Mosul issue. Moreover, the country is without many requirements for the life of a modern state. As regarding the harm that results from endorsing the treaty, it lasts only for four years, the term of the treaty as stated in its appendix. The newspaper assaulted those who said that Britain would not abandon Iraq and would not withdraw from it in case the assembly rejected the treaty.

On June 3, *Al-Mufid* published an article under the headline "The Ambiguous Situation", in which it warned of the danger of refusing the treaty with regard to the Mosul issue. It said, "If we make an advice in this regard, it is not because we do not admit the heavy restrictions the treaty and its attachments contain; rather, it is because we believe that the danger of the rejection is much greater than that of its endorsement and because we do not want to choose the lesser evil. Those who differ from us in this belief must remember that the homeland's body is on the autopsy table in the Istanbul Conference; so, what are we going to do?!"

Al-Iraq newspaper followed suit in the footsteps of *Al-Mufid*. It is interesting that it was published on June 9 under the headline "The Nation Holds its Representatives Accountable", a telegram from some secondary voters in Shatra declaring the withdrawal of their vote of confidence from Salim al-Khayun.

As for *Al-Awqat Al-Baghdadiyya* newspaper, it undertook another route: it followed the method of intimidation instead of that of rational conviction. The following is a sample of its method excerpted from an article it published on May 22:

> "Almost two months have passed as the founding assembly continues to look into the Iraqi-British treaty. We now heard that additional reports are being prepared for footnotes and long and wide discussions in the matter of refusing, amending or accepting the treaty with terms which aim at amending it in the future. But what is the use of all of this talk since it is now clear to the least intelligent person as clearly as the sun in midday that the country does not want

a treaty which is explained by its attachments? Therefore, let the members of the founding assembly express their views and reject the treaty or completely crush it, and let them know that the British themselves do not want the treaty. If the British are to remain in the country, and if they are included in the friendship and love in order to help the country tread the route of success, they would accept to stay, but this dream has come to an end: skepticism has replaced friendship; so, why should the British remain in this land? The most suitable for Britain's policy in Turkey, Persia and India is for the British to get out of Iraq without chit-chat. Thus, they entirely remove from them doubts of empirical greed. What we now ask is: will the British get out of Iraq if its people turn the tables upside down for them as their present situation seems to be? Trade with Iraq is insignificant, Iraq's grain, hides and wool are the worst in quality in the world, and the British companies in Iraq are not making any profit. It is possible cotton will be planted here in the future, but it is of a lower quality than that planted in the Sudan and the African colonies. It is also possible for companies to find oil, but we can get it in other countries without risking our capitals. So, our empire gains nothing from staying in Iraq. Let the members of the assembly, then, hurry and vote according to the people's wish, for it is time we got rid of the plots and trickeries. If the Iraqis do not accept the treaty and its attachments, let them state so, and let the British leave this land. We make a sure statement that there is no nation like the British nation that is pleased to get rid of problems of lowly countries and of a nation that is impossible to please with anything."

On June 2, the same newspaper wrote, saying, "The main issue for Iraq nowadays is not independence but the defence of Mosul against the Turks. Everyone must now and every day understand that if they do not ratify the treaty, it is likely they will lose Mosul. And if they ratify it, Britain will exert all its effort to keep the governorate of Mosul as part of Iraq.

Britain will not defend this governorate in case the treaty is not ratified with the knowledge that Iraq's present condition does not enable it to defend it."

On June 7, she wrote saying, "Finally, we want to say something to the people of Iraq: some representatives who scream against the treaty in reality scream against the government; why? They do so because they want to be cabinet ministers. If the assembly still does not wish to ratify the treaty and does not trust Great Britain, we do not expect the British government to help Iraq or to place its trust in it; Britain will then be free to do whatever it pleases."

On June 9, this newspaper published an article under exciting headlines: "Turkish plots in Baghdad; Amazing Reports; Only 48 Hours to save Mosul; The Country has to Choose Either Turkey's Despotism or freedom with British Help; How the Turks Misled the Representatives and the Public; Rejecting the Treaty Ends the Arab Issue and the Independence of the Arabs." The newspaper pointed out in its article what was being done by Turkey's supporters in Iraq: the dissemination of lies about the treaty and about the British, how the advocates of nationalism who were angry with the mandate in the Summer of 1922 were secretly trying to sell Mosul to the Turks. Also, the newspaper pointed out that the Turks were the ones who masterminded the Kirkuk incident in which many of Kirkuk's people were killed at the hands of Orthodox soldiers as we will discuss in the next chapter. The newspaper said, "We thought that the Iraqi nation is sensible, understanding, but we now think it is blind to the facts or is absolutely ignorant of them, for it no longer differentiates between false and true reports, and nothing is left for us except to articulate the painfully wounding reality."

On June 10, the newspaper published another threatening article. On that day, the warning that the high commissioner had issued to the king ended. The article was under exciting headlines such as "The Great Decision: Iraq may Either Win its Freedom and the Arab their Nationality or Lose it this Day." The newspaper stressed in its article its previous claim about a relationship between those who opposed the treaty and the Turks who wanted to occupy Iraq. It wondered: "Why are the Turks not kicked out of Baghdad?!" Then it pointed out the heavy terms in the treaty as the price which Britain gets in return for spending huge sums of money and sacrificing many lives of the British soldiers in order to protect Iraq; so, Britain had the right to insist on those terms in exchange for these sacrifices. Then the newspaper concluded its article with the following:

> "If the assembly refuses to ratify the treaty today, the Iraqis, Arabs and Kurds will have rejected an offer by Britain, and they will have themselves reneged on General [Stanley] Maude's promise. Britain will then be free and not obligated to defend Mosul. The representatives have a decreed duty which they must carry out on behalf of the citizens and of the country, and it is up to them to choose either to build the kingdom of Iraq or to destroy it. Each of their members becomes responsible before the Iraqi people and other nations for the final decision which he issues, the decision which must be made this day because Britain withdraws its detachment as soon as the clock rings on 12 today in the evening, and the issue of Iraq's future will be referred to Europe. So, the founding assembly may either win today and come out victorious for the benefit of the homeland, or it ends the life of a modern nation perhaps forever."

Dobbs Is Angry

The king was in a dilemma for which he was not envied. At midnight of June 10, the warning that Dobbs gave ended. The king was apprehensive lest the assembly should refuse to ratify the treaty that day, and he did not know what the consequence would be.

The king summoned the assembly members to meet with him at his mansion at 4:30 in the afternoon of June 9. When their number was complete, he stood to talk to them at length in order to convince them to ratify the treaty. We quote the last portion of his talk due to its importance:

> "When I read the treaty and its agreements [attachments], I felt what the assembly felt, and the nation felt it [too], but I

do not hide anything from you, and I do not want to hide what my chest conceals. I see that the country's situation is perilous; so we must not walk behind sentiments; rather, we must accept the judgment of reason. You are the people in charge, so I lift from myself the responsibility and lay it upon you. I do not tell you to accept or reject the treaty, but I say: do what you see as the most beneficial for the country's interest. If you want to reject it, do not leave Faisal hanging between the earth and the sky; rather, find a way for us other than the treaty, and you will see that we need funds and men to fight the Turks, to resist the British mandate and to stand in the face of the Iranians and others. I am before you in the field of the war and in that of politics. My past is well known, so do not lose what is in your hands. I thank the assembly for its stance, and I thank the committee for its efforts, for we thus gained reservations and explanations that are in the interest of Iraq, and we gained a clear promise from the high commissioner to amend the financial agreement and that we will soon enter into negotiations after the ratification to amend the rest of the articles, that is, if you agree to ratify it and to solve the dilemma."[1]

It seems that this talk by the king did not have a significant impact on the representatives, for the assembly was supposed to hold its next session at 9:00 am. When the hour came, it did not seem that the representatives were ready to attend. Two hours passed by in vain. The representatives kept going in and getting out as if they were reluctant to attend. At that time, a violent argument broke out with screaming and noise in the hall that led to the assembly, and Salim al-Khayun was seen at the head of a number of representatives as they were getting out of the assembly. Other representatives came to invite them to return and to insist on them till they were able to get them back. At 11:30 am, the quorum was complete in the hall, but a representative asked for the session to be delayed for a short while, so the president agreed to delay it for half an hour.

---

[1]*Al-Aalam Al-Arabi* newspaper of June 10, 1924.

When the session started at 12:30 pm, an argument erupted between two groups of representatives, one of which supported the suggestion of the representatives of the north to postpone the ratification of the treaty until after settling the Mosul issue, and the other supported al-Hashimi's proposal and that of his group for the necessity of amending the treaty prior to ratifying it. The prime minister was very much angered by all of that because he hoped the representatives would look into the matter of ratifying the treaty in its present condition, but he found them differing about two proposals, neither of which led to the anticipated outcome. The prime minister got out of the hall, where he contacted the king by phone and told him that things looked bad, then he returned to the hall to ask the president of the assembly to postpone the session till the next day, whereupon the president agreed immediately. The representatives started exiting like released birds, according to the expression of Capt. Holt, who was then present in the listeners' balcony.[1]

When Dobbs came to know about what happened in the assembly, he burst in outrage in unusual British conduct. It is worth mentioning in this regard that Dobbs was well known for the intensity of his outrage. Strange tales are narrated about him in this regard. It was rumoured that whenever he was angry with one of his officials, he would hurl the ink pot in his face. He once slammed a flower pot on the floor and crushed it because he did not like the way the flowers were planted in it.[2]

Ms Bell talked in a letter about Dobbs' anger when he heard what went on in the assembly. She said, "I hurried to tell Cornwallis about the matter by phone, so he shouted: 'Oh my God!' Then I went to Sir Henry [Dobbs] to tell him, and he was in a degree of anger the like of which I never witnessed in anyone else. As we were talking, the telephone's bell rang, and it was the king asking for a day's respite. Sir Henry Dobbs responded to him with his refusal, saying that he would visit him to ask him to dissolve the assembly at midnight if it could not be assembled in the afternoon." Ms Bell adds, saying, "Sir Henry kept getting angrier one moment after another, regarding the matter as having been arranged by

---

[1]Burgoyne (op. cit.), Vol. 2, p. 345.

[2][Harry] Sinderson, *Ten Thousand and One Nights: Memories of Iraq's Sherifian Dynasty*, London, U.K., 1973, p. 77.

the king, but this is not true. He kept taunting this and that till I suggested to him that we should go to eat lunch. Sir Henry is pitiful. He kept calming his anger down with a glass of iced beer."[1]

A Memorable Night

At 3:00 pm in the afternoon of that day, Ja`far al-`Askari went with Yasin al-Hashimi to the house of the British Commissioner in al-Karkh to meet Dobbs. When they both arrived, they found Dobbas about to leave. He looked askance at them and said that he was going to King Faisal to ask him to dissolve the founding assembly immediately since he did not expect anything good out of the assembly for the relations between Britain and Iraq.[2]

Al-`Askari left for his office in a hurry and kept trying to get the representatives together in the hope the assembly would meet in the evening and ratify the treaty before the warning's deadline. As for Dobbs, he reached the king's mansion at four o'clock. When he entered, he found Cornwallis sitting with him, so he submitted to the king a sheet of paper containing a warning asking him to dissolve the assembly starting at midnight that night and to issue instructions to the interior ministry to close the assembly's building immediately and to surround it with a police force sufficient to carry out this order. The king surrendered to this warning and summoned to the mansion the British adviser to the ministry of justice in order to prepare a law bill to dissolve the assembly.

Ja`far al-`Askari was meanwhile busy trying to get the representatives together, and he was able to bring some of them to the assembly's building, but Salim al-Khayun and his group stood at the assembly's door urging the representatives not to enter. At eight o'clock, al-`Askari telephoned the king, telling him that he could not get a sufficient number of representatives, requesting him to give him a day's respite. Dobbs refused to give him this respite, and the law bill to dissolve

---

[1]Burgoyne (op. cit.), Vol. 2, pp. 344-345.

[2]Abdul-Razzaq al-Hassani (op. cit.), Vol. 1, p. 185.

the assembly had already been prepared and was in the king's hands to sign.[1]

Ja`far al-`Askari returned anew to get the representatives together, exerting his utmost effort along this route as if he realized that his political fate was hanging on his success in it. He was assisted in this endeavour by his brother, Tahsin al-`Askari, who was then general director of the police and who mobilized all the police apparatus to search for the representatives everywhere and to bring them to the assembly. The king had sent his own bodyguard, Tahsin Qadri, to assist them.

Many means were used to bring the representatives to the assembly: sometimes requests, sometimes pleas and some other times strong insistence. Threats or violence may have also been used with some of them. Al-Hajj Naji al-Karradi has said in a talk with Ms Bell about that night that the police dragged him from his bed and put him in a car not knowing whether they were taking him to the guillotine or somewhere else.[2]

At 10:30 that night, 68 representatives could be collected, so they were lodged in the assembly's hall, and the session started over a meeting in which extreme tension prevailed.

It was a session the like of which is seldom found in the history of the world's parliamentary councils. Every member in the hall felt as if the whole world was watching him and would hold him accountable for what he did in that session. The balconies of the listeners were overcrowded with attorneys and others, and their eyes were fixed at the hall and their tongues ready to pour curses on the fathers of those who would agree to ratify the treaty. As for the cabinet ministers, they had left the seats assigned to them on the right side of the presidency podium and penetrated the ranks of the representatives, begging them to accept the treaty: "Folks, the country is in danger, use reason." Yasin al-Hashimi was playing his well-known game during that time, for he was outwardly opposing the treaty while covertly advocating its ratification. Al-Sa`doun, too, was also playing his game in blocking the ratification of the treaty out of spite of the king as well as his fellow Ja`far al-`Askari.

---

[1] Philip Ireland (op. cit.), p. 316.

[2] Burgoyne (op. cit.), Vol. 2, p. 348.

There were two reports in al-Sa`doun's hands: 1) the opposition's report which called for amending the treaty before ratifying it, and 2) the government's report, which called for ratifying the treaty first and then entering after that into negotiations to amend it. Al-Sa`doun submitted the opposition's report first, asking every member to stand up to express his opinion. Al-Sa`doun meant by that to intimidate those who supported the treaty from expressing their views under the looks of those who were sitting in the listeners' balconies.[1] But his plan failed: only 23 representatives supported the opposition's report. As for the government's report, it was supported by 37 representatives. Eight representatives abstained from voting.[2]

Among interesting anecdotes narrated in this regard is that an assembly member had promised Ms Bell to support the treaty, but at the time of voting, he took his rosary beads out of his pocket and sought Allah's advice through it, and the result was negative; Ms Bell finally felt disappointed with him.

Al-Hajj Naji al-Karradi was one of those eight representatives who abstained. He went to Ms Bell after that feeling timid and kept apologizing to her for not supporting the treaty. He justified it by narrating what happened to him when they dragged him out of his bed at night. Ms Bell accepted his excuse and kept pacifying him and promising him that she would visit him at his house to have supper with him on the rooftop under the rays of the full moon.[3]

When the session ended after the ratification of the treaty, some representatives who supported it were reluctant to go out of the assembly for fear someone would assassinate them; therefore, each of them was provided one or two policemen to protect him. But fear did not entertain Nouri al-Sa`eed, for he carried in his pocket a hand grenade. When he got out of the assembly, he accompanied in his car a representative who supported the treaty, namely Muzhir al-Hajj Sigab. Nouri took the grenade out of his pocket and said to Muzhir, "This can kill two hundred persons at once." Ms Bell says in her comment, "The presence of that

---

[1]*Ibid.*, Vol. 2, p. 346.

[2]Abdul-Razzaq al-Hassani (op. cit.), Vol. 1, pp. 187-189.

[3]Burgoyne (op. cit.), Vol. 2, p. 348.

bomb acted as a calming effect on Muzhir al-Hajj Sigab, but not so with me when I ride a car that violently shakes."[1]

Al-Awqat Al-Baghdadiyya newspaper of June 12 came out to say, "The ratifying of the treaty was generally received with indifference, and there was no sign of wailing or jubilation which we expected, so we heard none of that as we walked down the streets after completing the important event in the founding assembly. We also did not see or notice any group of youths armed with sticks, knives and pistols who made themselves visible to a great degree during the period of the assembly's discussions."

On June 18, Ms Bell wrote, saying, "When Sir Henry [Dobbs] sent a telegram about the treaty to London on June 11 asking to be informed whether it was acceptable, we did not get any answer. It is difficult to imagine, but we did not get an answer except on the 17th of the month. This is very inappropriate. Local newspapers started showing their scepticism about the British government's rejection of the treaty. The representatives who supported the treaty kept coming to me, and they were upset. I could not do anything other than give them an answer which was almost implausible: Aall the British government went on a holiday and did not yet look into the treaty. When the answer finally came, there was nothing in it other than a mere news report: the British government accepted the decision, without one word of appreciation of Sir Henry or congratulating him, being the man who had to undertake the serious decisions and who actually undertook the sound decisions that brought British policy this happy outcome. Sir Henry is very much in pain."[2]

Al-Hashimi From Negative To Positive

On June 13, the *Mufid* newspaper wrote attacking al-Hashimi and denounced his duplicity. It addressed him thus: "You, as we have come to know from reliable, trustworthy sources, have repeatedly stated to some British politicians and to your friends in the present administration as well as to others that what is best for Iraq is to ratify the treaty, and you urged many representatives through these methods to ratify it. This is

---

[1]*Ibid.*, Vol. 2, p. 346.

[2]*Ibid.*, Vol. 2, pp. 347-348.

something that cannot be denied because it is not impossible for us to prove it with much evidence. If the matter is as such, what prompted you to oppose it at the time of voting after you had supplied many of your fellows with pieces of advice in support of the treaty?"

On June 18, Ms Bell wrote, saying, "I expect Ja`far [al-`Askari] will be forced to let Yasin [al-Hashimi] enter the cabinet if he himself wants to do so. He is strong, and his strength is derived from the extremists' support for him. Moreover, he is less dangerous inside the administration than outside it. For almost a week, he was contemplating a change in his stance to support the treaty, and he started working in this direction, but he found out that he was unable to maintain his party members and that he would lose his respect among them. Despite his conviction that this would lead to a catastrophe, he rejected the treaty. We must state that they all did not believe that we would get out of the country; therefore, rejecting the treaty was not in their view that risky."[1]

On July 9, Ms Bell wrote, saying, "Ja`far al-`Askari's administration is staggering on its way to its grave, and the last action Sir Henry undertook was getting ready for the birth of a new administration. Yasin [al-Hashimi] Pasha is the one chosen to form the [new] administration. He is the most able man here from the standpoint of intelligence, but I look at the matter of his handling the post of head of the administration with scepticism. But I entertain myself by thinking that Sir Henry knows the matters more than me and that what he undertook is the best solution."[2]

It is worth mentioning that al-`Askari's administration did not fall in that period as Ms Bell had predicted; rather, it remained standing till the founding assembly completed the ratification of the constitution and the law for electing the representatives. On August 2, the founding assembly was dissolved after completing its job. On the same day, al-`Askari submitted his administration's resignation, which the king accepted and summoned Yasin al-Hashimi to form a new administration.

---

[1]*Ibid.*, Vol. 2, pp. 347-348.

[2]*Ibid.*, Vol. 2, pp. 348-349. [Original Arabic text provides page numbers 248 – 249, but this quite obviously is a typographical error. – Tr.]

Al-Hashimi took charge as deputy defence minister in addition to being the prime minister, while al-Sa`doun became interior minister, Sasson Hisqail the minister of finance, Rasheed Aali al-Gailani the minister of justice, Muzahim al-Pachachi the minister of labour and transport, Ibrahim al-Haidari, the minister of endowments, and Ridha al-Shibeebi, the minister of education.

The king wanted to assign the defence ministry to Nouri al-Sa`eed, but he did not succeed. He wanted to keep al-Hashimi distant from direct contact with the army; therefore, he asked for the creation of a new post in the defence ministry, which is that of deputy commander-in-chief, since the king himself is the commander-in-chief, and to assign the post to Nouri al-Sa`eed so the army's matters would go through him to al-Hashimi, and the king's request was implemented.

On August 5, Ms Bell wrote, saying, "Yasin [al-Hashimi] and Sasson [Hisqail] came to visit me on Monday. When Yasin shook hands with me, he said, 'We want to help you; we want to help you in particular.' I said to them that every administration is appointed by the king and is endorsed by the high commissioner. It has the right to ask for my assistance.' When they both wanted to leave, Yasin repeated his first statement with full seriousness, so I wrote him saying that he would of course, get my full assistance, but I did not add anything else. I have a very precise remark which is: the *Istiqlal* newspaper, which Ja`far [al-`Askari] had shut down during the time of the disturbances as the treaty was being discussed, jumped yesterday to the world of existence, taunting Ja`far's administration, accusing it of tyranny. The editor and main writer are now both in Yasin's pocket, and I am sure to a great extent that everything that appears in the *Istiqlal* newspaper is either inspired by Yasin or he agreed to it at the very least."[1]

---

[1]*Ibid.*, Vol. 2, pp. 349-350.

Conclusion

The Growth Of Political Awareness In Modern Iraq

The reader may notice from reviewing this part the appearance of political awareness in Iraq in a clear and strong way. It is worth mentioning that this awareness did not exist in Iraq at the beginning of this [twentieth] century. Religious awareness at the time was the one that took its place in people's minds. In fact, this shift, which is akin to a leap in political awareness, was a social phenomenon worthy of study. Regretfully, we do not see it studied by our writers and researchers despite its significance for understanding our present life. I submit the following brief study of that phenomenon, and perhaps this will encourage others to build on it.

It is known that the public during the Ottoman period did not like to interfere in politics and regarded it as being outside the field of their interest because on the one hand, politics was dangerous to them and, on the other hand, politics did not provide them with "bread". If you talk to one of them about politics, he will say to you, "This is not my job, man; I want to do something that provides me with bread." In this regard, an anecdote is narrated which took place during World War I. Its summary is this: a young man from among the people of al-Kadhimiyya was fond of reading newspapers and following up on war reports, and his father used to advise him against doing so but to no avail. One day, this youth went home shouting, "Warsaw fell!" He read it in the newspaper and was glad about it, so his father wanted to teach him a lesson that would deter him from keeping himself busy with such matters which were of no benefit, so he took him by the hand to a woman selling thistles in the market [as firewood] to whom he said, "Do you sell me a bundle of thistles in exchange for the fall of Warsaw?" The woman of course refused and jeered at him. It was then that the father turned to his son and said, "Look at this news which you brought how it is not worth a bundle of thistles!"

Moreover, the commoners were keen on respecting and courting the men of the government in order to thus shun their evil. This reflected itself on their vernacular axioms: "I call whomsoever marries my mother 'Uncle'"; "I serve one who loads watermelons in the scaffolder"; "If you need the dog, call it 'Hajji doggie'"; "Bring me something with embroidery [to wear] and say, 'Wear it in good health"; "The hands that you cannot cut off you should kiss"; "It is none of my business"; "What is in it for me?"; "The ruler is wise"; "What happened has happened, Allah grants the sultan victory," etc.

This tradition was clearly exemplified among the heads and dignitaries who were used to courting men of the government and putting their seals on every "dossier" those men requested of them, supplicating to Allah Almighty to support the creed and the state, Amen! The commoners became accustomed to flattering those prominent men as much as the latter flattered the rulers. It was a circle connected to other circles in which the low woo the one who is one degree above him, and so on. It is noticed that each of them respected the one who is above him outwardly while inwardly supplicating to Allah to annihilate him, Amen!

This is how people were up to the beginning of the twentieth century or, in a more precise statement, up to the year 1906. Since that year, events have kept happening successively in Iraq of the type that moves minds and stirs debates. Those events were able during a few years to transform the Iraqi people from being politically unaware to being very politically aware.

We discussed, in this volume and in some previous volumes, those events in detail, and we will try to briefly mention them again with some additions. We have numbered them chronologically so the reader may form a generally unified idea about them:

FIRST: the first event which attracted the Iraqis' attention to politics is called the "mashroota" [conditional] movement, i.e. the movement that demanded a constitution. In 1906, reports reached Najaf about the feud that was exacerbated in Iran between the supporters of the "mashroota" and the supporters of despotism. Soon the feud's infection moved to Najaf, so Mulla Kadhim al-Khurasani adopted the "mashroota" principle, while Sayyid Kadhim Yazdi adopted that of despotism, and people were split into two contending parties, each of which kept accusing the other of apostasy and of departing from Islam.

We must not forget that Najaf has an ancient history of debates. In the past, the debate in it revolved around issues of belief and of logic which had nothing to do with the existing reality, such as the issue of caliphate, for example, and who is the most worthy of all people for this [position] after the Prophet: Ali or Abu Bakr? When the "mashroota" movement came, the debate came out of its old framework and became realistic, touching on people's interests and problems of livelihood. The preachers and pulpit speakers began talking about politics as they used to talk about Ali and Abu Bakr in the past, and they may have linked the present to the past in order to come out with the result that they wanted.

Most commoners were supporters of despotism. As for the supporters of the "mashroota", they were mostly from the group called "the enlightened". This [group] started advocating some principles and modern concepts such as opening schools, reading newspapers, learning foreign languages, liberating women and such matters which the commoners used to regard as reprehensible or prohibitive. Someone told me that the newspapers used to reach them secretly, so they had to meet at someone's house secretly in order to read them. On leaving the house, they would hide the newspapers under their cloaks for fear a commoner or one of the latter's supporters from among the clergymen would see them, so he would accuse them of being followers of foreigners or of Masonry.

We do not need to say that the impact of this feud, which took place in Najaf, must have moved to other Shi'a cities, especially where there are holy Shrines. Many people there started talking about nothing in their assemblies or cafés other than this talk of despotism or of the "mashroota", as well as the conflict between Khurasani and Yazdi.

SECOND: In 1908, an incident took place that had a strong connection to the previous incident. On July 24 of that year, a report reached Baghdad that the Committee of Union and Progress (CUP) in Istanbul, the committee that called for a constitution in the Ottoman lands, had won. Iraq was shaken by this report, and signs of decorum and elation spread everywhere. On the walls, the slogan of the committee appeared: it is comprised of four words: Freedom, Justice, Equality and Brotherhood. Branches for the committee started opening in Baghdad and other cities to which the Afandis, dignitaries and chiefs belonged. Several newspapers appeared at the time, cursing the former regime and giving the people glad tidings of a new glorious era in which freedom would prevail, and all people would be equal before the law in their various creeds and social classes.

This wave of elation and optimism had to stir a reaction among the conservatives, for they regarded the new era as violating the Islamic Shari`a because it equalled the Muslims with the Christians and Jews and because it derived its constitution from the foreigners, whereas it must derive it from the speech of Allah. A society was founded in Baghdad in the name of "al-Mushawwir" to defend Muhammad's Shari`a and to resist irreligious ideologies. On November 13, an incident took place that acted like a spark that ignited a fire. Its summary is: that two Unionists, namely [poet] Ma`ruf al-Rusafi and Abdul-Lateef Thanyan, went to the Wazir Mosque facing the Sarai accompanied by some of their supporters. It so happened at that time that one of the pulpit preachers was preaching to people, so al-Rusafi took him down from the pulpit and took his place to read a party statement, then he delivered an enthusiastic speech in which he lauded the principles of the Committee of Union and Progress since it granted freedom and equality to people in their various creeds and social classes. Al-Rusafi hardly finished his speech and left the mosque with his companions when a rumour set out in the markets that the Unionists insulted the Islamic religion; therefore, members of the Mushawwir society met at a mosque and one of them issued a *fatwa* to execute al-Rusafi and his supporters by hanging. Then a demonstration came out of the mosque shouting, "O religion, O Muhammad!" It went towards the governor's home near al-Bab al-Sharqi, causing the closing down of markets for fear of looting. When the demonstrators reached the governor's house, their voices rose to taunt the apostates who reneged from the creed. They demanded the latter to be hanged. The governor had to instruct the police to arrest Ma`ruf al-Rusafi and Abdul-Lateef

Thanyan. Both men spent several days in jail, then they were released after people had calmed down.

THIRD: In late 1911, a political party was founded in Istanbul which opposed the "Union and Progress" party; it was the "Freedom and Coalition" party. Since then, a violent conflict erupted between both parties, the infection of which moved to Iraq, where its impacts appeared on the pages of newspapers, in government offices and in elections. The Afandis in Baghdad split into two contending groups: one was Unionist, and the other was Coalitionist.

Sayyid Talib al-Naqeeb played an important role during that phase. He, in the beginning, opened a branch for the Coalition Party in Basra, but in early 1913, he turned that branch into a party standing alone itself, which he called the "Reform Society" and kept calling for Arabism and Arab nationalism, strengthening his ties with advocates of Arabism in Lebanon and the non-centralism society in Egypt. The conflict as a result intensified between Sayyid Talib and the Unionists, and the latter started scheming against him, sending to Basra a strict leader named Farid Beg to put an end to him, but Sayyid Talib sent him someone who assassinated him on June 20, 1913, and the Unionists were unable to do anything to seek revenge against Sayyid Talib or to curb his reins.

Sayyid Talib had the personality that stirred the Iraqis' admiration, one that derived its roots from the Bedouin values, for he was "brave, generous" or, in other words, "a looter, a giver." When he was able to assassinate the Turkish leader, Farid Beg, his reputation among the Iraqis rose to its peak, and his name was on everyone's tongue, so much so that he was called "Iraq's pillar". Poets went to him to deliver their lauding poems according to the method used with ancient sultans, and he on his part, would shower them with his gifts. On the one hand, he used to impose tributes on the rich while, on the other, he was overly generous with poets and others.

The Unionists had no weapon against Sayyid Talib other than that of religion, for the nationalist call was regarded in those days as a plot of the unbelievers to divide the Muslims and to destroy the entity of the Ottoman state. Sulayman Faydhi, who was then secretary to Sayyid Talib, says that when he went to Mosul in 1913, he did not find in it anyone who believed in the Arab issue except very few individuals because the religious trend, which characterized the people of Mosul, stood as a barrier between them and rebelling against the Ottoman state which had Islamic characteristics and the sacred caliphate. For this reason, rumours and charges hovered over Sulayman Faydhi that he was advocating the reunification of the religious traditions and disobedience of the successor of the Messenger of Allah.[1]

FOURTH: In early November of 1914, the British started their attack on Iraq from the Faw area. It was then that exciting telegrams set out of Basra to the people of Iraq, saying: "The unbelievers are threatening Basra, the lands of Islam are in danger, help!" Those telegrams were read to the people at mosques, and callers read them loudly at marketplaces, while preachers and speakers kept charging people's sentiments with their enthusiastic speeches in which they stressed that if the British people occupied Iraq, they would demolish its mosques and holy Shrines, burn the Qur'an, violate women's sanctities and slaughter children. People believed these statements, and panic spread among them. Clergymen issued their *fatwas* that the Islamic lands must be defended and that *jihad* against the unbelievers must be declared. Many of them started making preparations to go to the war front to carry out this duty that the Islamic legislative system (Shari`a) mandated upon them.

Actually, the commoners also hated the Turkish government very much, hoping it would come to an end because of the woes of conscriptions which it imposed on them, the paper money and the confiscations, etc. When *jihad* was declared, they were confused: religion ordered them to defend the government. This is on the one hand. On the other hand, the circumstances of their reality prompted them to disobey the government. This is what happened to many of them: they shifted from the *jihad* position to that of rebellion during a short period of time. This became obvious in Najaf in a tangible way: we saw it as a centre for the *jihad* movement in the beginning, and then it became shortly thereafter a center for the rebellious movement. We also saw the tribes going to the war front in obedience to the command of the men of the

---

[1]Sulayman Faydhi, *Fi Ghamrat al-Nidal* (in the midst of struggle), Baghdad, Iraq, 1952, p. 121.

creed, but when they hardly saw the Turkish army vanquished, they fell on it with looting and killing.

FIFTH: The British had, shortly before and during the war, followed a policy with the Arabs of encouraging the nationalist, independent and liberation principles and the like in order to weaken and fragment the Ottoman state. When the British occupied Iraq, they started striking on these chords. Among what they declared in this regard was their famous statement: "We have come to you to liberate, not to conquer." It is worth mentioning that the British military men in Iraq were not pleased with this policy due to their belief that it opened the Iraqis' eyes and made them yearn for freedom and independence, and they would demand them both, causing the British problems in the future. But London's government insisted on sticking to this policy, spurred by some political and international motivations.

During the occupation, a young officer, namely Col. [Arnold Talbot] Wilson [1884 – 1940], strictly believed in the error of his government's policy in lavishing promises to the Iraqis. In his view, the Iraqis were ignorant folks who were not fit for self-rule, and it was their interest to remain under direct British rule till they learned the art of governance. The dispute between Wilson and his government about this subject intensified: London wanted to set up a national government in Iraq of an Arab appearance and a British essence, whereas Wilson wanted to establish a pure and fully British government. This conflict in policy led to the surfacing of a tense situation in Iraq to, which Sayyid Alwan al-Yasiri, one of the leaders of the 1920 Revolution, pointed out when he thus addressed one of the British governors: "We lived here for hundreds of years in a condition very distant from independence, but you finally came to us to give us promises of independence. You presented to us the idea of independence at a time when we did not ask you for it, nor did we dream of it, until you came and put the idea in our heads. Now, every time we demand independence, you jail us."[1]

---

[1][James Saumarez] Mann [1851 - 1928], *An Administrator in the Making, 1893 – 1920*, London, U.K., 1921, p. 392.

SIXTH: On November 30, 1918, London's government sent a telegram to Wilson asking him to hold a referendum in Iraq in order to get to know the type of government that the residents desired and the individual whom they wanted to be in charge of them. The telegram stressed to Wilson that the population's expression of opinion must be true. But Wilson found this order to be contrary to his own view, so he did not follow it to the letter and tried to be evasive in its regard. He issued his secret orders to the political governors in the governorates stressing on they to get from the population the views that supported the continuation of British rule and not permit opposite views to surface. The governors obeyed his order; therefore, the result of the referendum was that most residents asked for British rule in Iraq to continue. Only very few of them—in Baghdad, al-Kadhimiyya, Karbala and Najaf—asked for an Arab government over which one of the sons of Sherif Hussain would preside.

Actually, the referendum was a surprise that most Iraqis did not understand. It was the first time in Iraq's history that a government asked its subjects about the type of rule they desired. They could not believe what they heard when it was said to them that the country that conquered their land with the sword and spent a great deal of money, and sacrificed lives would, in truth, ask them such a question. This is something that they did not understand, nor did it cross their minds. When they found out that the matter was serious and that the rulers summoned them to ask them what they wanted, they kept asking each other: what is the purpose behind this question? There must be a secret behind it that they did not understand.

A dignitary declared it frankly when he addressed the governor who asked him the same question saying, "You are asking us, while you are the government, what type of rule we need. This is out of the ordinary. It is something which we never heard before. What do I have to do with this subject? If you appoint over us a Christian or a Jewish ruler or an Ethiopian slave, it would be for us a government anyway."[1] Mahdi al-Baseer, who was contemporary to the referendum and witnessed some of its events, says, "The time of the referendum was one of wonders, strange things, rumours and insinuations, and it was rumoured in the beginning that the government's purpose behind the referendum was to sift people's

---

[1]Atiyyah, *Iraq*, Beirut, Lebanon, 1973, p. 272.

minds so it would know who its friends and who its enemies were, so it would reward these and punish those according to the dictates of its interest."[1]

Anyhow, Wilson was pleased with the result of the referendum and sent a telegram to his government informing it of the good news: most Iraqis desired that direct British rule should continue. What is noticed is that in the reports that he sent to his government, Wilson stressed this point. He toured parts of Iraq, met with dignitaries and chiefs and listened to their views, and he found them all supplicating to Allah to sustain for them the shade of the "just" British government, Amen! So, they believed what they were saying, and he wrote about it to his government, then he slept sound!

SEVENTH: The small band that demanded Arab rule during the referendum is regarded as the seed from which the 1920 Revolution resulted, for it kept growing as time went by, and everyone who grumbled about the British people joined it.

People called members of that group "nationalists". As for those who were different from this group, they were in the public eyes, traitors and allies of the unbelievers. Poets started making enthusiastic poems about Prince Abdullah as the nationalists' candidate for Iraq's throne, so people would shout whenever they heard his name and would applaud him. Actually, they did not do that except to spite the British and to defy them. Had the British desired it, they would, of course, have shouted against it according to the principle that says, "One is keen about that from which he is prevented." Ms Bell was aware of this, but only when it was too late. She wrote on June 12, 1921, that is, several months after the Revolution, saying, "When they were last year shouting the name of Abdullah, it was not because he was in their views the best man; rather, they regarded shouting his name as going against the desire of the British."[2]

---

[1]Muhammed al-Baseer, *Tarikh al-Qadhiyya al-Iraqiyya* (history of the Iraqi issue), Baghdad, Iraq, 1923, p. 81.

[2]Burgoyne, *Gertrude Bell*, London, U.K., 1961, Vol. 1, p. 220.

The 1920 Revolution can anyway be regarded as one of the most important events in Iraq's modern history in as far as its effect in growing political awareness is concerned. It was like a public school teaching the people some principles and concepts which they found to be odd, such as "freedom", "independence", "nationalism," "patriotism", and the like. These concepts were, in the past, restricted within the scopes of the Afandis and those who were like them, whereas the public regarded them as matters which did not give them bread. So, when the revolution erupted, the situation changed in a stunning way: those concepts became the axis of the public's interest, and people kept talking about them, shouting for them day after day.

EIGHTH: The installation of Faisal as king in 1921 was hailed by the nationalists and the British at the same time. The nationalists regarded it as meeting their desire, which they had declared before, in choosing one of the sons of Sherif Hussain as king. As for the British, they thought that Faisal would be a pliant tool in their hands, similar to the emirs whom they installed in other kingdoms. But this auguring of both parties did not last long. Soon it became clear to each of them that it was wrong and that Faisal was not as they had imagined him to be.

Faisal tried his utmost to be thought of well by both parties: he kept showing each party that he was loyal to it. But this matter is very difficult, or it may be impossible, for nobody can coordinate between two opposite directions. If he, for a period of time, can do that, he will not be able to continue doing it till the end. Ireland says, "Faisal found himself as the balancing point between the British and the nationalists: on the one hand, he owed his throne to the British, while on the other hand, he needed the support of the nationalists so he could get true independence from the British government."[1]

To what extent was Faisal able to compromise between these opposite directions? This question is difficult to answer, and we may probably return to it in a forthcoming volume when we discuss Faisal's death. This is what made the British hide their intense grudge against him and think of deposing him. They regarded him as a traitor, an ingrate to

---

[1]Philip Ireland, *Iraq* (translated by Ja`far al-Khayyat), Beirut, Lebanon, 1949, p. 279.

their blessing. Destiny willed that Faisal was sick with an ulcer at this very time, so the high commissioner seized the opportunity, took the reins in his hand and started striking at the nationalist movement very hard until he silenced it and displaced its men. When Faisal was healed from his ailment, he found the movement on which he depended to have become fragmented. One of the leaders of the movement went to him to congratulate him on becoming healed, so Faisal asked him, "What have you done with the British? Have you changed your mind about getting them out of the country?" The man answered him immediately, saying, "They told us that *you* were expelled from the country," whereupon he remained silent.[1]

This was the beginning of an obvious change in Faisal's conduct. Since then, he became closer to the British than to the nationalists, but he did not completely abandon his old habit, for we found him resuming contact with the nationalists from time to time whenever he found the British being rigid towards him.

NINTH: When Faisal was getting close to the British in order to avoid problems, a second problem appeared before him from the other side, which was: the problem of pleasing the nationalists, foremost of which were the *mujtahids*. His relationship in the first year was good with the *mujtahids* and bad with the British, but now it turned to the contrary, becoming good with the British and bad with the *mujtahids*. Faisal exerted his effort to convince the *mujtahids* to take his circumstances into consideration, to have mercy on his condition, but to no avail. The *mujtahids*, especially Sheikh Mahdi al-Khalisi, regarded him as having reneged on his pledge to them and that he had sold himself to Satan, becoming a toy in the hands of the British. Al-Khalisi said in front of a crowd of people: "I have taken Faisal off just as I have taken off this ring of mine!"

During that period, a man who was regarded as a first-grade statesman returned from Istanbul to Iraq. He was Abdul-Muhsin al-Sa`doun. Quickly the British discovered in him the strong man who could solve for them the *mujtahids* problem and the Faisal problem at the same

---

[1]Ameen al-Rayhani, *Faisal I*, Beirut, Lebanon, 1958, p. 123.

time, so they handed over the matters to him and supported him. They said to him, "Do whatever you want. We are behind you."

Al-Sa`doun was of the view that dealing with the *mujtahids* problem would not be done except according to the method of Alexander of Macedonia, that is, by cutting off the knot instead of untying it. He was determined to banish the *mujtahids* to Iran in order to get rid of their continuous opposition and *fatwas* for good. Faisal expressed his concerns about this daring action, and the British were concerned about it, too, thinking that a revolution more powerful than that of 1920 would take place in Iraq as a result of banishing the *mujtahids*. But al-Sa`doun insisted on his stance and assured the sceptics that he was able to do it without anything that was feared taking place. Events showed that he was right.

The people had supported the *mujtahids* in their opposition, demonstrating full enthusiasm with such support, but as soon as they saw how the *mujtahids* were deported outside the borders, they returned to their old slogan: "I have nothing to do with it." They learned political awareness recently, but they were unable to forget their old habits. They, therefore, would become enthusiastic at one moment and cool down at another moment. This is one of the manifestations of social disharmony in them.

To sum up, these events, which we have already mentioned and which started before 1906, stirred in Iraq an unprecedented conflict and debate. We do not deny that Iraq had before then witnessed greater events than these and was invited to conflict, but they were of another type that differed from the one which we have witnessed during this period.

Iraqis' disputes were in the past conventional on which one grows since early childhood and maintains when he grows up, such as the dispute among religious sects, tribes, cities or quarters. The individual was then fanatical about his sect, tribe, home town or quarter, supporting it against its enemies due to the social legacy on which he grew up at home. It was a shame for him to swerve from this legacy or to act contrary to it. As regards the new events, they stirred in people a dispute of principles which was not linked to the customary traditional affiliations. Thus, we began to witness a strong dispute and argument among the sons of the same sect or quarter, and a dispute may take place among the brothers in the same house: this believes in the "mashroota" and that believes in despotism, or this is nationalist, and that is Ottoman, or this is *jihadi,* and that is escapee, or this is nationalist, and that is pro-government..., etc.

Training Period

The period we talked about, which extended from 1906 to 1923, has its significance in the development of political awareness in Iraq. We must not forget that when signs of political awareness began in 1906, it was within the cradle of religion and under its auspices. That is, it grew through religious awareness and did not stand on its own. When people debated a political issue, such as the constitution, for example, they did not want to know if the constitution was beneficial for or harmful to the public; rather, they wanted to know if it was [Islamically] permissible or prohibited: does it agree with the Islamic Shari`a or does it oppose it? People remained like that during the period when the clergymen were working in politics in Iraq.

Actually, it was an odd period that was distinguished due to some social phenomena particular to it. Among those phenomena is that many bread-earners and shop-keepers who never before cared about political issues became interested in them and felt enthusiastic about them. Take the example of Hassoun Abul-Jibin who was a grocer in the Sarai market in Baghdad. In his youth, he was like his father, avoiding politics and regarding them as earning no bread, but we saw him suddenly turning into a first-rate political enthusiast wearing shrouds, participating in demonstrations and shouting as loudly as he could: "Down with *Great Britain!*" We do not need to say that the reason behind the change in this man and his likes was religion and the *fatwas* of the clergymen; otherwise, this man would have maintained the tradition of his fathers and grandfathers of: "Why should I care?"

It seems that this period was necessary for the growth of political awareness in Iraq. Perhaps it was like a period of training and of accustoming the people to express an interest in politics. So, when this period ended with the banishment of the *mujtahids,* the people's training was completed, and they no longer needed the clergymen's *fatwas.* For this reason, we found them in 1924, when a discussion went on about the treaty, demonstrating and showing enthusiasm near the founding assembly as they used to do in the Haidar-Khana Mosque in 1920. They came out of their old shell and never to return to it!

Between The Afandis And The Mullas

It can be said that the banishment of the *mujtahids* in 1923 is one of the manifestations of the conflict between the *mullas* and the *afandis*. In other words, it was between clergymen and statesmen. This conflict was not new. Its roots extended to the 18th century when early signs of modern civilization started reaching the Islamic lands. The clergymen resisted that civilization and considered it as opposing the Islamic Shari`a, whereas the men of state were fond of it and regarded it as necessary for their nation so it could through it survive in the struggle of modern life.

It is worth mentioning that the *afandis* and the *mullas* in Iraq were allies during the 1920 Revolution and in the short period that followed it, but this alliance was temporary, and it is not in its nature to last long. Each of these two groups had its own mentality which opposed that of the other. The *mullas* wanted to implement the Islamic Shari`a on political matters, whereas the *afandis* wanted to keep religion away from politics. When they were allied, and in agreement for a short period of time, it was due to a common interest among them. And when that interest started tilting, when the *afandis* won positions which they sought, the difference started appearing between both groups and kept intensifying day after day.

Some *afandis* who were far-sighted realized early in time the extent of the gap that separated them in their thinking from the *mullas*. In a letter dated November 3, 1920, Ms Bell quoted a viewpoint expressed by Abdul-Majeed al-Shawi in this regard, saying:

> "The Shi`as' problem may be the greatest in this land. We discussed this problem last evening during a banquet which I held at my house. Abdul-Majeed Beg said: 'What will you do if the senior *mujtahid* issues his *fatwa* that the Shi`a individual must not be a member of the legislative council as long as the government is under the British mandate, knowing that the *mujtahid*'s speech is regarded as Allah's speech? Suppose the council started discussing the coining of

a law, then the *mujtahid* issues a *fatwa* saying that that law violates the Shari`a and must be rejected without taking anything else into consideration. Imagine the Pope in Italy practising a secular authority and hindering every action the government does. How will the situation be? The solution, as time passes by, will be as what occurred in Italy: there, they started looking at the Pope as they would at a silly old man. But we here are yet to reach that phase'."[1]

One may ask: why did the Shi`a clergymen set themselves apart by opposing the government in those days while their Sunni fellows remained silent? In order to answer this question, we have to go back to what we stated in Volume Three of this series about the Shi`a *ijtihad* system. A Shi`a *mujtahid* depends for his livelihood on the religious dues his followers give him; therefore, he is forced, in order to maintain his livelihood and status, to be strongly connected to the public masses, feeling what they feel, standing by their side against their rulers. As for the Sunni clergyman, he is like a government official who depends for his livelihood on his salary, which he receives at the start of every month; therefore, he is mostly forced to be supportive of the government in whatever it does.

A Turning Point

The banishment of the *mujtahids* in 1923 was like a turning point in political awareness in Iraq. The *mujtahids* leaving politics left the field empty for the *afandis* to do as they pleased: a group of them assumed the reins of government, while another group held the reins of opposition, and they kept handling the matter among them like the wind wheel with which children play during the Eid: up and down.

There is a big difference between the *mujtahids'* opposition and that of the *afandis*. An *afandi* chooses the route of opposition in order to reach authority. As for the *mulla*, he does not think of reaching authority, nor does he want it; rather, he chooses the route of opposition in order to

---

[1]Burgoyne (op. cit.), Vol. 2, pp. 168-169.

raise through it his religious status among the masses. He knows that if he assumes a position of authority, he will lose that status immediately and people will condemn him and say about him that he traded his religion for this world. He becomes in the eyes of the people, an *afandi* despite maintaining his black or white turban!

This means that the *mullas* were using the opposition as an end goal because it raised their social status in people's eyes. As for the *afandis*, they used it as a means towards another end: reaching authority. An *afandi* realized that if he remained outside authority for a long period of time, he would lose his social status and become one of the retired café-goers.

It is noticed that the *afandis* during the monarchy period used to shift their political positions time and over again. If they are outside power, they become enthusiastic opponents calling for freedom and full independence and accusing the rulers of injustice and treason. But as soon as they hold the reins of authority, they forget what they said and adopt the same route of those whom they only yesterday used to criticize.

Some *afandis* did not hesitate, when opposing, to use any means that would get them to reach their goal regardless of the dire consequences that could result from them. This became quite clear after Faisal's death when his weak, inexperienced son ascended to the throne: a group of them would resort to stirring the tribes, while another group would resort to stirring the army, as a third group would resort to plots and schemes. In all of this, they claimed that they wanted to save the country from injustice and disintegration. But when they reach authority, people will not find in their time any difference from what it used to be before.

This led to many administrations changing in the monarchy period in Iraq. These, in turn, led to magnifying political awareness in it. Every coup or violent cabinet shake-up had to stir interest in public circles and open their eyes to political issues, stirring among them arguments and disputes about them.

A Worthwhile Objection

We stop at this limit in this study which we will try to complete in a forthcoming volume of this series. Here, reference must be made to a worthwhile objection which I think some readers may direct at this study.

The reader may become amazed and may wonder when he sees me talking about the conflict between the *afandis* and the *mullas*, for example, whereas the thinkers nowadays are busy with the subject of the feud between the bourgeois and the proletariats, for example, or between the reactionaries and progressives or other facets of the struggle about which there is so much talk on the pages of newspapers and books these days.

In reality, I differ in the view from those who talk about such subjects, but I see that we must not forget at the same time the nature of our society, its conditions and class compositions. I remember I was one day in an assembly that included some professors, and the discussion revolved around the Iraqi society and its class composition, so I pointed out in my discussion to the *afandis* as the ones who, in the beginning of this century, used to form a distinctive social class which thought of itself as being higher than the rest of people and had its own traditions and zeal. One of the attendants objected, absolutely denying the term "class" for the *afandis*. I noticed that the reason behind his objection was due to the fact that he did not find in the foreign books in which he reviewed anything that pointed this out or discussed it.

It may be right to say that many of our writers and thinkers are of this type: they have in their minds ready "yardsticks" which they derived from foreign sources, and they have used them as stagnant ideological matrixes which they applied to their society and history regardless of the numerous differences between this society and other societies.

We notice this clearly in some studies which have surfaced about the 1920 Revolution, especially those made recently by Russian researcher [L.N.] Kotlov.[1] This [Russian] author has a "yardstick" in his mind that he

---

[1] Refer to his book about the 1920 Revolution which Abdul-Wahid Karam translated. [I, Translator of this book, am sure that the author is actually referring

wants to apply to Iraqi society in general and to the 1920 Revolution in particular. He kept trying hard to look for information that agreed with his matrix while overlooking the information which differed from it. He was finally able to bring us a study about our own society, which made it look as though it is different from the society in which we live.

In his study, Kotlov wants to prove, first of all, that the Iraqi society was, before the 1920 Revolution, controlled by the feudal system and that those who undertook the revolution were masses from among the farmers, Bedouins, workers and craftsmen. Then he retracts, saying that the leadership of the Revolution was in the hands of tribal sheikhs, clergymen and national bourgeois.

Had the 1920 Revolution taken place in a land distant from us, perhaps it would have been right for us to believe in what Kotlov said because we do not know much about that land. But the revolution happened in our homeland, and we saw many of those who participated in it and came to know some of them and socialized with them. I do not know how the revolution erupted against feudalism while the tribal sheikhs and the clergymen were the ones who led it!

There is no room here to simplify this subject, for we researched it thoroughly in the fifth volume of this series which we hope will soon be published. At any rate, what we call for is that our study must be social, stemming from the reality of our life. But this does not mean that we must close our minds with regard to the various studies that take place in the world. We are supposed to be enlightened by such studies rather than be restricted by them.

---

to this source: Kotlov, L.N. *Natsional'no-osvoboditel'noe vosstanie 1920 g.v hake.* Moscow, 1958. –Tr.]